# SPANISH
# FOR THE
# PROFESSIONS

# SPANISH FOR THE PROFESSIONS

## Health Care, Law Enforcement, Education, Welfare, Business

### A Manual and a Workbook

**Jorge A. Santana**
California State University, Sacramento

987654321

Copyright 1981 by Jorge A. Santana - Random House
Second Edition 1988 - Hispanic Press
Third Edition 1995

LIBRARY OF CONGRESS CATALOGING IN PUBLICATION DATA

Santana, Jorge A
    Spanish for the Professions.
    Bibliography: p. 155
    1.  Spanish language-Conversation and phrase book.    I  Title.
PC4121.S24    468.3'421    80-22364

ISBN: 1-881781-03-8

Cover Photos:

Medicine-  Dr. José Herrera and Elizabeth Santana
Social work- Mari Angeles de Rose
Law Enforcement- Jan Bejar
Education- Beatriz Hernández
Travel- Ileana Romo de Vivar
Business- Cindy Santana

**TO ORDER ADDITIONAL COPIES:**

**SPANISH FOR THE PROFESSIONS**
**1548 37th St.**
**Sacramento, CA 95816-6704**
**(916) 455-8003**

Manufactured in the United States of America
Printed by Griffin Printing

# Preface

The goal of *Spanish for the Professions* is to meet the long-standing need for a text to train students in the use of Spanish in professional activities. With the increasing number of Hispanics living in the United States and the growing importance of bilingual education, the practical uses of such a text — and of university-level courses in this subject area — are readily apparent.

*Spanish for the Professions* is geared to the needs of professionals or persons planning to become professionals in fields that cater to Spanish-speaking persons. Although only five areas are covered — health care, law enforcement, welfare, education, and business — persons involved in other professions could well benefit from the material presented. Instructors should also note that the contents of the various chapters complement each other. Thus, the chapter on health care is of interest not only to those directly involved in the medical professions, but also to law-enforcement officials who frequently face medical emergencies and to school employees who are concerned for the health of their students.

This text presupposes a beginner's knowledge of Spanish. The "Capítulo preliminar" provides a brief review of major points of Spanish grammar and of some basic vocabulary; it can easily serve as a self-contained refresher course for students who need to review basic Spanish-language skills before focusing their attention on their areas of professional interest. In addition, the "Capítulo preliminar" offers practice in basic interview skills common to all professions. The five chapters with specific professional content emphasize conversation, vocabulary building, and realistic drills that are directly applicable to work situations. Grammar is presented in the context of realistic professional needs.

The ability to communicate with patients or clients is developed in the type of exercise that constitutes the bulk of the drill materials: the true-to-life interview situation. Professionals should be able not only to ask for information, but also to interpret and record that information. For this reason, many exercises suggest that two students work together in a role-playing situation in which one acts as the professional and the other as the client. Roles should be reversed frequently, so that students will have the chance to understand and practice the vocabulary and grammatical structures of both roles.

I am grateful to Thalia Dorwick and Eirik Børve for their constructive criticism of the manuscript, and to my students, whose help and encouragement during the development and classroom testing of the manuscript were invaluable.

# About the Author

Jorge A. Santana  is a Professor of Spanish at California State University, Sacramento.  He received his B.A. and M.A. from California State University, San Diego and his Ph. D. from the Universidad Complutense de Madrid where he was a Fulbright Scholar and a Del Amo Foundation recipient.  Professor Santana is editor of the literary journal *Explicación de textos literarios*  and is co-autor of *Lecturas españolas* and  *Antología comentada del modernismo*. His most recent book is the historical anthology *La adivinanza a través de 500 años*.   He specializes in Mexican and Chicano literature and culture, as well as teaching Spanish for the Professions. He has taken many student groups to Spain, Mexico and Guatemala / Costa Rica. Professor Santana was born in Rosarito, Baja California, Mexico, and has lived in the United States since he was four years old.

# Acknowledgments

I gratefully acknowledge the advice and suggestions offered by Dr. Fausto Avendaño, and the typing of the original manuscript by Eva Martínez-Torres.
My special thanks to Ms. Angélica Ulloa for her assistance on the Second Edition and Ms. Gabriela Rodarte for her assistance on the Third Edition.

# Índice general

# SPANISH
# FOR THE
# PROFESSIONS

# CAPÍTULO PRELIMINAR

El español básico/
Basic Spanish

# 1 EL ALFABETO Y LA PRONUNCIACIÓN / Alphabet and Pronunciation

**El alfabeto:** A  B  C  *CH*  D  E  F  G  H  I  J  K  L  *LL*  M
N  Ñ  O  P  Q  R  *RR*  S  T  U  V  W  X  Y  Z

**Vocales:** Spanish vowels are never silent; they are always pronounced. (Exception: the *u* in *que, qui.*)

| | |
|---|---|
| A (as in *a*tomic) | Ana, mamá, papá, Castro, Sara, cama |
| E (as in *e*pidermis) | pelo, pecho, estafa, asesino, reo, vena |
| I (as in pol*i*ce) | delito, lista, libro, quito, Cristina, Irma |
| O (as in *o*ver) | robo, codo, ombligo, atraco, boca, soborno |
| U (as in r*u*le) | nuca, hurto, vacuna, apuntes, Cantú, buscar |

**Diptongos:** In Spanish, a diphthong is a combination of a strong vowel (**a, e, o**) and a weak vowel (**i, u**), or of two weak vowels in the same syllable.

| | | | | |
|---|---|---|---|---|
| seis | Aurora | reino | oir | baile |
| ciudad | cuidado | suicidar | Luis | Guillermo |

**Consonantes:**

**B/V**    After a pause or after **m** or **n**, like English *b:*

boca, blusa, beber, vena, volante, verdura, también, nombre, ombligo, un vaso, un viejo, un vago

In all other cases, a weaker sound in between English *b* and *v:*

abierto, abuelo, obedecer, cubrir, pavo, favor

**C**    Like English *k* before **a, o**, and **u:**

cara, cobro, cura, cofre, cabeza, codo, cuarto

Like English *s* before **e** and **i:**

ceja, cinco, cerca, cinturón, cita, obedecer, once

**CH**    As in *ch*ill:

muchacho, fichar, chofer, fecha, chaqueta, cachete

**GE/JE**    As in *h*air:

gestionar, emergencia, ejercicio, ejemplo, jefe, eje

**GI/JI**    As in *h*eat:

gitano, ginebra, giro, girar, jitomate, jinete, jirafa

H        Always silent in Spanish:

        hora, hospital, herido, huella, hambre, almohada, cohete

J        Like English *h*:

        manejar, jefe, jugar, mejorar, juez, hijo, Vallejo

LL       Like English *y* in *yes*:

        llamar, apellido, llevar, tobillo, lluvia, allí

Ñ        Like English *ny* in ca*ny*on:

        señalar, reñir, riñón, niña, señor, ñoño, niño

QU       Like English *k*:

        que, aquí, turquesa, quince, quitar, queja, toque

R        At the beginning of a word, trilled like Spanish rr:

        repetir, rico, riña, reo, rueda, redondo, rubio

        In all other cases, like English *tt* in Be*tt*y:

        ahora, pero, cero, nuera, martes, abril, número

RR       Trilled:

        interrogar, cerrar, arrestar, ahorrar, correr, borracho

Z        Like English *s*:

        zona, zapato, azul, plaza, mezcla, taza, marzo

## PRÁCTICA

**A.**  Pronounce the following Hispanic place names.

| | | | | |
|---|---|---|---|---|
| Albuquerque | San Antonio | El Cajón | Reno | La Jolla |
| Las Pulgas | Mariposa | Mesilla | Truchas | Canutillo |
| Sierra | Socorro | Cimarrón | Portillo | La Jara |
| El Camino | Manteca | San José | El Monte | Los Ángeles |

**B.**  **Palabras homófonas:** words that are identical or nearly identical in sound.

| | | |
|---|---|---|
| azar - asar | cauce - cause | pillo - pío |
| baca - vaca | hablando - ablando | sexta - cesta |
| casa - caza | leyes - lees | tuvo - tubo |

**C.**  **Trabalenguas/Tongue twisters**

Tres tristes tigres tragaron tres tazas de trigo en un triste trigal.

A mí me mima mi mamá; mi mamá a mí me mima.

El tamal que me enviaste,
aunque no sé con quién,
no está mal, porque está bien,
y está bien porque es tamal.

El Arzobispo de Constantinopla se quiere desarzobisconstantinopolitanizar;
el desarzobisconstantinopolitanizador que le desarzobisconstantinopolitanice
buen desarzobisconstantinopolitanizador será.

## 2 NOMBRES Y APELLIDOS HISPÁNICOS / Hispanic First and Last Names

Continue practicing Spanish pronunciation by saying the following common Hispanic names. Those followed by an * are commonly mispronounced by non-Spanish speakers.

### Nombres de hombre

| | |
|---|---|
| Agustín | Joaquín* |
| Alberto | Jorge* |
| Andrés | José |
| Ángel* | Juan |
| Antonio | Manuel |
| Carlos | Miguel |
| Francisco | Pedro |
| Gregorio | Rafael |
| Guillermo* | Ramón |
| Javier* | Víctor |

### Nombres de mujer

| | |
|---|---|
| Alicia | Irma |
| Ana | Margarita |
| Beatriz | María (abbreviation M$^a$) |
| Cecilia | Marta |
| Consuelo | Patricia |
| Cristina | Rosario |
| Delia | Sara |
| Ester | Soledad |
| Gloria | Susana |
| Guadalupe | Teresa |

### Apellidos

| | | | | |
|---|---|---|---|---|
| Aguilar | Delgado | Jiménez | Ortiz* | Vallejo |
| Aguirre | Díaz | Juárez | Pérez | Vargas |
| Álvarez | Fernández | López | Preciado | Velasco |
| Andrade | Fuentes | Macías | Rodríguez | Velásquez* |
| Barrios | García | Martínez* | Sánchez | Vera |
| Burgos | González | Méndez | Sandoval* | Villa |
| Caballero | Gutiérrez | Mendoza | Soto | Zamora |
| Cantú | Hernández | Morales | Tapia | Zapata |
| Castro | Herrera | Muñoz* | Torres | Zúñiga* |

### Order of surnames

The system of Hispanic surnames is much more elaborate than that of the English-speaking world. The following chart illustrates the order of Hispanic names and surnames.

| | FIRST NAME | MIDDLE NAME | FATHER'S NAME | MOTHER'S NAME |
|---|---|---|---|---|
| When | Juan | José | Sánchez | Ortiz |
| marries | Ana | María | Gutiérrez | López |

her married name will be:

**Ana María Gutiérrez de Sánchez**

Juan and Ana's children will write their names as follows, with the mother's surname coming last:

**Antonio Sánchez Gutiérrez**

**Elvia Sánchez Gutiérrez**

If Ana María became a widow, she would write her name:

**Ana María Gutiérrez Viuda de Sánchez**

Hispanic names are not always this complex, since many Spanish surname persons have Anglicised the pronunciation and/or spelling of their names, or may use only their father's or husband's name. When both surnames are used, a name is alphabetized by the husband's or father's surname: **Gutiérrez de Sánchez, Ana María; Sánchez Gutiérrez, Antonio.**

## PRÁCTICA

**A.** If **Soledad Velásquez Martínez** marries **Guillermo Ortiz Vallejo**, what will her married name be? What will be the surnames of their son **Pablo**?

**B.** Locate the mother and father of each child in the list of **Parents**.

| Children | Parents |
|---|---|
| Delia López Castro | Victor Castro Andrade |
| | Cecilia Castro Soto |
| Carlos Castro López | Irma Soto Castro |
| | Ana López Andrade |
| Rosario Díaz Soto | Antonio López Soto |
| | Ramón Díaz Andrade |

# 3 PRONOMBRES PERSONALES / Personal Pronouns

| | SINGULAR | | PLURAL |
|---|---|---|---|
| yo | I | nosotros/as | we |
| tú | you | vosotros/as | you (*used mainly in Spain*) |
| él | he | ellos | they (*masc., masc./fem.*) |
| ella | she | ellas | they (*fem.*) |
| usted (Ud.) | you (*sir, madam*) | ustedes (Uds.) | you (*ladies and gentlemen*) |

## PRÁCTICA

**A.** Tell which personal pronouns you would use to refer to different persons and groups of people in the class, and which you would use to speak directly to them. For example: use **ellas** to refer to three women, **Uds.** to address them directly.

**B.** Would you use **tú** or **usted(es)** to address these persons?

1. a client whom you have just met

2. a five-year-old child brought into the emergency room of the hospital where you are working

3. a husband and wife who have come to apply for welfare benefits

4. an elementary school class

# 4 REPASO DE VERBOS / Verb Review

Conjugation model charts for regular -**ar**, -**er**, and -**ir** verbs are given on pages 10–12. Stem-changing verbs and irregular verbs are presented throughout the text, where appropriate; they are also listed in Appendix II.

## PRÁCTICA

**A.** Using the verb charts as a model, complete a copy of the blank chart on page 13 with the conjugation of the following verbs:

| -ar | -er | -ir |
|---|---|---|
| comprar | beber | abrir |
| ganar | correr | recibir |

# -AR VERBS: HABLAR

| MODO INFINITIVO | | | | | |
|---|---|---|---|---|---|
| | yo | tú | él/ella/Ud. | nosotros | ellos/ellas/Uds. |
| 1. Infinitivo | hablar | | | | |
| 2. Gerundio | hablando | | | | |
| 3. Participio | hablado | | | | |

| MODO INDICATIVO | yo | tú | él/ella/Ud. | nosotros | vos. | ellos/ellas/Uds. |
|---|---|---|---|---|---|---|
| 4. Presente | hablo | hablas | habla | hablamos | | hablan |
| 5. Imperfecto | hablaba | hablabas | hablaba | hablábamos | | hablaban |
| 6. Pretérito | hablé | hablaste | habló | hablamos | | hablaron |
| 7. Presente perfecto | he hablado | has hablado | ha hablado | hemos hablado | | han hablado |
| 8. Pluscuamperfecto | había hablado | habías hablado | había hablado | habíamos hablado | | habían hablado |
| 9. Futuro | hablaré | hablarás | hablará | hablaremos | | hablarán |
| 10. Futuro perfecto | habré hablado | habrás hablado | habrá hablado | habremos hablado | | habrán hablado |

| MODO CONDICIONAL | yo | tú | él/ella/Ud. | nosotros | | ellos/ellas/Uds. |
|---|---|---|---|---|---|---|
| 11. Condicional simple | hablaría | hablarías | hablaría | hablaríamos | | hablarían |
| 12. Condicional perfecto | habría hablado | habrías hablado | habría hablado | habríamos hablado | | habrían hablado |

| MODO SUBJUNTIVO | yo | tú | él/ella/Ud. | nosotros | | ellos/ellas/Uds. |
|---|---|---|---|---|---|---|
| 13. Presente del subj. | hable | hables | hable | hablemos | | hablen |
| 14. Imperfecto del subj. | hablara | hablaras | hablara | habláramos | | hablaran |
| 15. Presente perfecto | haya hablado | hayas hablado | haya hablado | hayamos hablado | | hayan hablado |
| 16. Pluscuamperfecto | hubiera hablado* | hubieras hablado | hubiera hablado | hubiéramos hablado | | hubieran hablado |

| MODO IMPERATIVO | | tú | él/ella/Ud. | nosotros | | ellos/ellas/Uds. |
|---|---|---|---|---|---|---|
| 17. Positivo | | habla | hable | hablemos | | hablen |
| 18. Negativo | | no hables | no hable | no hablemos | | no hablen |

*hubiese hablado, hubieses hablado, etcétera

# -ER VERBS: COMER

| MODO INFINITIVO | | | | | | |
|---|---|---|---|---|---|---|
| 1. Infinitivo | comer | | | | | |
| 2. Gerundio | comiendo | | | | | |
| 3. Participio | comido | | | | | |

| MODO INDICATIVO | yo | tú | él/ella/Ud. | nosotros | vos. | ellos/ellas/Uds. |
|---|---|---|---|---|---|---|
| 4. Presente | como | comes | come | comemos | | comen |
| 5. Imperfecto | comía | comías | comía | comíamos | | comían |
| 6. Pretérito | comí | comiste | comió | comimos | | comieron |
| 7. Presente perfecto | he comido | has comido | ha comido | hemos comido | | han comido |
| 8. Pluscuamperfecto | había comido | habías comido | había comido | habíamos comido | | habían comido |
| 9. Futuro | comeré | comerás | comerá | comeremos | | comerán |
| 10. Futuro perfecto | habré comido | habrás comido | habrá comido | habremos comido | | habrán comido |

| MODO CONDICIONAL | yo | tú | él/ella/Ud. | nosotros | vos. | ellos/ellas/Uds. |
|---|---|---|---|---|---|---|
| 11. Condicional simple | comería | comerías | comería | comeríamos | | comerían |
| 12. Condicional perfecto | habría comido | habrías comido | habría comido | habríamos comido | | habrían comido |

| MODO SUBJUNTIVO | yo | tú | él/ella/Ud. | nosotros | vos. | ellos/ellas/Uds. |
|---|---|---|---|---|---|---|
| 13. Presente del subj. | coma | comas | coma | comamos | | coman |
| 14. Imperfecto del subj. | comiera | comieras | comiera | comiéramos | | comieran |
| 15. Presente perfecto | haya comido | hayas comido | haya comido | hayamos comido | | hayan comido |
| 16. Pluscuamperfecto | hubiera comido* | hubieras comido | hubiera comido | hubiéramos comido | | hubieran comido |

| MODO IMPERATIVO | yo | tú | él/ella/Ud. | nosotros | vos. | ellos/ellas/Uds. |
|---|---|---|---|---|---|---|
| 17. Positivo | | come | coma | comamos | | coman |
| 18. Negativo | | no comas | no coma | no comamos | | no coman |

*hubiese comido, hubieses comido, etcétera

# -IR VERBS: VIVIR

| MODO INFINITIVO | yo | tú | él/ella/Ud. | nosotros | vos. | ellos/ellas/Uds. |
|---|---|---|---|---|---|---|
| 1. Infinitivo | vivir | | | | | |
| 2. Gerundio | viviendo | | | | | |
| 3. Participio | vivido | | | | | |
| **MODO INDICATIVO** | | | | | | |
| 4. Presente | vivo | vives | vive | vivimos | | viven |
| 5. Imperfecto | vivía | vivías | vivía | vivíamos | | vivían |
| 6. Pretérito | viví | viviste | vivió | vivimos | | vivieron |
| 7. Presente perfecto | he vivido | has vivido | ha vivido | hemos vivido | | han vivido |
| 8. Pluscuamperfecto | había vivido | habías vivido | había vivido | habíamos vivido | | habían vivido |
| 9. Futuro | viviré | vivirás | vivirá | viviremos | | vivirán |
| 10. Futuro perfecto | habré vivido | habrás vivido | habrá vivido | habremos vivido | | habrán vivido |
| **MODO CONDICIONAL** | | | | | | |
| 11. Condicional simple | viviría | vivirías | viviría | viviríamos | | vivirían |
| 12. Condicional perfecto | habría vivido | habrías vivido | habría vivido | habríamos vivido | | habrían vivido |
| **MODO SUBJUNTIVO** | | | | | | |
| 13. Presente del subj. | viva | vivas | viva | vivamos | | vivan |
| 14. Imperfecto del subj. | viviera | vivieras | viviera | viviéramos | | vivieran |
| 15. Presente perfecto | haya vivido | hayas vivido | haya vivido | hayamos vivido | | hayan vivido |
| 16. Pluscuamperfecto | hubiera vivido* | hubieras vivido | hubiera vivido | hubiéramos vivido | | hubieran vivido |
| **MODO IMPERATIVO** | | | | | | |
| 17. Positivo | | vive | viva | vivamos | | vivan |
| 18. Negativo | | no vivas | no viva | no vivamos | | no vivan |

*hubiese vivido, hubieses vivido, etcétera

PRÁCTICA

| | yo | tú | él/ella/Ud. | nosotros | vos. | ellos/ellas/Uds. |
|---|---|---|---|---|---|---|
| **MODO INFINITIVO** | | | | | | |
| 1. Infinitivo | | | | | | |
| 2. Gerundio | | | | | | |
| 3. Participio | | | | | | |
| **MODO INDICATIVO** | | | | | | |
| 4. Presente | | | | | | |
| 5. Imperfecto | | | | | | |
| 6. Pretérito | | | | | | |
| 7. Presente perfecto | | | | | | |
| 8. Pluscuamperfecto | | | | | | |
| 9. Futuro | | | | | | |
| 10. Futuro perfecto | | | | | | |
| **MODO CONDICIONAL** | | | | | | |
| 11. Condicional simple | | | | | | |
| 12. Condicional perfecto | | | | | | |
| **MODO SUBJUNTIVO** | | | | | | |
| 13. Presente del subj. | | | | | | |
| 14. Imperfecto del subj. | | | | | | |
| 15. Presente perfecto | | | | | | |
| 16. Pluscuamperfecto | | | | | | |
| **MODO IMPERATIVO** | | | | | | |
| 17. Positivo | | | | | | |
| 18. Negativo | | | | | | |

**B.** Working with another student, ask and answer the following questions, using these personal pronouns in your answers: **yo, nosotros, Ud., ellas, él, Uds., tú.** Change the question by using the words given in parentheses.

1. ¿Quién compra *la casa*? (*la medicina, el seguro, los libros*)

2. ¿Quién bebe *agua*? (*leche, cerveza, café*)

3. ¿Quién abre *la botella*? (*la puerta, el armario, el sobre*)

**C.** Working with another student, ask and answer the following questions, changing the verb forms and personal pronouns as indicated.

1. ¿Cuánto dinero gana *Ud.*? (*él, tú, ellas, nosotros*)

2. ¿Corre *ella* a la cita? (*nosotros, Ud., tú, Jorge*)

3. ¿Cuándo reciben *ellos* el cheque? (*yo, María, Ud., ella, tú*)

**D.** Repeat exercise C in the preterite, imperfect, and future tenses.

## 5 ADJETIVOS DEMOSTRATIVOS / Demonstrative Adjectives

The demonstrative adjectives point out specific nouns: *this* pencil, *that* apple. They show the distance of persons, places or objects from the speaker: 1) *this/these*; 2) *that/those*; 3) *that/those* (farther away or quite distant).

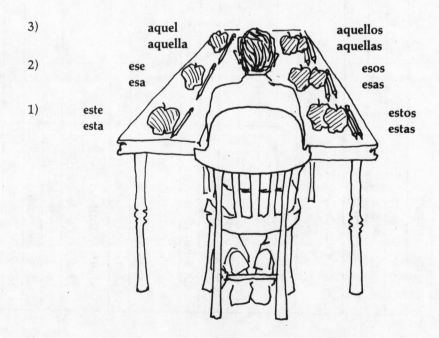

| | | |
|---|---|---|
| 3) | **aquel** / **aquella** | **aquellos** / **aquellas** |
| 2) | **ese** / **esa** | **esos** / **esas** |
| 1) | **este** / **esta** | **estos** / **estas** |

# PRÁCTICA

**A.** Working with another student, ask and answer the following questions. Use all forms of the demonstrative adjectives: **este, ese, aquel.**

1. ¿De quién es _____ lápiz?

   _____ lápiz es mío.

2. ¿De quién es _____ manzana?

   _____ manzana es tuya.

3. ¿De quién son _____ lápices?

   _____ lápices son de ella.

4. ¿De quién son _____ manzanas?

   _____ manzanas son de ellos.

**B.** Working with another student, ask and answer the questions in exercise A, using items from your field of interest.

*General Interest:* carro (coche, automóvil), documentos, botella, solicitudes

*Health Care:* receta, radiografías, jarabe, barbitúricos

*Law Enforcement:* motocicleta, huellas, reloj, zapatos

*Education:* nota, libretas, mesabanco, libros

*Welfare:* fábrica, herramientas, equipo, gastos

*Business:* empresa, cuentas, banco, intereses

# 6 ADJETIVOS POSESIVOS / Possessive Adjectives

**Possessive adjectives: singular object**

| | |
|---|---|
| Él es **mi** hermano. | *He is my brother.* |
| Éste es **tu** número de seguro. | *This is your insurance number.* |
| Éste es **su** número de teléfono. | *This is his (her, your, their) telephone number.* |
| Es **nuestro** número de teléfono/ **nuestra** casa. | *It's our telephone number/ our house.* |

**Possessive adjectives: plural object**

| | |
|---|---|
| Ellos son **mis** hermanos. | *They are my brothers.* |
| Éstos son **tus** números de seguro. | *These are your insurance numbers.* |
| Éstos son **sus** números de teléfono. | *These are his (her, your, their) telephone numbers.* |
| Son **nuestros** números de teléfono/ **nuestras** casas. | *They are our telephone numbers/ our houses.* |

## PRÁCTICA

Working with another student, use the vocabulary from exercise 5.B to ask and answer questions with **¿De quién es/son . . .?**, according to the model.

*Model:*   *¿De quién es* el equipo?

       *Es mi (tu, su, nuestro . . .) equipo.*

# 7 MIEMBROS DE LA FAMILIA / Family Members

| | | | |
|---|---|---|---|
| **abuela** | grandmother | **nuera** | daughter-in-law |
| **abuelo** | grandfather | **padrastro** | stepfather |
| **cuñada** | sister-in-law | **padre (papá)** | father (dad) |
| **cuñado** | brother-in-law | **padres** (*m pl*) | parents |
| **esposa** | wife | **parientes** (*m pl*) | relatives |
| **esposo** | husband | **prima** | cousin |
| **hermana** | sister | **primo** | cousin |
| **hermano** | brother | **prometida (novia)** | fiancée |
| **hija** | daughter | **prometido (novio)** | fiancé |
| **hijo** | son | **sobrina** | niece |
| **madrastra** | stepmother | **sobrino** | nephew |
| **madre (mamá)** | mother (mom) | **suegra** | mother-in-law |
| **nieta** | granddaughter | **suegro** | father-in-law |
| **nieto** | grandson | **tía** | aunt |
| **novia** | girlfriend | **tío** | uncle |
| **novio** | boyfriend | **yerno** | son-in-law |

## PRÁCTICA

**A.** Working with another student, ask and answer the following questions, substituting as many family members as possible from the list, as well as names from **Nombres y apellidos hispánicos.**

*Singular model:*   ¿Cómo se llama su _____?

           Mi _____ se llama _____.

     ¿Cómo se llama su *abuela*?            *What's your grandmother's name?*

     Mi *abuela* se llama *Alicia*.            *My grandmother's name is Alicia.*

*Plural model:*   ¿Cómo se llaman sus _____?

           Mis _____ se llaman _____ y _____.

     ¿Cómo se llaman sus *hermanas*?        *What are your sisters' names?*

     Mis *hermanas* se llaman *Ana* y        *My sisters' names are Ana and*
       *Rosita.*                               *Rosita.*

**B.** Working with another student, ask and answer questions based on the model, using **Tomás** as your reference point. Vary the family members.

*Model:* ¿Quién es (¿Cómo se llama) *el abuelo* de Tomás?

*El abuelo* de Tomás es (se llama) *Francisco.*

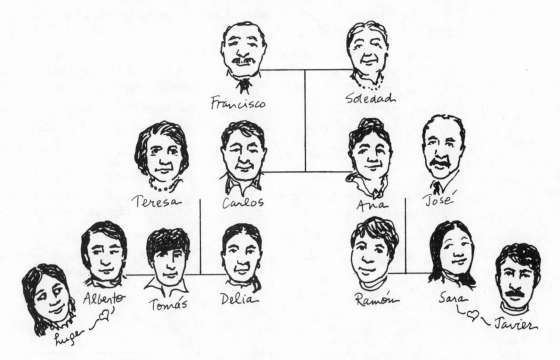

**C.** Add last names to the family tree members given in exercise B. Then, working with another student, ask and answer questions such as: **¿Cuál es el apellido de Delia?** Provide complete names for married female members of the family.

# 8 DÍAS DE LA SEMANA / Days of the Week

Note that the days of the week are not capitalized in Spanish.

**domingo  lunes  martes  miércoles  jueves  viernes  sábado**

1. Hoy (*today*). Hoy es lunes.

2. Mañana (*tomorrow*). Mañana es martes.

3. Pasado mañana (*day after tomorrow*). Pasado mañana será miércoles.

4. Ayer (*yesterday*). Ayer fue domingo.

5. Anteayer/antier/antes de ayer (*day before yesterday*). Antier fue sábado.

The definite article expresses *on* with days of the week: **el/los lunes** (*on Monday/Mondays*).

## PRÁCTICA

**A.** Using any day of the week as **hoy**, say sentences 1-5, changing the names of the days as needed.

**B.** Working with another student, ask and answer the following questions, using different days of the week.

1. ¿Para qué día es su cita con el (médico, abogado, maestro, trabajador social, jefe)?

   Mi cita es para el _____.

   *What day is your appointment with the (doctor, lawyer, teacher, social worker, director)?*

   *My appointment is on/for _____.*

2. ¿Cuándo llamo para la cita?

   Llame para la cita el _____.

   *When do I call for the appointment?*

   *Call for the appointment on _____.*

3. ¿Para cuándo es su cita?

   Mi cita es para (hoy, mañana, pasado mañana, el _____).

   *When is your appointment?*

   *My appointment is for (today, tomorrow, the day after tomorrow, _____).*

4. ¿Para cuándo fue su cita?

   Mi cita fue para (ayer, antes de ayer, antier, el _____).

   *When was your appointment?*

   *My appointment was for (yesterday, the day before yesterday, _____).*

# 9 PRONOMBRES POSESIVOS / Possessive Pronouns

The following chart illustrates the forms and uses of possessive pronouns, using singular and plural objects.

|  | MINE | YOUR(S) | HIS/HERS/ITS/ YOURS/THEIRS | OUR(S) |
|---|---|---|---|---|
| Este documento es *mío.* Éste es *mío.* | mío | tuyo | suyo | nuestro |
| Esta solicitud es *mía.* Ésta es *mía.* | mía | tuya | suya | nuestra |
| Estos papeles son *míos.* Éstos son *míos.* | míos | tuyos | suyos | nuestros |
| Estas huellas son *mías.* Éstas son *mías.* | mías | tuyas | suyas | nuestras |

## PRÁCTICA

Working with another student, ask and answer the following questions, using possessive pronouns that refer to: yourself, yourself and a friend, Juana and Ramón, your partner, Ramón.

1. ¿De quién es este documento?

2. ¿De quién es esta solicitud?

3. ¿De quién(es) son estos papeles?

4. ¿De quién(es) son estas huellas?

# 10 NÚMEROS CARDINALES / Cardinal Numbers

| | | | |
|---|---|---|---|
| 1 uno | 11 once | 21 veinte y uno | 200 doscientos/as |
| 2 dos | 12 doce | 22 veinte y dos | 300 trescientos/as |
| 3 tres | 13 trece | 30 treinta | 400 cuatrocientos/as |
| 4 cuatro | 14 catorce | 40 cuarenta | 500 quinientos/as |
| 5 cinco | 15 quince | 50 cincuenta | 600 seiscientos/as |
| 6 seis | 16 diez y seis | 60 sesenta | 700 setecientos/as |
| 7 siete | 17 diez y siete | 70 setenta | 800 ochocientos/as |
| 8 ocho | 18 diez y ocho | 80 ochenta | 900 novecientos/as |
| 9 nueve | 19 diez y nueve | 90 noventa | 1000 mil |
| 10 diez | 20 veinte | 100 cien/ciento | 2000 dos mil |

In Spanish, the indefinite article is not used with **mil: Tengo mil dólares.** Nº is the abbreviation for **número** (*number*). Years are expressed as follows:

1981    mil novecientos ochenta y uno

## PRÁCTICA

**A.** Say the following numbers aloud in Spanish. Try to avoid looking at their spelled forms, given to the right.

| | |
|---|---|
| 2 - 12 | dos - doce |
| 3 - 13 | tres - trece |
| 60 - 70 | sesenta - setenta |
| 148 | ciento cuarenta y ocho |
| 200 muchachos | doscientos muchachos |
| 200 muchachas | doscientas muchachas |
| 500 | quinientos |
| 756 | setecientos cincuenta y seis |
| 999 | novecientos noventa y nueve |
| 100 | ciento |
| 100 pacientes | cien pacientes |
| 102 | ciento dos |
| 3000 | tres mil |

**B.** Say the following numbers aloud in Spanish. Then have someone say them to you in Spanish while you practice writing them down as numbers: **quince ⟶ 15.**

| 43 | 65 | 113 | 479 | 904 | 503 | 1949 | 1957 | 1515 |
|----|----|-----|-----|-----|-----|------|------|------|
| 67 | 72 | 469 | 782 | 555 | 717 | 1971 | 1966 | 2314 |
| 76 | 32 | 707 | 675 | 873 | 999 | 1923 | 1049 | 5754 |
| 32 | 54 | 550 | 856 | 504 | 973 | 1944 | 1981 | 3847 |

**C.** Working with another student, ask and answer the following questions, varying the numbers. Practice writing down the numbers as they are said.

1. ¿Cuál es su número de teléfono?

   Mi número de teléfono es 443-56-87 (cuatrocientos cuarenta y tres, cincuenta y seis, ochenta y siete).*

   *What's your phone number?*

   *My phone number is four four three, five six eight seven.*

2. ¿Cuál es su número de seguro social?

   Mi número de seguro social es 357-60-6789 (trescientos cincuenta y siete, sesenta, seis mil setecientos ochenta y nueve).*

   *What's your social security number?*

   *My social security number is three five seven, sixty, six seven eight nine.*

3. ¿Cuál es el número de su casa?

   El número de mi casa es 666.

   *What's your house number?*

   *My house number is 666.*

*As in English, there are many ways to say phone numbers and social security numbers in Spanish.

# 11 EL VERBO TENER / The Verb to Have

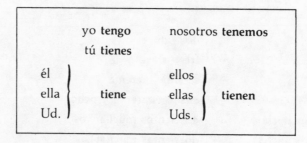

|  |  |  |
|---|---|---|
| yo **tengo** | nosotros **tenemos** | |
| tú **tienes** | | |
| él | ellos | |
| ella } **tiene** | ellas } **tienen** | |
| Ud. | Uds. | |

**Idiomatic uses of tener:**

| tener . . . años | to be . . . years old |
|---|---|
| calor | warm, hot |
| frío | cold |
| hambre | hungry |
| miedo | afraid |

| | |
|---|---|
| **razón** | right, correct |
| **sed** | thirsty |
| **sueño** | sleepy |
| **tener ganas de** + *infinitive* | to feel like (doing something) |
| **tener que** + *infinitive* | to have to (do something) |

## PRÁCTICA

**A.** Working with another student, ask and answer the following questions, using **tener.**

1. ¿Tiene Ud. su (documento, recibo, tarjeta de identificación, mica)?

   *Do you have your (document, receipt, I.D. card, immigration card)?*

2. ¿Cuánto dinero tiene su (miembro de la familia)?

   *How much money does your (family member) have?*

3. ¿Cuántos (carros, hijos, empleos) tiene Ud.?

   *How many (cars, children, jobs) do you have?*

4. ¿Cuánta (medicina, gasolina) tiene Ud.? ¿Mucha o poca?

   *How much (medicine, gasoline) do you have? A lot or a little?*

5. ¿Cuántas (hijas, botellas, recetas) tiene Ud.?

   *How many (daughters, bottles, prescriptions) do you have?*

**B.** Working with another student, ask and answer questions based on the following phrases, using **tener** idioms.

1. ¿Cuántos años _____ tú?

   *How old are you?*

   ¿Cuántos años tiene tu (miembro de la familia)?

   *How old is your (family member)?*

2. ¿_____ calor en el verano?

   *_____ warm in the summer?*

   ¿con este abrigo?

   *in this coat?*

3. ¿_____ frío en el invierno?

   *_____ cold in the winter?*

   ¿en las montañas?

   *in the mountains?*

4. ¿_____ ganas de comprar algo?

   *_____ feel like buying something?*

   ¿beber algo? ¿recibir algo?

   *drinking something? receiving something?*

5. ¿_____ hambre todos los días?

   *_____ hungry every day?*

   ¿en el restaurante?

   *at the restaurant?*

6. ¿_____ miedo de la oscuridad?

   *_____ afraid of the dark?*

   ¿de los fantasmas?

   *of ghosts?*

7. ¿_____ que comer? ¿beber?

   *_____ have to eat? to drink?*

   ¿hablar? ¿trabajar? ¿dormir?

   *to speak? to work? to sleep?*

8.  ¿_____ razón siempre?                    _____ *always right?*

9.  ¿_____ sed en el desierto?               _____ *thirsty in the desert?*

      ¿en este momento?                        *right now?*

10. ¿_____ sueño a las once de la            _____ *sleepy at eleven at night?*
    noche? ¿en este momento?                   *right now?*

      ¿_____ sueño después de comer?         _____ *sleepy after eating?*

# 12  MESES DEL AÑO Y PRETÉRITO DE NACER / Months of the Year and Preterite of to Be Born

Note that the months of the year are not capitalized in Spanish.

| enero | abril | julio | octubre |
|-------|-------|-------|---------|
| febrero | mayo | agosto | noviembre |
| marzo | junio | se(p)tiembre | diciembre |

el **primero** de julio   *the first of July*
el **cinco** de marzo   *the fifth of March*

| Preterite of **nacer** | |
|-------------|-------------|
| **nací** | nacimos |
| **naciste** | |
| **nació** | nacieron |

## PRÁCTICA

Working with another student, ask and answer questions based on the following phrases, using the months of the year and **nacer.**

1.  ¿Qué mes viene después de _____?          *What month follows _____?*

   ¿Qué mes viene antes de _____?          *What month comes before _____?*

2.  ¿En qué mes nació su (miembro de            *When was your (family member) born?*
    la familia)?

   Mi _____ nació en _____.              *My _____ was born in _____.*

3. ¿En qué mes nació Ud.?

Yo nací en el mes de _____.

*When were you born?*

*I was born in the month of _____.*

4. ¿En qué fecha naciste tú?

Yo nací el _____ de _____ de
19_____.

*What is your birth date?*

*I was born the _____ of _____,
19_____.*

5. ¿En qué fecha nació su hijo/a?

Mi hijo/a nació el _____ de _____
de 19_____.

¿En qué fechas nacieron sus
hijos/as?

Mis hijos nacieron el _____ de
_____ de 19_____ y el _____ de
_____ de 19_____.

*When was your son/daughter born?*

*My son/daughter was born on the
_____ of _____, 19_____.*

*When were your children born?*

*My children were born on the _____
of _____, 19_____, and the _____
of _____, 19_____.*

6. ¿Dónde nació Ud.?

Yo nací en _____.

*Where were you born?*

*I was born in _____.*

# 13 NÚMEROS ORDINALES / Ordinal Numbers

| | | | |
|---|---|---|---|
| **primero/a** | first | **sexto/a** | sixth |
| **segundo/a** | second | **séptimo/a** | seventh |
| **tercero/a** | third | **octavo/a** | eighth |
| **cuarto/a** | fourth | **noveno/a** | ninth |
| **quinto/a** | fifth | **décimo/a** | tenth |

Before masculine singular nouns, **primero** and **tercero** shorten to **primer** and **tercer** respectively: **primer médico**, **tercer documento**.

## PRÁCTICA

**A.** Working with another student, ask and answer questions based on the following phrases, using the ordinal numbers.

1. ¿Es su primera visita aquí?

Sí, es mi primera visita aquí.

No, es mi cuarta visita aquí.

*Is this your first visit here?*

*Yes, it's my first visit here.*

*No, it's my fourth visit here.*

2. ¿Es su _____ infracción?

Sí/no, es mi _____ infracción.

*Is it your _____ citation?*

*Yes/no, it's my _____ citation.*

3. ¿Es su _____ operación?

Sí/no, es mi _____ operación.

*Is it your _____ operation?*

*Yes/no, it's my _____ operation.*

4. ¿Cuál es su primer nombre?                *What is your first name?*

   Mi primer nombre es _____.               *My first name is _____.*

5. ¿Es su primera vez aquí?                  *Is it your first time here?*

   Sí/no, es mi _____ vez aquí.             *Yes/no, it's my _____ time here.*

# 14 INTERROGATIVOS / Interrogatives

All interrogative words have a written accent mark in Spanish.

| ¿Cómo? | *How?* |

¿Cómo se llama Ud.?                          *What is your name?*
¿Cómo está Ud.?                              *How are you?*

| ¿Cuándo? | *When?* |

¿Cuándo nació Ud.?                           *When were you born?*
¿Cuándo trabajó allí?                        *When did you work there?*

| ¿Cuál? ¿Cuáles? | *Which (one)? Which (ones)?* |

¿Cuál es su hijo?                            *Which (one) is your child (son)?*
¿Cuál es su apellido?                        *What is your last name?*
¿Cuáles son sus hijos?                       *Which (ones) are your sons (children)?*
¿Cuáles son sus síntomas?                    *What are your symptoms?*

| ¿Qué? | *What?* |

¿Qué edad tiene?                             *How old are you?*
¿Qué desea?                                  *What would you like?*
¿Qué tiene para mí?                          *What do you have for me?*

| ¿Quién? ¿Quiénes? | *Who?* |

¿Quién es su padre?                          *Who is your father?*
¿Quién tiene el documento?                   *Who has the document?*
¿Quiénes son sus padres?                     *Who are your parents?*
¿Quiénes viven en su casa?                   *Who lives at your house?*

| ¿A quién? | *Whom?* |

¿A quién llamamos en caso de emergencia?     *Whom do we call in case of emergency?*
¿A quién quiere ver Ud.?                      *Whom do you wish to see?*

| ¿De quién? | *Whose?* |

¿De quién es el automóvil?                   *Whose car is it?*
¿De quién son estas llaves?                  *Whose keys are these?*

| | |
|---|---|
| **¿Por qué?** | *Why?* |
| ¿Por qué no trabaja Ud.? | *Why don't you work?* |
| ¿Por qué solicita ayuda? | *Why are you applying for help?* |
| **¿Cuánto?** | *How much?* |
| ¿Cuánto gana Ud.? | *How much do you earn?* |
| ¿Cuánto pesa Ud.? | *How much do you weigh?* |
| **¿Cuántas veces?** | *How often? How many times?* |
| ¿Cuántas veces toma esto por día? | *How many times per day do you take this?* |
| ¿Cuántas veces por día se marea? | *How many times a day do you get dizzy?* |
| **¿Dónde?** | *Where?* |
| ¿Dónde está su esposo? | *Where is your husband?* |
| ¿Dónde le duele? | *Where does it hurt you?* |
| **¿A dónde?** | *Where (to)?* |
| ¿Adónde va Ud.? | *Where are you going?* |
| ¿Adónde mandamos la cuenta? | *Where do we send the bill?* |

## PRÁCTICA

**A.** Practice reading the preceding questions aloud.

**B.** Answer all of the preceding questions. Listen to the answers that other students in the class give, and try to write down the information as they say it, as if you were interviewing them.

**C.** Working with another student, ask and answer the questions. The person asking the questions should record the information given.

## 15 LOS USOS DEL VERBO SER / The Uses of the Verb to Be (ser)

| | |
|---|---|
| soy | somos |
| eres | |
| es | son |

**I.** to express ORIGIN: **ser** + **de** + *place of origin*

Note that the names of certain countries require the use of the definite article.

| la Argentina | Chile | el Japón | la República Dominicana |
| Bolivia | Ecuador | México | El Salvador |
| Brasil | España | Nueva York | Sud América |
| California | los Estados Unidos | Paraguay | Texas |
| Colombia | Guadalajara | el Perú | Uruguay |
| Cuba | Guatemala | Puerto Rico | Venezuela |

## II.   with NATIONALITY and REGIONAL ADJECTIVES

These adjectives correspond to the places given in section A. Note that nationality and regional adjectives are not capitalized in Spanish.

| argentino/a | chileno/a | japonés(a) | dominicano/a |
| boliviano/a | ecuatoriano/a | mexicano/a | salvadoreño/a |
| brasileño/a | español(a) | neoyorquino/a | sudamericano/a |
| californiano/a | estadounidense | paraguayo/a | texano/a |
| colombiano/a | tapatío/a | peruano/a | uruguayo/a |
| cubano/a | guatemalteco/a | puertorriqueño/a | venezolano/a |

## PRÁCTICA

Working with another student, ask and answer questions based on the model, using places of origin and nationality and regional adjectives.

*Model:*   ¿Es Ud. de _____?

Sí, soy (adjective).

## III.   to express PROFESSIONS

The names of some professions can refer to men or women, depending on which article is used: **el/la policía.** The names of other professions have a masculine and a feminine form: **el maestro, la maestra**

| **abogado/a** | lawyer | **empacador(a)** | packer |
| **albañil** | bricklayer | **enfermero/a** | nurse |
| **banquero** | banker | **jardinero/a** | gardener |
| **cajero/a** | teller, cashier | **juez** | judge |
| **campesino/a** | farm worker | **mecánico/a** | mechanic |
| **cocinero/a** | cook | **mecanógrafo/a** | typist |
| **comerciante** | business person | **mesero/a** | waiter/waitress |
| **contador(a)** | bookkeeper | **plomero** | plumber |
| **criado/a** | servant | **policía** | police officer |
| **doctor(a)** | doctor | **secretario/a** | secretary |

## PRÁCTICA

Working with another student, ask and answer questions based on the model, using the names of professions. The indefinite article (**un/una**) is not needed.

*Model:*   ¿Es Ud. _____?

Sí, soy _____.

## IV. with COLORS

| | | | |
|---|---|---|---|
| amarillo/a | yellow | gris | grey |
| anaranjado/a | orange | morado/a | purple |
| azul | blue | negro/a | black |
| blanco/a | white | rojo/a | red |
| café | brown | verde | green |
| color de rosa | pink | | |

## PRÁCTICA

Working with another student, ask and answer questions based on the model, using colors and items from your field of interest.

*Model:* ¿De qué color es su _____?

Mi _____ es rojo y blanco.

*General Interest:* carro, casa, libros, flores

*Health Care:* cápsulas, jarabe, polvo, receta

*Law Enforcement:* celda, barba, julia, cofres

*Education:* mesabanco, cuadernos, bandera, pizarra

*Welfare:* taller, fábrica, regalo, autobús

*Business:* carta, billete, tienda, tarjeta de crédito

## V. to express the MATERIAL of which something is made

| | | | | | |
|---|---|---|---|---|---|
| algodón (m) | cotton | hierro | iron | piedra | stone |
| aluminio | aluminum | lana | wool | plástico | plastic |
| cobre (m) | copper | madera | wood | plata | silver |
| cuero | leather | metal (m) | metal | seda | silk |
| fibra | fiber | oro | gold | tela | cloth |
| goma | rubber | papel (m) | paper | vidrio | glass |

## PRÁCTICA

Working with another student, ask and answer questions based on the model, using the names of materials and items from your field of interest.

*Model:* ¿De qué material es su _____?

Mi _____ es de *plástico y metal.*

*General Interest:* televisor, carro, lámpara, tarjeta de crédito

*Health Care:* curita, báscula, termómetro, zapatos

*Law Enforcement:* suéter, neumático, camisa, barba

*Education:* libro, bandera, escritorio, pluma

*Welfare:* herramienta, ropa, mica, dinero

*Business:* caja fuerte, factura, dulce, disco

**VI.**   to tell TIME

¿Qué hora es?  ⎱
                 *What time is it?*
¿Qué horas son? ⎰

**Es la una.**   *It is one o'clock.*      **Son las dos.**   *It is two o'clock.*
**A la una.**    *At one o'clock.*         **A las dos.**     *At two o'clock.*

## PRÁCTICA

Working with another student, ask and answer the following questions.

1. ¿Qué hora es?

2. ¿Qué horas son?

3. ¿A qué hora es su cita?

**VII.**   with PERMANENT CHARACTERISTICS

| | | | |
|---|---|---|---|
| **alegre** | happy | **nuevo/a** | new |
| **amable** | kind, nice | **odioso/a** | despicable, hateful |
| **bueno/a** | good | **simpático/a** | nice |
| **malo/a** | bad | **triste** | sad |
| **mentiroso/a** | deceitful | **vivo/a** | bright, quick |

## PRÁCTICA

Working with another student, ask and answer questions based on the model, using the preceding adjectives and some of the nouns of profession. The use of **siempre** in these sentences conveys the idea of permanency; it implies that, as a rule, these characteristics are part of someone's personality.

MODEL:   ¿Es siempre *simpático* su *jefe*?

¿Es Ud. siempre *amable*?

**VIII.**   to IDENTIFY persons, places, or things

**Éste es mi esposo.**          *This is my husband.*
**Ése es mi barrio.**           *That's my neighborhood.*
**Aquel formulario es mío.**    *That application is mine.*

## PRÁCTICA

Working with another student, ask and answer questions based on the model, using **ser** to identify these persons or objects: **niño**, **rayos equis**, **carro**, **texto**, **solicitud**, **cheque**, **clientes**.

*Model:*   ¿De quién es este _____?

Este _____ es mío.

## 16 LOS USOS DEL VERBO ESTAR / The Uses of the Verb to Be (estar)

| | |
|---|---|
| estoy | estamos |
| estás | |
| está | están |

**I.** to express LOCATION

Mi esposa está en casa.
El recibo no está aquí.
Nuestros ahorros están en el banco.

*My wife is at home.*
*The receipt isn't here.*
*Our savings are in the bank.*

### PRÁCTICA

Working with another student, ask and answer questions based on the model, using items from your field of interest.

*Model:* ¿Dónde está el _____?

El _____ está en el _____.

*General Interest:* clase, dinero, profesor, barrio

*Health Care:* farmacia, clínica, laboratorio, enfermeras

*Law Enforcement:* cárcel, fiador, celda, juez

*Education:* cuaderno, bandera, biblioteca, textos

*Welfare:* fábrica, solicitudes, taller, psiquiatra

*Business:* banco, tienda, cheque, cajera

**II.** to describe a person's MENTAL STATE or CONDITION

| | | | |
|---|---|---|---|
| **alegre** | happy | **indiferente** | indifferent |
| **borracho/a** | drunk | **molesto/a** | upset |
| **calmado/a** | calm | **nervioso/a** | nervous |
| **cariñoso/a** | affectionate | **preocupado/a** | worried |
| **contento/a** | content | **risueño/a** | smiling, pleasant |
| **enojado/a** | angry | **triste** | sad |

### PRÁCTICA

Working with another student, ask and answer questions based on the model, using the preceding adjectives and some of the nouns of profession. The use of **ahora** in these sentences implies that the conditions or states described are temporary.

*Model:* ¿Cómo está el _____ ahora?

El _____ está _____ ahora.

**III.** to describe PHYSICAL STATES

**Health:** bien (*well*), enfermo/a (*sick*), sano/a (*healthy*)
**Climate:** bonito (*nice out*), lloviendo (*raining*), nublado (*cloudy*)
**Temperature of objects:** caliente (*hot, warm*), frío/a (*cold*), templado/a (*warm*)

## PRÁCTICA

Working with another student, ask and answer the following questions.

1. ¿Cómo están los niños (pacientes, sospechosos, estudiantes, clientes)?

2. ¿Cómo está afuera?

3. ¿Está frío/a (la sopa, el termómetro, la celda)?

**IV.** with the gerund, to form the PROGRESSIVE TENSES

| | |
|---|---|
| Yo **estoy/estaba** estudiando. | *I am/was studying.* |
| Tú **estás/estabas viviendo** en esta ciudad. | *You are/were living in this city.* |
| Él/ella **está/estaba bebiendo** demasiado. | *He/she is/was drinking too much.* |

## PRÁCTICA

Working with another student, ask and answer the following questions.

1. ¿Qué está Ud. buscando?

    Estoy buscando (los rayos equis, el carro, la clínica, el formulario, las facturas).

    *What are you looking for?*

    *I'm looking for the (X-rays, car, clinic, application, bills).*

2. ¿Dónde estaban viviendo Uds.?

    Estábamos viviendo en (esa ciudad, el campo, un apartamento, una casa pequeña).

    *Where were you living?*

    *We were living in (that city, the country, an apartment, a small house).*

# 17 PREGUNTAS Y RESPUESTAS BÁSICAS PARA SOLICITUDES / Basic Questions and Answers for Applications

**A.** Practice reading the following questions aloud.

**B.** Answer all of the following questions. Listen to the answers that other students in the class give, and try to write down the information as they say it, as if you were interviewing them.

**C.** Working with another student, ask and answer the questions. The person asking the questions should record the information given by his/her partner on the form on pages 37–38.

## I.  GENERAL INTEREST

1. ¿Cómo se llama Ud.?                           *What's your name?*
   Me llamo _____.
   ¿Cuál es su nombre?                            *What's your name?*

2. ¿Cuál es su domicilio?                         *What's your address?*
   ¿Dónde vive Ud.?                               *Where do you live?*
   ¿En qué calle vive?                            *What street do you live on?*
   ¿En qué ciudad vive?                           *What city do you live in?*
   Vivo en _____.

3. ¿Cuál es su número de teléfono?               *What's your telephone number?*
   Mi número de teléfono es _____.

4. ¿Cuál es su número de seguro                   *What's your social security number?*
   social?
   Mi número de seguro social es

   _____.

5. ¿Cuántos años tiene?                           *How old are you?*
   Tengo _____ años.

6. ¿Cuándo nació Ud.?                             *When were you born?*
   ¿En qué fecha nació?                           *What is your date of birth?*
   Nací el _____ de _____ de
   19_____.

7. ¿Dónde nació Ud.?                              *Where were you born?*
   Yo nací en _____.

8. ¿Es casado/a, soltero/a, viudo/a,             *Are you married, single, widowed,*
   divorciado/a, separado/a?                      *divorced, separated?*
   Soy _____.

9. ¿Cómo se llama su esposo/a?                    *What is your spouse's name?*
   Mi esposo/a se llama _____.

10. ¿Vive con su esposo/a?                    *Do you live with your spouse?*

    _____ vivo con mi esposo/a.

11. ¿Tiene Ud. hijos?                         *Do you have any children?*

    _____ tengo hijos.

    ¿Cuántos?                                 *How many?*

    Tengo _____ hijos.

    ¿Qué edad tienen?                         *What are their ages?*

    Tienen _____ y _____ años.

12. ¿Dónde trabaja?                           *Where do you work?*

    Yo trabajo en/para _____.

    ¿Qué puesto tiene Ud.?                    *What do you do? What is your job?*

    Soy _____.

13. ¿Para qué hora es su cita?               *When is your appointment?*

    Mi cita es para la(s) _____.

## II.  HEALTH CARE

14. ¿Es ésta su primera visita?              *Is this your first visit?*

    _____, ésta es mi _____ visita.

15. ¿Tiene Ud. seguro de salud, de           *Do you have health, accident, or hos-*
    accidente o de hospital?                  *pital insurance?*

    _____, tengo seguro de _____.

16. ¿Es Ud. alérgico/a a (el polen, las      *Are you allergic to (pollen, bee stings,*
    picaduras de abeja, la leche, el          *milk, dust)?*
    polvo)?

    _____, soy alérgico/a a(l) _____.

17. ¿A quién llamamos en caso de             *Whom do we call in case of emer-*
    emergencia?                               *gency?*

    Pueden llamar a (pariente, domi-
    cilio).

18. ¿Cuánto pesa Ud.?                         *How much do you weigh?*

    Peso _____ libras.

19. ¿Cuánto mide Ud.?                         *How tall are you?*

    Mido _____ pies _____ pulgadas.

20. ¿Dónde le duele?                          *Where do you hurt?*

    Me duele(n) _____.

21. ¿Qué problema tiene?                      *What is your problem?*

    No duermo. No tengo apetito.
    Me duele(n) _____.

22. ¿Qué enfermedades ha tenido?

He tenido (varicela, sarampión, tos ferina, paperas).

*What diseases have you had?*

*I've had (chicken pox, measles, whooping cough, mumps).*

23. ¿A quién mandamos la cuenta?

Pueden mandar la cuenta a (pariente, domicilio).

*To whom do we send the bill?*

## III. LAW ENFORCEMENT

24. ¿A qué velocidad iba Ud.?

Yo iba a _____ millas por hora.

*How fast were you going?*

25. ¿Es ésta su primera infracción?

_____, ésta es mi _____ infracción.

*Is this your first violation?*

26. ¿Ha estado bebiendo?

_____, he estado bebiendo.

*Have you been drinking?*

27. ¿Qué ha bebido Ud.?

He bebido (vino, cerveza, n° de tragos).

*What have you been drinking?*

*I've been drinking (wine, beer, number of drinks).*

28. ¿Tiene alguna identificación?

_____, tengo (una licencia de manejar, un pasaporte, una mica).

*Do you have any identification?*

*_____, I have (a driver's license, a passport, a green card).*

29. ¿Quién es el propietario del coche?

(Nombre) es el dueño del coche.

*Who is the owner of the car?*

30. ¿En cuánto valora lo robado?

Valoro lo robado en _____ dólares.

*What is the value of the stolen goods?*

31. ¿A qué hora cree que se cometió el robo?

Creo que el robo tomó lugar por la (mañana, tarde, noche).

*At what time do you think that the robbery took place?*

32. ¿Hubo algún testigo?

_____, hubo _____ testigos.

*Were there any witnesses?*

33. ¿Por dónde entraron los ladrones?

Entraron por (la ventana, la puerta, el sótano).

*How did the robbers enter?*

*They came in through (the window, the door, the basement).*

## IV. EDUCATION

34. ¿Qué nota es ésta?

Es la nota de (tardanza, permiso, del médico).

*What's this note?*

*It's the (late, permission, doctor's) slip.*

35. ¿Cuántas veces has faltado a la
    escuela?

    He faltado _____ veces.

*How many times have you missed classes?*

36. ¿Qué tarea estás entregando?

    Estoy entregando la tarea de
    (matemáticas, lectura, ciencia, historia).

*What homework are you turning in?*
*I'm turning in the (math, reading, science, history) homework.*

37. ¿Qué nota recibiste en el último
    examen?

*What grade did you get on the last exam?*

38. ¿Hasta qué página tienes que leer?

    Tengo que leer hasta la página
    _____.

*What page do you have to read to?*

39. ¿Qué carrera quieres estudiar?

    Quiero estudiar la carrera de (abogado, doctor, maestro).

*What career are you interested in studying for?*

40. ¿Cuándo fue tu última visita al
    dentista?

    Mi última visita al dentista fue el
    _____ de _____ de 19_____.

*When was your last visit to the dentist?*

41. ¿Qué vacunas te faltan por poner?

    Me faltan por poner la vacuna
    de(l) (polio, difteria).

*What vaccinations do you still need to get?*
*I still need to get my (polio, diphtheria) shot.*

42. ¿En qué nivel de lectura vas?

    Voy en el _____ nivel.

*What reading level are you in?*

43. ¿Sabes tus tablas de (sumar, multiplicar, restar, dividir)?

    _____, sé las tablas de _____.

*Do you know your (addition, multiplication, subtraction, division) tables?*

## V.  WELFARE

44. ¿Desde cuándo no trabaja?

    No trabajo desde hace _____
    meses.

    No trabajo desde el mes de _____.

*When did you work last?*
*I haven't worked for the past _____ months.*
*I haven't worked since (month).*

45. ¿Cuál fue su último empleo?

    Mi último empleo fue con _____.

*What was your last job?*

46. ¿Cuánto dinero gana (ganó) por
    semana/mes/año?

    Gano (gané) _____ por _____.

*How much money do (did) you earn per week/month/year?*

47. ¿Tiene Ud. transportación propia?    *Do you have your own transportation?*
    \_\_\_\_\_, tengo (carro, bicicleta, motocicleta).
    ¿Maneja Ud.?    *Do you drive?*
    \_\_\_\_\_ manejo.

48. ¿Qué gastos tiene Ud.?    *What expenses do you have?*
    Tengo gastos de (casa, seguro, unión, carro, utilidades/servicios municipales, deudas/drogas\*).    *I have (house, insurance, union, car, utilities, debt) expenses.*

49. ¿Qué servicio solicita?    *What service do you want?*
    Solicito (dinero en efectivo, ayuda médica, estampillas para comida).    *I need (cash, medical aid, food stamps).*

50. ¿Es Ud. dueño/a de su casa?    *Do you own your own home?*
    \_\_\_\_\_ soy dueño/a de mi casa.

51. ¿Tiene Ud. cuenta de ahorros?    *Do you have a savings account?*
    \_\_\_\_\_ tengo cuenta de ahorros.
    ¿Cuánto dinero tiene?    *How much money do you have in it?*
    Tengo \_\_\_\_\_ dólares.

52. ¿Qué ayuda está recibiendo ahora?    *What aid are you getting now?*
    Estoy recibiendo \_\_\_\_\_.

## VI. BUSINESS

53. ¿Qué tipo de cuenta quiere abrir?    *What type of account do you want to open?*

    Quiero abrir una cuenta (de ahorros, corriente).    *I want to open a (savings, checking) account.*

54. ¿Es Ud. el único titular de la cuenta?    *Is the account only in your name?*
    No, mi \_\_\_\_\_ también es titular.

55. ¿Con cuánto dinero quiere abrir su cuenta?    *How much money do you want to open your account with?*
    Quiero abrir la cuenta con \_\_\_\_\_ dólares.

56. ¿Quiere Ud. esa cantidad en efectivo, giro o cheque del banco?    *Do you want that amount in cash, money order or bank draft?*
    Quiero esa cantidad en \_\_\_\_\_.

57. ¿Cuál es el número de su cuenta?    *What is your account number?*
    El número de mi cuenta es \_\_\_\_\_.

\*In Mexico, *to have debts* is commonly expressed as **tener drogas.**

58. ¿Cómo quiere pagar?

Quiero pagar (con tarjeta de crédito, con dinero en efectivo, por
cheque).

*How do you want to pay?*

*I want to pay (with my credit card, in cash, by check).*

59. ¿Por qué devuelve este artículo?

Porque (está muy grande/pequeño,
no me queda, no me gusta el
color).

*Why are you returning this item?*

*Because (it's too big/small, it doesn't fit me, I don't like the color).*

60. ¿De qué color prefiere el artículo?

Lo prefiero en _____.

*In what color would you prefer it?*

61. ¿Cuánto dinero me ofrece por ello?

Le ofrezco _____ dólares.

*How much money will you give me for it?*

*I'll offer you _____ dollars.*

62. ¿Quiere su cambio en billete
grande o pequeño?

Quiero mi cambio en billete
_____.

*Do you want your change in large or small bills?*

## PRÁCTICA

The following are key words that should suggest questions similar to the preceding ones. Working with another student, formulate interview questions based
on the key words. Refer to the list of questions, if necessary.

*Model:*   ¿nombre? ——→ ¿Cómo se llama Ud.?

### I.   GENERAL INTEREST

1. ¿teléfono?
2. ¿estado civil?
3. ¿seguro social?
4. ¿domicilio?
5. ¿edad?
6. ¿fecha de nacimiento?
7. ¿lugar de nacimiento?
8. ¿hijos?
9. ¿cita?

### II.   HEALTH CARE

1. ¿estatura?
2. ¿alergia?
3. ¿la cuenta?
4. ¿enfermedades?
5. ¿dolor?
6. ¿nº de visita?
7. ¿emergencia?
8. ¿peso?
9. ¿seguro de salud?

### III.   LAW ENFORCEMENT

1. ¿testigos?
2. ¿bebido?
3. ¿identificación?
4. ¿velocidad?
5. ¿nº de infracción?
6. ¿tipo de bebida?
7. ¿propietario del coche?
8. ¿valor de lo robado?
9. ¿lugar de entrada?

### IV.   EDUCATION

1. ¿fecha de visita al
   dentista?
2. ¿nivel de lectura?
3. ¿página de lectura?
4. ¿tipo de nota?
5. ¿nº de faltas?
6. ¿nota del examen?
7. ¿carrera?
8. ¿vacuna?
9. ¿tablas?

## V. WELFARE

1. ¿transportación?
2. ¿último empleo?
3. ¿dueño de casa?

4. ¿salario?
5. ¿gastos?
6. ¿sin trabajo?

7. ¿servicio solicitado?
8. ¿cuenta de ahorros?
9. ¿ayuda recibida?

## VI. BUSINESS

1. ¿billete de cambio?
2. ¿tipo de cuenta?
3. ¿cantidad de depósito?

4. ¿titulares?
5. ¿n° de cuenta?
6. ¿color?

7. ¿forma de pago?
8. ¿oferta de dinero?
9. ¿por qué devolver?

## I. GENERAL INTEREST

Nombre _____

Domicilio _____

Número de teléfono _____ Seguro Social _____

Edad _____ Fecha de nacimiento _____

Lugar de nacimiento _____

Casado _____ Soltero _____ Viudo _____ Divorciado _____ Separado _____

Nombre de esposo/a _____ ¿Vive en casa? No _____ Sí _____

Número de hijos _____ Edades _____ Lugar de trabajo _____

_____ Tipo de trabajo_____

Hora de cita _____.

## II. HEALTH CARE

Número de visita médica _____ Seguro de: salud _____ accidente _____

hospital _____ Alergias _____

Nombre y domicilio de persona a llamar en caso de emergencia: _____

_____

Peso _____ Estatura _____ ¿Tiene dolores? _____

Problemas médicos _____

Enfermedades que ha tenido_____

Domicilio para mandar la cuenta _____

## III. LAW ENFORCEMENT

Velocidad _____ mph N° de infracción _____ ¿Bebido? _____ Sí_____ No_____

Tipo de bebida _____ Identificación _____ licencia de manejar _____

pasaporte _____ mica _____ Propietario del coche _____

Valor de lo robado _____ Hora del suceso _____ a.m. _____ p.m. _____

Testigos_____Lugar de entrada_____

## IV. EDUCATION

Nota de _____ tardanza _____ permiso _____ médico. Nº de faltas _____

Tarea entregada _____ Nota del último examen _____

Página de lectura_____ Carrera_____

Fecha de visita al dentista_____ de_____ de_____ Vacunas_____

Nivel de lectura _____ Tablas de _____ sumar _____ multiplicar _____

restar _____ dividir _____.

## V. WELFARE

No trabaja desde _____

Último empleo _____ Sueldo: Cantidad _____ por _____

¿Tiene transportación propia? No _____ Sí _____, carro _____ motocicleta _____

bicicleta _____ Gastos: casa _____ seguro _____ unión _____ deudas _____

utilidades (servicios municipales) _____

Servicio que solicita: dinero en efectivo _____ estampillas para comida _____

ayuda médica _____ ¿Es dueño/a de su casa? No _____ Sí _____

Cuenta de ahorros: No _____ Sí _____ Cantidad _____ ¿Qué ayuda recibe ahora? _____

_____

## VI. BUSINESS

Tipo de cuenta _____ ahorros _____ corriente. Titulares _____

Cantidad depósito _____ Devolución en _____ Nº de cuenta _____

Forma de pago _____ Razón por devolución del artículo _____

Color _____ Oferta de dinero _____ Billete de cambio _____

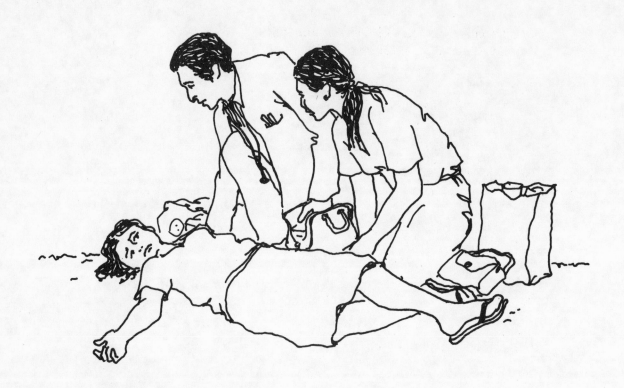

# CAPÍTULO 1

## La medicina/
## Health Care

# 1 DIÁLOGO /
## Dialog

### Una emergencia en la calle

*Enfermera:* Aquí, *doctor*, venga pronto. Hay un *accidente*. Una señorita *está boca arriba* sobre la calle. Creo que está *herida* — hay mucha *sangre*.

*Doctor:* ¿Una señorita? Y, ¿qué le pasa? (Pasan a la calle.) ¿*Se ha caído* o la *han atropellado*? ¡Ay! ¡Cuánta sangre y la señorita no *se queja*! No *se mueva*, señorita, le vamos a *ayudar*.

*Dolores:* ¡Ayyy, ayyy! ¿Dónde estoy? ¿Qué es esto? ¡Sangre! ¡Mi sangre! *Me voy a morir*. ¡Cómo me *duele*! ¡Ayúdenme!

*Enfermera:* (muy tranquila) *Cálmese*, señorita. Aquí está el doctor Jiménez para ayudarle. No *se preocupe*. No es nada *serio*. Dígame, ¿qué le pasó?

*Doctor:* (a la enfermera) Shh, no *moleste* a la *paciente*. ¡*Qué lástima*, pobrecita, cómo *sufre*! Enfermera, tráigame el *maletín*. ¡Es una *emergencia*! (Sale la enfermera.)

*Dolores:* Doctor, ¡ayúdeme! Mire toda la sangre. Me duele mucho. Me voy a morir. Por favor, ¡ayúdeme doctor!

*Doctor:* *Tranquila*, cálmese. Ud. no se va a morir. Tenemos que *examinar* unas cosas primero. ¿Dónde *siente* el *dolor*? ¿Le duele el *pie*? ¿Quizá los *dedos del pie*? ¿Es el *tobillo*? La *pierna* no está *rota*.

*Dolores:* ¡Ayyy, tengo miedo! No aguanto ver sangre. ¡Cuánto me duele! ¡Me voy a morir!

*Enfermera:* Doctor, aquí está su maletín. ¿Cómo está la paciente?

*Doctor:* No sé todavía. Ya veremos. Por favor, señorita, trate de mover las piernas . . . sí, todo me parece estar bien.

*Dolores:* ¡Ayyy! No, doctor, allí no, más arriba. Me duele más arriba.

*Doctor:* ¿Más arriba? ¿Será la *espina dorsal*?

*Enfermera:* Doctor, yo creo que . . .

*Doctor:* (interrumpiéndola) Shh, yo creo que el dolor está en la *mano*. ¿Le duele la *muñeca*? . . . ¿o el *codo*? ¿Tal vez el *brazo*?

*Dolores:* No, doctor, me duele la *espalda*. Es un dolor *agudo*.

*Enfermera:* ¿La espalda? Con razón. Mire, doctor, ella se ha caído sobre una bolsa de comida. No es sangre. Se ha roto una botella de salsa de tomate.

## PRÁCTICA

A. Working with two other students, practice the dialog aloud, concentrating on pronunciation and fluency. As you become more proficient, try to vary some of the elements of the dialog.

*Model:*　Una señorita está boca arriba sobre la calle. Creo que está herida . . . ⟶

　　　　　*Un señor* está boca arriba sobre la calle. Creo que está *herido.*

**B.**　Translate the dialog into English. Then compare your translation with the one given in the Appendix (page 168).

**C.**　Translate the English text of the dialog into Spanish, without consulting the original as you work. Then compare your translation with the Spanish version given here.

# 2 VOCABULARIO MÉDICO DEL DIÁLOGO / Medical Vocabulary from the Dialog

**el accidente**　accident
**aguantar**　to endure
**agudo/a**　sharp
**atropellar**　to run over
**ayudar**　to aid, help
**el brazo**　arm
**caerse (me caigo)**　to fall down
**calmarse**　to calm down
**el codo**　elbow
**el dedo (del pie)**　finger (toe)
**el/la doctor(a)**　doctor
**doler (ue)**　to hurt
**el dolor**　pain
**la emergencia**　emergency
**el/la enfermero/a**　nurse
**la espalda**　back
**la espina dorsal**　spinal column
**estar boca arriba**　to be face up
**examinar**　to examine
**herido/a**　wounded, hurt

**el maletín**　(doctor's) bag
**la mano**　hand
**molestar**　to bother
**morirse (ue)**　to die
**moverse (ue)**　to move
**la muñeca**　wrist
**el/la paciente**　patient
**el pie**　foot
**la pierna**　leg
**preocuparse**　to worry
**¡Qué lástima!**　What a shame!
**quejarse**　to complain
**romper (roto/a)**　to break (broken)
**la sangre**　blood
**sentir (ie)**　to feel; to regret
**serio/a**　serious
**sufrir**　to suffer
**el tobillo**　ankle
**tranquilo/a**　calm; relax (*command*)

## PRÁCTICA

**A.**　Fill in the blanks with the proper form of words from the list.

1. El __rodillo__ , los __pies__ del pie y el __tobillo__ son partes de la pierna.

2. La __espina__ __dorsal__ es parte de la espalda.

3. La __muñeca__ , los __codos__ , la __mano__ y el __dedo__ son partes del brazo.

4. No se __preocupe__ , señor, no es nada serio.

5. Lo siento, esta mujer va a __morir__ , pues tiene heridas muy graves. ¡Cómo está __emergencia__ !

6. El doctor lleva su equipo en el _maletín_. Lo necesita cuando _examina_ a los _pacientes_. La enfermera le _ayuda_.

7. Después del _accidente_, el enfermero dijo que el chofer no debía _moverse_, pues tenía una pierna rota y le salía mucha _____. También le _____ mucho la espina dorsal.

8. El paciente se _queja_ de un dolor _agudo_ en la espalda. Fue llevado en ambulancia a la sala de _____.

9. El coche _atropella_ al peatón anoche.

**B.** Give the antonym (opposite) of these words.

1. nacer _morir_
2. levantarse
3. boca abajo _boca arriba_

4. no tolerar
5. dejar en paz _molestar_

**C.** Give a synonym (word similar in meaning) for these words.

1. calmado
2. médico
3. accidentado
4. tranquilizarse

5. quebrar
6. grave
7. ¡Qué pena!

# 3 LA ANATOMÍA HUMANA—EL CUERPO HUMANO / Human Anatomy—The Human Body

**I.** Identify these general areas of the body on the drawing.

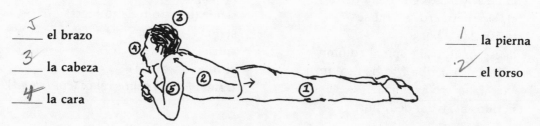

_5_ el brazo
_3_ la cabeza
_4_ la cara

_1_ la pierna
_2_ el torso

**II.** Give the English equivalent of these words. To what general area of the body are these body parts related?

_Model:_ El hombro es parte del torso.

1. la cadera
2. la cintura
3. el codo
4. el corazón
5. el costado
6. los dedos
7. los dedos del pie

8. la espalda
9. la espina dorsal
10. la espinilla
11. el estómago
12. el hígado
13. el hombro
14. el hueso

15. la mano
16. la muñeca
17. el muslo
18. los nudillos
19. el ombligo
20. la pantorrilla
21. **el pecho (seno)**

22. los pechos
23. el pie
24. la planta (del pie)
25. los pulmones

26. el puño
27. el riñón
28. la rodilla
29. la sentadera / nalga

30. el talón
31. la uña
32. la tráquea
33. la clavícula

III. Identify these body parts on the drawings.

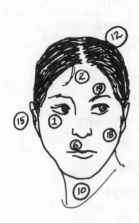 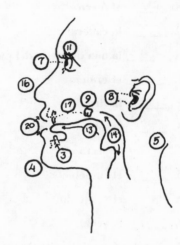

_____ la barbilla/la piocha

_6_ la boca

_12_ el cabello

_____ la ceja

_10_ el cuello

_3_ el diente

_____ las encías

_10_ la garganta

_20_ los labios

_13_ la lengua

_____ la mejilla/el cachete

_____ la muela

_16_ la nariz

_____ la niña

_____ la nuca

_8_ el oído

_11_ el ojo

_7_ la oreja

_____ el pelo

_____ las pestañas

IV. Más vocabulario. Match the Spanish words with their English equivalents.

1. _u_ la piel

2. _f_ el intestino

3. _v_ el tendón

4. _d_ la clavícula

5. _____ el bazo

6. _____ la costilla

7. _k_ el pene

8. _ch_ el pulmón

9. _____ la vesícula biliar

10. _g_ el vientre/útero/matríz

11. _w_ el esófago

12. _ñ_ la vejiga

a. toenail

b. armpit

c. windpipe

ch. lung

d. shoulder blade

e. bladder

f. intestine

g. uterus

h. vein

i. artery

j. womb

k. penis

13. _____ la escápula                    l.  cervix

14. _____ la coronilla                   ll. testicle

15. __i____ la arteria                     m. rectum

16. __s____ el dedo índice                 n.  gall bladder

17. __c____ la tráquea                      ñ.  skull

18. __g____ el útero                        o.  instep

19. _____ la cadera                       p.  thyroid

20. _____ la uña del dedo del pie         q.  hip

21. __v____ el cráneo                       r.  tendon

22. __p____ la tiroides                     rr. spleen

23. _____ el sobaco / la  axila           s.  index finger

24. __m____ el recto                        t.  collar bone

25. _____ el empeine                      u.  skin

26. __ll___ el testículo                    v.  crown of the head

27. __h____ la vena                         w.  esophagus

28. __i____ el cervix/cuello de la matríz   x.  rib

## PRÁCTICA

A.  Listen as another student completes the following sentences with a part of the
    body. Then indicate that part of your body. Note that the possessive adjectives
    (**mi, tu** . . .) are not used.

1. Déjeme ver el/la _____.

2. Ahora voy a examinar los/las _____.

B.  Working with another student, ask and answer the following questions, using
    parts of the body from the preceding lists. In these sentences, **doler** is used with
    indirect object pronouns (**me, le**) to indicate that a part of the body is painful *to*
    someone.

1. ¿Dónde le duele?

   Me duele el/la _____.

   Me duelen los/las _____.

2. ¿Desde cuándo le duele el/la _____?

   Me duele el/la _____ desde _____.

3. ¿Desde cuándo le duelen los/las _____?

   Me duelen los/las _____ desde _____.

# 4 VERBOS RELACIONADOS CON LA SALUD / Verbs Related to Health

I.   **Verbos básicos / Basic Verbs**

| | | | |
|---|---|---|---|
| **aliviar** | to alleviate | **mejorar(se)** | to get better |
| **cortar** | to cut | **molestar** | to bother, to annoy |
| **curar** | to cure | **morir(se)** | to die |
| **examinar** | to examine | **operar** | to operate (on) |
| **fracturar** | to fracture, to break | **sanar** | to cure |
| **lastimar** | to harm, to hurt | | |

## PRÁCTICA

Complete each series of sentences (A-D) with the verbs indicated, first in the present tense, then in the preterite, imperfect, and future tenses.

**A.**   **aliviar, curar, examinar, lastimar, molestar, operar**

In this model, the subject of the sentence (**el doctor**) acts on or directly affects another person (**el paciente**).

*Model:*   El doctor cura al paciente.        *The doctor cures the patient.*

1. Yo _____ al enfermo.

2. Tú _____ a la anciana.

3. Él/ella/Ud. _____ al niño.

4. Nosotros _____ a la señora Martínez.

5. Ellos/ellas/Uds. _____ al paciente.

**B.**   **cortarse, curarse, examinarse, lastimarse, mejorarse, morirse, sanarse**

In this model, the verb (**se cura**) is used reflexively, reflecting the action back to the subject (**el paciente**). The reflexive pronouns (**me, te, se, nos**) correspond to the subject.

*Model:*   El paciente se cura.        *The patient gets well (cures himself).*

1. Yo me _____ en el hospital.

2. Tú te _____ en casa.

3. Él/ella/Ud. se _____ en la clínica.

4. Nosotros nos _____ poco a poco.

5. Ellos/ellas/Uds. se _____ en el sanatorio.

**C.**   **cortarse, curarse, examinarse, fracturarse, lastimarse**

In this model, the action of the verb affects a part of the body. Note the use of the reflexive pronouns—not the possessive, as in English—to express possession.

*Model:*   El paciente se cura la pierna.        *The patient cures his leg.*

1. Yo me _____ la cadera.

2. Tú te _____ la muñeca.

3. Él/ella/Ud. se _____ el dedo.

4. Nosotros nos _____ el tobillo.

5. Ellos/ellas/Uds. se _____ la pierna.

### D. cortar, examinar

In this model, the subject (**el médico**) acts on a part of his patient's body. Note that the patient is indicated with indirect object pronouns.

*Model:*    El médico le examina el brazo.      *The doctor examines his arm.*

1. El doctor me _____ el brazo.

2. La enfermera te _____ el pie.

3. La médico le _____ la mejilla.

## II. Verbos adicionales / Additional Verbs

Give the English equivalent of these verbs.

| | | |
|---|---|---|
| 1. **abortar** | 15. **enjuagar** | 29. **parir (dar a luz)** |
| 2. **afeitar (se)** | 16. **enyesar** | 30. **prevenir** |
| 3. **aplicar** | 17. **evitar** | 31. **reposar** |
| 4. **bañar** | 18. **frotar** | 32. **respirar** |
| 5. **beber** | 19. **hinchar (se)** | 33. **sangrar** |
| 6. **bostezar** | 20. **hospitalizar** | 34. **sentir (se) (ie)** |
| 7. **crecer (crezco)** | 21. **internar** | 35. **soplar** |
| 8. **descansar** | 22. **inyectar** | 36. **tocar** |
| 9. **descoyuntar** | 23. **limpiar (se)** | 37. **torcer** |
| 10. **diagnosticar** | 24. **masticar** | 38. **toser** |
| 11. **digerir (se)** | 25. **morder (ue)** | 39. **tragar (tragué)** |
| 12. **dislocar** | 26. **ordenar** | 40. **tratar** |
| 13. **enfermar (se)** | 27. **orinar** | 41. **vendar** |
| 14. **engordar** | 28. **padecer** | 42. **vomitar** |

## PRÁCTICA

**A.**   What part of the body are the preceding verbs most closely associated with, if any?

**B.**   Using ten of the preceding verbs, write ten questions about medical situations in the present, preterite, or imperfect tenses. Then write ten more questions using ten different verbs in any tense. Answer the questions of other students as they read them aloud, or ask and answer questions with a partner.

## III. Expresiones médicas con estar / Medical Expressions with estar

| | |
|---|---|
| **estar a dieta** | to be on a diet |
| **estar inconsciente** | to be knocked out (out cold) |
| **estar pachucho/a** (*Spain*) | to be under the weather |
| **estar recuperándose** | to be on the road to recovery |
| **estar reviviéndose** | to be coming around |

## PRÁCTICA

**A.**   Write one question for each of the preceding expressions. Answer the questions of other students as they read them aloud, or ask and answer questions with a partner.

**B.**   Restate the questions you wrote in exercise A in the preterite and imperfect tenses.

# 5 MANDATOS / Commands

*Enfermera:*   Señor Martínez, por favor, *pase. Sígame. Quítese* los zapatos y *súbase* a la báscula. *No se mueva.* Hmmm... bien, ciento treinta y cinco libras. *Bájese* y *póngase* los zapatos. *Venga* conmigo. *Entre* en este cuarto. *Siéntese* allí. Le voy a tomar la temperatura. *Abra* la boca. *Sujete* el termómetro debajo de la lengua por un momento. *Súbase* la manga. Le voy a tomar la presión. No haga un puño. Mejor *suéltelo. Afloje* el puño por completo. Gracias. Vamos a ver cómo está el termómetro. *Suéltelo.* Tiene un poco de fiebre. Ahora voy a examinar su garganta. *Abra* la boca completamente. *Diga* «ahh...» *Dígalo* otra vez. No parece estar roja. *Desvístase* de todo menos su ropa interior. *Cuélguela* allí. El doctor no tardará en venir.

## PRÁCTICA

**A.**   Perform the preceding scene with another student who will play the part of Mr. Martínez. Instead of memorizing the commands as given in the scene, focus on the infinitives and on the logical sequence of actions.

pasar ⟶ seguir (i) ⟶ quitarse ⟶ subirse ⟶ moverse (ue) ⟶ bajarse ⟶
ponerse ⟶ venir (ie) ⟶ entrar ⟶ sentarse (ie) ⟶ abrir ⟶ sujetar ⟶
subirse ⟶ hacer ⟶ soltar (ue) ⟶ aflojar ⟶ soltar (ue) ⟶ abrir ⟶
decir (i) ⟶ desvestirse (i) ⟶ colgar (ue)

When you can perform the skit as written, Mr. Martínez should become less cooperative and not respond as readily to your commands. Change your commands to correspond to his behavior.

**B.** Perform the same scene with «Jaimito», a 9-year-old, using informal (**tú**) commands.

**C.** Working with another student, write a skit related to medicine or dentistry in which a minimum of ten different commands are used: at the therapist's, at the radiologist's, and so on.

# 6 PERSONAL DEL HOSPITAL Y ESPECIALISTAS / Hospital Personnel and Specialists

With the exception of **doctor(a)** and **enfermero(a)**, the names of the following hospital personnel can refer either to men or women: **el/la anestesista, el/la cardiólogo.**

**anestesista** anaesthetist
**cardiólogo (corazón)** cardiologist
**cirujano** surgeon
**dermatólogo (piel)** dermatologist
**doctor(a)** doctor
**doctor(a) de cabecera** family doctor
**enfermero/a** nurse
**ginecólogo (enfermedades de la mujer)** gynecologist
**internista (medicina interna, glándulas internas)** internist
**médico** physician
**neurólogo (tejido nervioso, cerebro)** neurologist

**oculista (ojos)** oculist
**odontólogo/dentista (dientes)** dentist
**oftalmólogo (enfermedades de los ojos)** ophthalmologist
**otorrinolaringólogo (nariz, garganta y oídos)** ear, nose, and throat doctor
**pediatra (niños)** pediatrician
**pedicuro (pies)** podiatrist
**psiquiatra/siquiatra** psychiatrist
**quiropráctico (huesos)** chiropractor
**radiólogo (rayos equis)** radiologist
**tocólogo (partos)** obstetrician
**urólogo (vías urinarias)** urologist

All of these medical specializations can be expressed as follows:

**doctor de + área:** Quiero ver al **doctor de niños.**

Since many patients will not be familiar with the more technical terms for the specialists, it is also useful to learn the simpler form.

## PRÁCTICA

**A.** The following pictures review the list of specialists. With a little imagination you should be able to determine the specialist.

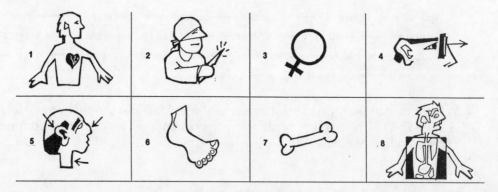

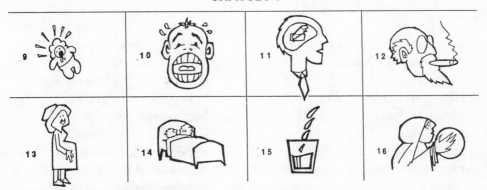

# 7 EDIFICIOS Y LUGARES / Buildings and Places

la **clínica**  clinic
el **consultorio**/la **consulta**  doctor's office
el **edificio**  facility, building
la **enfermería**  infirmary
la **farmacia/botica**  pharmacy
la **guardería**  nursery
el **hospicio para ancianos**  nursing home
el **hospital**  hospital
el **laboratorio**  lab(oratory)

el **pabellón/sala**  ward
el **piso**  floor
la **recepción**  front desk
la **sala de emergencia/urgencia**  emergency room
la **sala de espera**  waiting room
la **sala de operaciones**/el **quirófano**  operating room
el **salón**  lounge
el **sanatorio**  sanatorium

## PRÁCTICA

**A.** Working with another student, ask and answer the following questions, using vocabulary from the list of buildings and places.

1. ¿Está la internista en el/la _____?

   No, está en el/la _____.

2. ¿Va a hablar con el cirujano en el/la _____?

   No, le voy a hablar en el/la _____.

**B.** Explain the function of the following places, as if you were talking to a patient: **la farmacia, la guardería, el hospicio para ancianos, el pabellón, la sala de emergencia, el sanatorio.**

# 8 ENFERMEDADES / Diseases

la **alergia**  allergy
la **amigdalitis/anginas**  tonsillitis
la **apendicitis**  appendicitis

la **artritis**  arthritis
el **asma**  asthma
el **ataque cardíaco**  heart attack

el **ataque cerebral**  stroke
la **bronquitis**  bronchitis
el **cáncer**  cancer
el **catarro/resfriado**  cold
el **coágulo de sangre**  blood clot
el **cólico**  colic
la **diabetes**  diabetes
la **enfermedad venérea**  venereal disease
la **epilepsia**  epilepsy
la **fiebre escarlatina**  scarlet fever
la **gripe/gripa**  flu
la **hepatitis**  hepatitis
la **hernia**  hernia

el **infarto**  infarct
la **influenza**  flu
la **jaqueca**  migraine headache
la **laringitis**  laryngitis
las **paperas**  mumps
la **parálisis**  paralysis
la **peritonitis**  peritonitis
la **poliomielitis**  polio
la **pulmonía**  pneumonia
el **reumatismo/reuma**  rheumatism
el **sarampión**  measles
la **tosferina**  whooping cough
la **tuberculosis**  tuberculosis
la **varicela**  chicken pox

## PRÁCTICA

**A.**  Explain or define the preceding illnesses as if you were explaining them to a patient. Tell what part(s) of the body the illness affects. Use the following adjectives in your descriptions, as necessary.

| | | | |
|---|---|---|---|
| **adolorido/a** | sore | **grave** | serious |
| **agudo/a** | sharp | **hinchado/a** | swollen |
| **anormal** | abnormal | **inflamado/a** | inflamed |
| **congestionado/a** | congested | **irritado/a** | irritated |
| **crónico/a** | chronic | **prematuro / a** | premature |
| **estreñido/a** | constipated | **repentino/a** | sudden |
| **frecuente** | frequent | **roto/a** | broken |

**B.**  Working with another student, ask and answer the following questions, using vocabulary from the list of illnesses and the verbs **tener** (*to have*) and **padecer** (*to suffer*).

1.  ¿Qué enfermedades ha tenido Ud.?

    He tenido _____ y _____ y _____.

2.  ¿Qué enfermedades ha tenido su hijo/a (madre/padre)?

    Mi _____ ha tenido _____ y _____ y

    _____.

3.  ¿Padece Ud. de _____?

    _____ yo padezco de _____.

4.  ¿Desde cuándo padece de _____?

    Padezco de _____ desde _____.

**Otras enfermedades y síntomas / Other Illnesses and symptoms**

Give the English equivalent of the following diseases or medical conditions.

| | | |
|---|---|---|
| 1. el aborto | 18. el envenenamiento | 35. la palpitación |
| 2. el acné / las espinillas | 19. la esquizofrenia | 36. la peca / mancha |
| 3. el achaque | 20. la fractura | 37. la piedra de la vesícula |
| 4. el alcoholismo | 21. la gonorrea | 38. el pie de atleta |
| 5. la ampolla | 22. la hemorragia | 39. la pleuresía |
| 6. la anemia | 23. la herida | 40. la pus |
| 7. el calambre | 24. las herpes | 41. la rabia |
| 8. el cambio de vida | 25. la hinchazón | 42. la roncha |
| 9. el choque (stroke) | 26. la infección | 43. el sida |
| 10. la deshidratación | 27. el insomnio | 44. la sífilis |
| 11. la desnutrición | 28. la intoxicación | 45. la solanera* |
| 12. la difteria | 29. la leucemia | 46. el tétano |
| 13. la distrofia muscular | 30. el lunar | 47. la torcedura |
| 14. el dolor de muelas | 31. el mal de mar | 48. la tos |
| 15. el eczema | 32. la menstruación | 49. la úlcera |
| 16. el embarazo | 33. el mezquino | 50. la verruga |
| 17. la enfermedad nerviosa | 34. la narcomanía | 51. la viruela |

*Quemadura de sol (Mex.)/Insolación (Spa.)

## PRÁCTICA

Give a definition of each of the preceding conditions and diseases. Then present your definitions to another student, who will identify the disorder from your description.

## 9 DROGAS Y MEDICAMENTOS / Drugs and Medicines

| | |
|---|---|
| 1. el agua oxigenada  hydrogen peroxide | 18. el hielo  ice |
| 2. el alcohol  alcohol | 19. la inyección  shot |
| 3. la aspirina  aspirin | 20. el jarabe  cough syrup |
| 4. los barbitúricos  barbiturates | 21. la jeringa  syringe |
| 5. la cápsula  capsule | 22. el laxante / purga  laxative |
| 6. la cinta adhesiva  tape | 23. la marihuana  marijuana |
| 7. el condón  condom | 24. la jeringa  syringe |
| 8. la crema  cream | 25. la pastilla / la gragea  pill, sugar-coated pill |
| 9. la curita / tirita  band-aid | 26. la penicilina  penicillin |
| 10. las drogas  drugs | 27. el polvo (talco)  powder, dust |
| 11. el enema / la lavativa  enema | 28. la pomada  salve |
| 12. los estupefacientes / alucinógenos  hallucinogenic drugs | 29. la prescripción / receta  prescription |
| 13. las gárgaras (hacer)  gargle | 30. la puntada  stitch |
| 14. la gasa  gauze | 31. el suero  serum |
| 15. la gota  drop | 32. el supositorio  suppository |
| 16. los guantes desechables  disposable gloves | 33. la venda  bandage |
| 17. la heroina  heroin | 34. la vitamina  vitamin |

## PRÁCTICA

**A.** Working with another student, ask and answer the following questions, using vocabulary from the list of medicines and drugs. Use the verb **poner** with medicines that are applied externally (band–aids, salves, . . .) and **tomar** with medicines taken internally. Exception: **echar** is used with powders, talc, etc.

1. ¿Qué se está poniendo?

   Me estoy poniendo _____.

2. ¿Qué está tomando?

   Estoy tomando _____.

3. ¿Quién le puso el/la _____?

   La enfermera me puso el/la _____.

4. ¿Qué le recetó el médico a Ud.?

   El médico me recetó _____.

5. ¿Qué medicina está tomando ahora?

   Estoy tomando _____ tres veces por día.

6. ¿Compró Ud. el/la _____ en la farmacia?

   Sí, compré el/la _____ en la farmacia.

**B.** Give the English equivalent of the following prescription instructions. Then, using the prescription instructions, explain to a patient how to use one of the drugs or medicines from the preceding list.

1. **aplicar sobre el área afectada**

2. **(cuatro) veces por día**

3. **manténgase fuera del alcance de niños**

4. **media cucharada**

5. **media cucharadita**

6. **uso externo**

7. **uso interno**

8. **vía oral**

9. **vía rectal**

## 10   LESIONES Y SUS CONSECUENCIAS / Injuries and Their Consequences

| | |
|---|---|
| **el arañazo/rasguño** scratch | **la contusión** bruise |
| **el callo** corn | **la cortadura/cortada** cut |
| **la cicatriz** scar | **el chichón** lump |

**el dolor** pain
**la fiebre/calentura** temperature, fever
**la fractura** break, fracture
**el golpe** concussion
**el grano/granito** pimple
**la herida** wound
**la hinchazón** swelling
**la inflamación** inflammation, swelling
**el juanete** bunion

**la llaga** sore
**la mordedura / mordida** bite
**el ojo morado** black eye
**la quemadura** burn
**el quiste** cyst
**la rozadura** abrasion
**el sarpullido** rash
**la torcedura** sprain

## PRÁCTICA

A.    Working with another student, ask and answer the following questions, using vocabulary from the preceding list.

   1. ¿Qué tipo de lesión / herida causa un:

        mosquito? _____            perro? _____

        boxeador? _____            martillo? _____

   2. ¿Qué tipo de lesión / herida causa(n)

        unos zapatos apretados? _____      unas espinas de rosa? _____

        unos pañales? _____      agua caliente? _____

   3. ¿Cuál es el resultado de tener contacto con el fuego? _____

B.    Create five similar question and answer patterns, and practice them with another student.

C.    **Un repaso / A review.**   Name the parts of the body indicated on the drawings below. Then name as many illnesses or medical conditions as you can that affect that part of the body, and the kinds of treatment or medicine used to correct the condition.

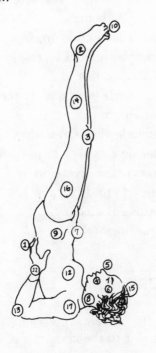
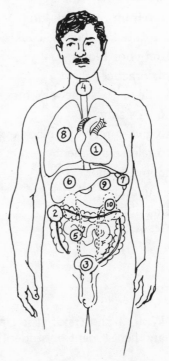

# 11 EXPRESIONES MISCELÁNEAS / Miscellaneous Expressions

| | |
|---|---|
| 1. to set a bone | poner el hueso en posición |
| 2. to put on a cast | enyesar |
| 3. I'm afraid there's no hope (for him/her). | No hay esperanza de que se salve. |
| 4. There's nothing else we can do. | No podemos hacer más. |
| 5. We'll change your room. | Le cambiaremos de cuarto. |
| 6. Please put out your cigarette/pipe/ cigar. | Por favor, apague su cigarro/pipa/ puro. |
| 7. I'll make your bed. | Le voy a hacer (tender) su cama. |
| 8. Brush your teeth. | Lávese (cepíllese) los dientes. |
| 9. Open your mouth (very wide). | Abra la boca (completamente/muy abierta). |
| 10. Keep it open. | Manténgala abierta. |
| 11. He/she vomited. | Él/ella vomitó/devolvió/depuso. |
| 12. to pass wind (gas) | echarse aires |
| 13. to have gas | tener gases |
| 14. Do you feel like (eating)? | ¿Tiene ganas de (comer)? |
| 15. to go to the bathroom | ir al excusado |
| 16. a sharp pain | un dolor agudo |
| 17. I feel sore all over. | Me siento adolorido/a. |
| 18. intensive care | cuidado intensivo |
| 19. He's/she's on the wagon. | Ha dejado de beber. |
| 20. I'm not into drinking. | Ya no le entro a la bebida. |
| 21. to refrain from drinking | dejar de beber |
| 22. a bad ticker (heart), back | me falla el corazón, la espalda |
| 23. iron poor blood | anemia, le falta hierro |
| 24. malpractice | mala práctica |
| 25. to tie or fix someone's tubes | arreglarle para que no tenga niños |
| 26. to be sickly | ser enfermizo/a |
| 27. to give someone a black eye | ponerle el ojo morado |
| 28. to release a patient | dar de alta al/a la paciente |
| 29. to give a shot | poner una inyección |
| 30. incubation period | el período de incubación |
| 31. first aid | primeros auxilios |
| 32. Get well! | Que mejore! |

## PRÁCTICA

Write a short skit using at least ten of the above expressions. Working with another student or students, present your skit to the class.

# 12 REPASO DEL CAPITULO
## Anatomía, Verbos, Enfermedades, Síntomas, Sinónimos

### A. ANATOMIA (PARTES DEL CUERPO)

**Posibles respuestas:**

muslo; corazón; esófago; empeine; intestino delgado; la tiroides; codo; rodilla; dientes; vejiga; puño; intestinos; garganta; cráneo; venas; escápula; coronilla; tráquea; recto; nuca; cabeza; costilla; clavícula; muñeca; espinilla; pulmón; tendón; encías; pantorrilla; barbilla o piocha; huesos o dientes; costado o torso; pene y testículos; útero o matriz; bazo e hígado; niña o pupila; hígado, riñón y bazo; arterias.

1. El músculo más fuerte del cuerpo humano. _____.
2. Parte del cuerpo donde se encuentran las costillas. _____o_____.
3. Hueso anterior de la pantorrilla. _____.
4. Donde se desarrolla el feto. _____o_____.
5. Parte superior de la cabeza. _____
6. Hueso que protege el cerebro. _____
7. Hueso que le quitaron a Adan para formar a Eva. _____
8. Organo que bombea la sangre. _____
9. Parte del cuerpo en la que se usa el sombrero. _____
10. Parte del cuerpo detrás del cuello. _____
11. Parte de la boca que se inflama cuando duelen los dientes. _____
12. Parte de la cara debajo de la boca. _____o_____
13. Parte de la pierna entre la rodilla y el tobillo. _____
14. Organos que destruyen células rojas viejas. _____e_____
15. Organo que guarda la orina. _____
16. El arco o puente del pie. _____
17. Partes del cuerpo que requieren calcio para fortificarse. _____o_____
18. Organo necesario para la respiración. _____
19. Conducto entre la faringe y el estómago. _____
20. Parte del cuerpo que se inflama cuando se tiene catarro. _____
21. Parte del brazo en la cual se usa el reloj. _____
22. Se forma al cerrar la mano. _____
23. Glándula que mantiene las hormonas del cuerpo y controla el metabolismo _____
24. Parte del ojo que cambia de tamaño. _____0_____
25. Tubo respiratorio para los pulmones. _____
26. Organo que saca las vitaminas de la comida. _____
27. Organos que purifican la sangre. _____, _____,_____
28. Unicos huesos que se ven. _____
29. Parte del cuerpo que se usa para doblar el brazo. _____
30. Parte del cuerpo que se usa para doblar la pierna. _____
31. Los dos órganos reproductivos del hombre: _____ y _____
32. Un ligamento pegado al hueso es un _____
33. El hueso en la parte posterior del hombro es. _____
34. La _____ es el hueso que se considera el más débil del ser humano.
35. Las _____ llevan la sangre al corazón.
36. Una cavidad que se encuentra entre las dos nalgas. _____
37. Las _____ transportan la sangre dentro del corazón al resto del cuerpo.
38. Uno es grueso y el otro es delgado y forman parte del estómago_____.

## B. VERBOS

**Posibles respuestas:**
diagnosticar; bosteza; enyesar; descoyuntar; digerir.

1. Cuando uno tiene mucho sueño a veces _____
2. El doctor examina al paciente para _____ el malestar.
3. _____ es sinónimo de "dislocar".
4. Le tuvieron que _____ el brazo porque se lo fracturó.
5. Después de comer, uno debe relajarse para que la comida se pueda _____

## C. ENFERMEDADES y SINTOMAS

**Posibles respuestas:**
calambre; piedras; ampolla; acné; úlcera; chichón; cáncer; pecas; gragea; anemia; aspirina; amigdalitis; alergia; fractura; leucemia; laringitis; narcomanía; gripe; gasa; hemorragia; hielo; rabia; paperas; penicilina; morado; epilepsia; diabetes; insomnio; jarabe; bronquitis; cicatriz; enfermedad venérea; curita o tirita; contusión o moratón; receta o prescripción; purga o laxante; ronchas o sarpullido; menopausa o cambio de vida; hemorragia o hematoma; infección o infectar; pneumonia o pulmonía; polio, parálisis o distrofia muscular; barbitúricos, estupefacientes y alucinógenos; sarampión, varicela y rubeola; pulmonía; bronquitis; asma y alergias.

1. Manchas pequeñas de la piel._____
2. Enfermedad de la piel, caracterizada por la formación de granitos pequeños._____
3. Contracción involuntaria de un músculo. _____
4. Rotura de un hueso. _____
5. Vejiga formada por la elevación de la epidermis. _____
6. Cesación natural de la menstruación a cierta edad. _____ o _____
7. El resultado de estar en contacto con los gérmenes de una enfermedad. _____ o _____
8. Un cáncer de la sangre. _____
9. El abuso de las drogas con hábito. _____
10. Depósitos minerales en la vesícula. _____
11. Inflamación de la piel, con un cambio de color. Usualmente a causa de una alergia. _____ o

    _____
12. Desintegración gradual del tejido del estómago. _____
13. Una enfermedad acompañada por fiebre y frío. _____
14. Empobrecimiento de la sangre. _____
15. Flujo de sangre. _____
16. Una píldora dulce. _____
17. Se toman para dolores de cabeza. _____
18. Inflamación de las amígdalas. _____
19. Bulto que se forma a causa de un golpe en la cabeza o en la frente. _____
20. Medicina que sirve para relajar los intestinos. _____ o _____
21. Enfermedad infecciosa que resulta de una mordedura de perro. _____
22. Enfermedad que causa hinchazón de las glándulas de la garganta._____
23. Enfermedad que causa la pérdida del uso de las cuerdas vocales. _____
24. La pérdida del uso de los músculos desde nacimiento. _____ , _____ o

    _____
25. Medicamento tradicional para curar sífilis. _____
26. Cuando uno tiene este tipo de llaga, la piel se pone morada y negra. _____ o

    _____
27. Tela absorbente que se usa para vendar. _____
28. Enfermedades que causan dificultad al respirar. _____ , _____ , _____ y

_____
29. Enfermedad caracterizada por excesiva secreción de orina cargada de azúcar. _____
30. Cuando una persona no puede dormir. _____
31. Infiltración de un tejido por la sangre. _____ o _____
32. Enfermedad causada por la inflamación de los bronquios. _____
33. Enfermedad caracterizada por la congestión aguda de un lóbulo pulmonar. _____ o
_____
34. Término genérico que se aplica a todo tumor maligno. _____
35. Enfermedad convulsiva que se manifiesta por violentas descargas neuromusculares. _____
36. Enfermedad infecciosa, contagiosa, y caracterizada por una erupción semejante a la viruela.
_____ , _____ y _____
37. Se usa para cubrir una herida en un dedo. _____ o _____
38. Líquido espeso que alivia la tos. _____
39. Señal que queda después de cerrarse una herida. _____
40. Adjetivo como resultado obtenido después de haber recibido un golpe en el ojo. _____
41. La heroína y muchos otros narcóticos forman parte de esta familia de drogas potentes. _____ ,
_____ y _____
42. Se necesita para adquirir ciertas drogas consideradas muy potentes. _____ o _____
43. El herpe y el sífilis forman parte de esta familia de enfermedades trasmitidas sexualmente.
_____
44. La hipersensibilidad natural producida por substancias en un organismo. _____
45. Se usa para bajar la hinchazón. _____

## D. SINONIMOS

**Posibles respuestas:**
afeitar; agudo; axila; barbilla; botica; deponer o devolver; descoyuntar; médico; mejilla; mejorar o
sanar; mordida; niña; padecer; parir o "aliviarse"; pastilla; pelo; prescripción; purga; rasguño;
reposar; resfriado; seno; sentadera; temperatura o calentura.

| | | |
|---|---|---|
| 1. dar a luz. | 2. cachete | 3. aliviar |
| 4. rasurar | 5. piocha | 6. descansar |
| 7. intenso, fuerte | 8. sufrir | 9. sobaco |
| 10. farmacia | 11. catarro | 12. receta |
| 13. pupila | 14. dislocar | 15. píldora |
| 16. pecho | 17. cabello | 18. doctor |
| 19. fiebre | 20. laxante | 21. arañazo |
| 22. nalga | 23. mordedura | 24. vómito |

The following are key words that should suggest questions similar to the
preceding ones. Working with another student, formulate interview questions
based on the key words. Refer to the list of questions if necessary.

| | |
|---|---|
| 1. síntomas actuales | 16. tuberculosis |
| 2. la cabeza | 17. visita al dentista |
| 3. función de brazos | 18. pies |
| 4. hinchazón | 19. dolores estomacales |
| 5. los pulmones | 20. problemas nerviosos |
| 6. la respiración | 21. el ano |
| 7. cuidado intensivo | 22. la ingle |
| 8. el corazón | 23. bulto |
| 9. el hígado | 24. medicamentos |
| 10. el riñón | 25. cirugía |
| 11. las articulaciones | 26. reacción adversa |
| 12. el examen médico completo | 27. órganos sexuales |
| 13. el peso | 28. antibióticos |
| 14. rayos equis | 29. lunar |
| 15. vómitos de sangre | 30. los ojos |

# CAPÍTULO 2

## El orden público/
## Law Enforcement

# 1 DIÁLOGO / Dialog

### Informe para un robo de carro

**Sr. Sandoval:** Por favor, ¿es Ud. el *agente* Ramírez? Me han dicho que aquí *se denuncia* el *robo* de un *carro.*

**Agente Ramírez:** Sí, yo soy el encargado de tomar los *datos* necesarios. Vamos a ver . . . ¿Me puede decir su nombre y domicilio completo?

**Sr. Sandoval:** Sí, soy Manuel Sandoval Gutiérrez. Vivo en la *calle* El Cerrito, número 1483, de esta ciudad.

**Agente Ramírez:** ¿Es Ud. el *dueño* del *automóvil*?

**Sr. Sandoval:** Sí, lo soy.

**Agente Ramírez:** ¿Ha traído el *papel* de *propiedad* del carro?

**Sr. Sandoval:** No. Lo dejé en casa y el *papel de la matrícula* está en la *guantera* del *coche.*

**Agente Ramírez:** Bueno, no importa. ¿Dónde le *robaron* el carro?

**Sr. Sandoval:** Estaba *estacionado* en la calle El Monte, *esquina* con la calle Madera. Tenían que habérselo robado entre las once y las doce de la mañana.

**Agente Ramírez:** ¿De qué *marca* y *año* es su carro?

**Sr. Sandoval:** Es un Ford, 1975.

**Agente Ramírez:** ¿Se acuerda del *número de la placa* (*chapa/matrícula/ licencia*)?

**Sr. Sandoval:** Sí, es la 083 MTZ de este estado.

**Agente Ramírez:** ¿Qué valor le pone?

**Sr. Sandoval:** Lo *valoro* en unos $5,500, pues tiene algunos *accesorios* de valor.

**Agente Ramírez:** ¿Qué accesorios tiene?

**Sr. Sandoval:** Tiene un *radio* y *cassette* con una *antena* al lado derecho de enfrente. Ahh, además tiene unas *llantas* (unos *neumáticos*) nuevas en *ruedas* especiales. Las llantas son *anchas de carreras.*

**Agente Ramírez:** ¿De qué color es su coche?

**Sr. Sandoval:** Es de dos colores. El color predominante es amarillo ligero con el *techo* café oscuro. Encima tiene una *parrilla* (*baca*) de aluminio.

**Agente Ramírez:** ¿De cuántas *puertas* es?

**Sr. Sandoval:** Es de dos puertas y la puerta derecha *tiene un abollón* (*está chocada*).

**Agente Ramírez:** ¿Estaba *cerrado con llave*?

**Sr. Sandoval:** No. Dejé *ventanas* abiertas y por descuido las llaves *puestas.*

**Agente Ramírez:** ¿Está *asegurado* su carro?

*Sr. Sandoval:* Sí, está asegurado con la *compañía* American Auto Insurance.

*Agente Ramírez:* ¿Hay otros *indicios* o *marcas* que nos puede dar Ud. para *localizar* su auto?

*Sr. Sandoval:* No. Bueno. . . ya que lo pienso, uno de los *faroles delanteros* está roto.

## PRÁCTICA

A. Working with another student, practice the dialog aloud, concentrating on pronunciation and fluency. As you become more proficient, try to vary some of the elements of the dialog.

   *Model:* Vivo en la calle El Cerrito, número 1483, de esta ciudad . . . ⟶
   Vivo en la calle *Las Pasas*, número *1829*, de esta ciudad.

B. Translate the dialog into English. Then compare your translation with the one given in the Appendix (pages 168–169).

C. Translate the English text of the dialog into Spanish, without consulting the original as you work. Then compare your translation with the Spanish version given here.

# 2 VOCABULARIO DEL DIÁLOGO / Vocabulary from the Dialog

**el abollón** dent
**el accesorio** accessory
**el/la agente** officer
**la antena** antenna
**el año** year
**asegurar** to insure
**el automóvil** automobile
**la baca** luggage rack
**el carro** car
**el cassette** cassette
**cerrar (ie) con llave** to lock
**el coche** car
**la compañía** company
**la chapa** license plate
**el dato** information
**delantero/a** front
**denunciar** to report
**el/la dueño/a** owner
**la esquina** corner

**estacionar** to park
**estar chocado/a** to be dented
**el farol** headlight
**la guantera** glove compartment
**el indicio** detail, indication
**la licencia** license
**localizar** to find, to locate
**la llanta (ancha de carreras)** (wide racing) tire
**la marca** mark; brand
**la matrícula** registration
**el neumático** tire
**el número de la placa** license number
**el papel de propiedad** proof of ownership
**la parrilla** luggage rack
**la puerta** door
**puesto/a** in place, placed

| | |
|---|---|
| **el radio**  radio | **el techo**  roof, top |
| **robar**  to rob, steal | **el valor**  value |
| **el robo**  robbery, theft | **valorar**  to value, to be worth |
| **la rueda**  rim | **la ventana**  window |

## PRÁCTICA

**A.**  Fill in the blanks with the proper form of words from the list.

1. Para que nadie entre al coche es necesario cerrar la _____ con llave.

2. Las _____ o los _____ están hechos de goma (hule).

3. Para llevar cosas encima del automóvil es necesario tener una _____ o una _____.

4. Por la noche es necesario poner los _____.

5. Un carro se identifica exteriormente por los números y las letras de la _____ (la _____, la _____, la _____).

6. El _____ de coches en muchos casos se debe al descuido.

7. En la _____ de metal se puede poner una _____ _____ _____ _____.

8. La _____ sirve para guardar los papeles de _____ y de la _____.

9. Una cosa que no es equipo estándar del coche es un _____.

10. Si uno tiene una póliza de seguro, su carro está _____.

**B.**  Give the antonym (opposite) of these words.

| | |
|---|---|
| 1. suelo | 4. menospreciar |
| 2. trasero | 5. abrir con llave |
| 3. perder | 6. estar en buenas condiciones |

**C.**  Give a synonym (word similar in meaning) for these words.

| | | |
|---|---|---|
| 1. señal | 7. lo que vale | 13. cinta |
| 2. receptor | 8. empresa | 14. modelo |
| 3. aparquear | 9. información | 15. cruce |
| 4. propietario | 10. representante | 16. situado |
| 5. dar información | 11. fecha de fabricación | 17. quitar |
| 6. cristal | 12. golpe | |

# 3 PERSONAL, VERBOS Y SUSTANTIVOS RELACIONADOS CON EL ORDEN PÚBLICO / Personnel, Verbs, and Nouns Related to Law Enforcement

| Personal | Equivalente inglés | Sustantivo | Verbo |
|---|---|---|---|

## I. Agentes de la ley / Law Enforcers

| Personal | Equivalente inglés | Sustantivo | Verbo |
|---|---|---|---|
| 1. el / la abogado | *lawyer* | | abogar |
| el / la licenciado (a) | | | |
| 2. el alcalde / la alcaldesa | *mayor* | la alcaldía | |
| 3. el / la cherif | *sheriff* | | |
| 4. el / la defensor (a) | *defender* | la defensa | defender (ie) |
| 5. el / la detective | *detective* | | |
| el / la inspector (a) | | inspección | inspeccionar |
| 6. el / la fiscal | *district attorney* | la fiscalía | fiscalizar |
| 7. el / la guardia | *guard* | | guardar |
| 8. el / la jefe de policía | *police chief* | jefatura | |
| 9. el / la juez | *judge* | juzgado / juicio | juzgar |
| 10. el jurado | *jury* | juramento | jurar |
| 11. el patrullero | *patrol officer* | la patrulla | patrullar |
| 12. la policía | *police force* | | |
| 13. el policía / la agente de policía | *officer* | | |
| 14. el policía de tránsito / la agente de tránsito | *traffic officer* | el tránsito | transitar |
| 15. el / la procurador (a) | *attorney general* | la procuraduría | procurar |
| 16. el / la secretario (a) de tribunal | *clerk of the court* | | |

## II. Violadores de la ley / Criminals

| Personal | Equivalente inglés | Sustantivo | Verbo |
|---|---|---|---|
| 1. el / la asaltador (a) | | | |
| el / la asaltante | *assailant* | el asalto (con lesión) | asaltar |
| 2. el / la asesino (a) | *assassin* | el asesinato | asesina |
| 3. el / la atracador (a) | *bank robber, holdup artist* | el atraco | atracar |
| 4. el / la bígamo (a) | *bigamist* | bigamia | |
| 5. el / la borracho (a) | *drunk* | borrachera | emborrachar |
| 6. el / la concusionario (a) | *extortionist* | | |
| 7. el / la conspirador (a) | *conspirator* | la conspiración | conspirar |
| 8. el / la contrabandista | *dealer in contraband* | el contrabando | "contrabandear" |
| 9. el / la criminal | *criminal, felon* | el delito, el crimen el delito menor | |

| Personal | Equivalente inglés | Sustantivo | Verbo |
|---|---|---|---|
| 10. el / la chantajista | blackmailer | el chantaje | "chantajear" |
| 11. el / la difamador (a) | libeler | la difamación | difamar |
| 12. el / la drogadicto (a) | drug addict | la drogadicción | endrogar |
| 13. el / la ebrio (a) | inebriate | la embriaguez | embriagar |
| 14. el / la estafador (a) | swindler, embezzler | la estafa | estafar |
| 15. el / la extorsionista | extortionist | la extorción | extorsionar |
| 16. el / la falsificador (a) | counterfeiter, forger | la falsificación | falsificar |
| 17. el / la hampón (a) | | | |
| | gangster | | |
| el / la mafioso (a) | | la mafia | |
| 18. el / la homicida | murderer | el homicidio | matar |
| 19. el / la incendiario (a) | arsonist | el incendio provocado | incendiar encender (ie) |
| 20. el / la ladrón (a) | thief, robber, burglar | el robo, el hurto | robar, hurtar |
| 21. el / la mutilador (a) | mutilator | la mutilación | mutilar |
| 22. el / la perjuro (a) | perjurer | el perjuro | perjurar |
| 23. el / la raptor (a) | kidnapper | el raptor | raptar |
| 24. el / la recluso (a) | prisoner, | | recluir |
| el / la reo | inmate, convict | | |
| 25. el / la saboteador (a) | saboteur | el sabotaje | sabotear |
| 26. el / la secuestrador (a) | kidnapper | el secuestro | secuestrar |
| 27. el / la sobornador (a) | briber | el soborno (la mordida) | sobornar |
| 28. el / la terrorista | terrorist | el terror | aterrar |
| 29. el / la traficante de drogas | drug pusher | el tráfico de drogas | traficar drogas |
| 30. el / la violador (a) | rapist | la violación | violar |

## II. Personal misceláneo / Miscellaneous Personnel

| Personal | Equivalente inglés | Sustantivo | Verbo |
|---|---|---|---|
| 1. el / la acusado (a) | accused | la acusación | acusar |
| el / la acusador (a) | | | |
| 2. el cadáver | corpse | | |
| 3. el / la conductor (a) | | | |
| | driver | | conducir |
| el / la chofer | | | |
| 4. el / la demandado (a) | defendant | la demanda | demandar |
| el / la demandante | plaintiff | | |
| 5. el / la fiador (a) | bondsperson | la fianza | fiar |
| 6. el / la inocente | innocent | la inocencia | |
| 7. el / la médico forense | coroner | | |
| 8. el / la notario público | notary public | notaría | |
| 9. el / la testigo | witness | el testimonio | atestiguar |
| 10. el / la víctima | victim | | |
| 11. el pandillero | gang member | la pandilla | |

## PRÁCTICA

**A.** The following pictures review the previous lists. With a little imagination you should be able to determine the **person**, **noun** and **verb**. Some pictures can have several possibilities and are listed as a), b), c), etc.

## REPASO GRAFICO DEL PERSONAL, VERBOS Y SUSTANTIVOS

1. a)
   b)

2.

3. a)
   b)

4. a)

5. a)
   b)

6.

7.

8.

9.

10. a)
    b)

11.

12.

13.

14.

15. a)
    b)
    c)

**B.** Complete the sentences in a logical way, putting the verb in boldface into the indicated tense. Remember that verbs ending in -**car**, -**gar**, and -**zar** have a spelling change in the preterite: -**qué**, -**gué**, -**cé**.

1. Preterite: **abogar**       Ayer yo . . . en . . .

2. Present: **defender**       El defensor . . .

3. Preterite: **juzgar**       Yo lo . . .

4. Preterite: **atracar**      La razón por la cual yo . . . fue . . .

5. Preterite: **endrogar**     Anoche no me . . . porque . . .

6. Preterite: **embriagar**    Me . . . el sábado porque . . .

7. Preterite: **falsificar**   Si yo . . . los documentos fue porque . . .

8. Present: **incendiar**      A veces los niños . . .

9. Present: **recluir**        Me . . . del mundo porque . . .

10. Preterite: **traficar**    El año pasado yo . . . con drogas porque . . .

11. Present: **conducir**      Yo . . . a . . .

**D.** Supply the missing word—personnel, noun, verb—according to the model.

Model:  atracador  _____  atracar ⟶

atracador  _____el atraco_____  atracar

1. juez  _____  juzgar
2. _____  la procuraduría  procurar
3. _____  el chantaje  chantajear
4. el estafador  _____  estafar
5. _____  la embriaguez  embriagar
6. la perjura  _____  perjurar
7. el terrorista  el terror  _____
8. la falsificadora  _____  falsificar
9. el defensor  la defensa  _____
10. _____  el asalto  asaltar
11. el asesino  _____  asesinar
12. _____  la conspiración  conspirar
13. la difamadora  _____  difamar
14. el extorsionista  la extorsión  _____
15. el mutilador  _____  mutilar
16. el raptor  _____  raptar
17. la saboteadora  _____  sabotear
18. el sobornador  _____  sobornar
19. _____  la acusación  acusar
20. _____  el testimonio  atestiguar

**E.** Give the personnel that correspond to these words.

1. la alcaldía
2. inspeccionar
3. la fiscalía
4. guardar
5. tránsito
6. patrullar
7. emborrachar
8. el contrabando
9. el crimen
10. el homicidio
11. el robo
12. la violación
13. la demanda
14. fiar

# 4  INSTITUCIONES Y EDIFICIOS / Institutions and Buildings

**el bufete**  lawyer's office
**el calabozo**  jail

**la cárcel**  jail
**la celda**  jail cell

la comandancia   police station
el correccional   reformatory
la delegación de policía   police station
el departamento de tránsito   traffic
   control department
la jefatura de policía   police station

el juzgado   court
el Palacio de Justicia   courthouse
el penal   prison
la prisión   prison
la procuraduría   Attorney General's office
la sala del tribunal   courtroom

## PRÁCTICA

Working with another student, ask and answer the following questions, using vocabulary from the preceding list.

1. ¿Dónde está el/la _____?

   El/la _____ está allí.

2. ¿Me puede decir dónde está el/la _____?

   Sí, el/la _____ se encuentra en (la calle, la avenida, el edificio).

# 5 MÁS VERBOS RELACIONADOS CON EL ORDEN PÚBLICO / More Verbs Related to Law Enforcement

1. **acusar**  to accuse
2. **apuñalar**  to stab
3. **arrestar**  to arrest
4. **atropellar**  to run over
5. **capturar**  to capture
6. **castigar**  to punish
7. **colgar (ue) / ahorcar**  to hang
8. **comparecer (comparezco)**  to appear
9. **confiscar**  to confiscate
10. **degollar (ue)**  to slash the throat
11. **delatar / denunciar**  to denounce, to report
12. **demandar**  to sue
13. **detener (ie)**  to detain
14. **disparar**  to shoot
15. **ejecutar**  to execute
16. **electrocutar**  to electrocute
17. **encarcelar**  to jail
18. **fichar**  to book
19. **forzar (ue)**  to force
20. **golpear**  to hit
21. **herir (ie)**  to wound
22. **huir**  to flee
23. **infringir (infrinjo)**  to violate, break the law
24. **interrogar**  to question
25. **investigar**  to investigate
26. **maltratar**  to mistreat, abuse
27. **manejar**  to drive
28. **matar**  to kill
29. **multar**  to fine
30. **parar**  to stop, detain
31. **pasar**  to pass
32. **registrar**  to search (false cognate)
33. **revisar**  to check up
34. **sentenciar**  to commit, to sentence
35. **suicidarse**  to commit suicide

## PRÁCTICA

A. Without using the infinitive or a word derived from it, make up ten definitions for the verbs from the preceding list. Present your definitions to your classmates, who will guess the verb.

*Model:*  Sujetar a alguien. ⟶ detener

**B.** Complete the following sentences in as many ways as possible, using the preterite tense of verbs from the preceding list.

1. El abogado _____ a la demandada.

2. El policía _____ al homicida.

3. La conductora _____ a la niña.

4. El ladrón _____ en el juzgado.

5. El hombre _____ al viejo.

6. La testigo _____ al chantajista.

7. El juez _____ a la contrabandista.

8. El violador _____ a la mujer.

9. El policía de tránsito _____ al conductor.

10. El asaltador _____ a la agente de policía.

**C** Using **forzar, herir, huir** and **infringir** write questions about law enforcement situations in the present, preterite, or imperfect tenses. Answer the questions of other students as they read them aloud, or ask and answer questions with a partner.

# 6 LA VOZ ACTIVA Y LA VOZ PASIVA / Active and Passive Voice

| La voz activa | La voz pasiva |
|---|---|
| El asesino **asesina** a la señora. | La señora **es asesinada por** el asesino. |
| El policía **capturó** al reo. | El reo **fue capturado por** el policía. |
| Las señoras **denunciarán** al abogado. | El abogado **será denunciado por** las señoras. |

## PRÁCTICA

Fill in the blanks in the first column with names from the list of **personal** and verbs from the list in section 5, using the present, preterite or future tense. Then change the sentences to the passive voice. **Remember:** Agreement in number and gender.

| Active voice | Passive voice |
|---|---|
| *Model:* El abogado <u>interroga</u> al ⟶ <br> <u>acusado</u> . | *El acusado es interrogado por el abogado.* |
| 1. El detective _____ al _____. | _____ |
| 2. La juez _____ a la _____. | _____ |
| 3. Los policías _____ a los _____. | _____ |
| 4. El ladrón _____ a las _____. | _____ |

5. La policía _____ al _____.                    _____

6. La víctima _____ a la _____.                  _____

7. Las mujeres _____ al _____.                   _____

8. El jurado _____ al _____.                     _____

9. El chofer _____ al _____.                     _____

10. La testigo _____ a la _____.                 _____

Some objects can also be used:

**El policia dispara la pistola.     La pistola es disparada por el policia.**

---

# 7 LA DESCRIPCIÓN DE UN SOSPECHOSO: ROPA / Describing a Suspect: Clothing

## I. Ropa / Clothing

el abrigo/sobretodo  (over)coat
el anillo  ring
la blusa  blouse
el bolsillo  pocket
el bolso/la bolsa  purse
los calcetines  socks
la camisa  shirt
la camiseta  undershirt, T-shirt
el collar  necklace
la corbata  tie
el chaleco  vest
la chaqueta  jacket
la falda  skirt
la gabardina/el impermeable  raincoat
las gafas oscuras  sunglasses
el gorro/la cachucha  cap
los lentes/anteojos, las gafas
    eyeglasses
las lentillas/pupilentes, los lentes de
    contacto  contact lenses

los pantalones  pants
los pantalones cortos  shorts, cutoffs
los pantalones vaqueros  jeans
la peluca/el pelo postizo  wig
los pendientes/aretes/zarcillos
    earrings
las pestañas postizas  false eyelashes
la pulsera  bracelet
el reloj  watch
el saco  sportscoat
las sandalias  sandals
el sombrero  hat
el suéter  sweater
los tenis  tennis shoes
el traje  suit
el vestido  dress
las zapatillas  slippers
los zapatos  shoes
los zapatos con tacones  high heels

## II. Patrones, diseños, tonos y materiales / Patterns, Designs, Shades, and Materials

1. **ajedrezado / a (cuadrado)** checkered
2. **de algodón** cotton
3. **de un color chillón / chillante** a loud color
4. **de un color ligero** a light color, pastel
5. **de color oscuro** a dark color
6. **con lunares** polka dots
7. **con tipo escocés** plaid

8. **las franjas / rayas/ listas** stripes
9. **de lana** wool
10. **de manga corta** shortsleeved
11. **de manga larga** long sleeved
12. **de material sintético** synthetic
13. **de mezclilla** denim
14. **de pana** corduroy

## PRÁCTICA

**A.** Describe each of the following persons as accurately as you can. Pay particular attention to the differences between them.

**B.** Describe the clothing of a classmate without naming him or her. The class will tell you whom you are describing based on your description.

**C.** Ask a student to leave the classroom. While he or she is outside, work with your classmates to describe the clothing he or she was wearing, answering the question: **¿Cómo estaba vestido/a el/la sospechoso/a?** Answer: **El sospechoso vestía/tenía puesto/llevaba . . .**

---

# 8  LA DESCRIPCIÓN DE UN SOSPECHOSO: APARIENCIA FÍSICA /
## Description of a Suspect: Physical Appearance

---

**I.    Adjetivos / Adjectives**

**alto/a**  tall
**bajo/a (chaparro)**  short

**barbudo/a**  bearded
**bien dotada**  buxom

bonito/a  pretty
cabezón(a)  with a large head
cojear  to limp
cojo/a  lame
con una cicatriz en . . .  with a scar
    on . . .
débil  weak
delgado/a  slim
enano/a  midget, little
enorme  gigantic
esbelto/a  slender

de estatura mediana  medium height
feo/a  ugly
flaco/a  skinny
gordo/a  fat
grueso/a  fat
guapo/a  handsome, cute, good-
    looking
joven  young
sin barba/barbilampiño  clean shaven
viejo/a  old

## II. Pelo / Hair

bigote  mustach
calvo/a  bald
canoso (entrecano)  grey hair
melenudo/a (greñudo)  long hair
pelirrojo/a  redhead

pelo corto  short hair
pelo largo  long hair
la peluca  wig
rubio/a  blond
pelo castaño  chestnut hair, brunette

## III. Raza, color / Race, Color

blanco/a  Caucasian, white
latino/a  Latin
negro/a  black

oriental  oriental
de tez blanca  of light complexion
trigueño/a  olive skinned

## IV. Sexo / Sex

hombre/varón/masculino  male
mujer/hembra/femenina  woman

homosexual  homosexual
lesbiana  lesbian

## PRÁCTICA

A.  Give the antonym (opposite) of these words.

| | | | |
|---|---|---|---|
| 1. gordo | 4. alto | 7. enana | 10. barbudo |
| 2. guapo | 5. pelo largo | 8. moreno | 11. joven |
| 3. rubia | 6. calvo | 9. negra | 12. mujer |

B.  Each member of the class should bring in a color photo of a person from a magazine. Put all of the photos together (on a table, on the wall, etc.). Choose a photo at random and describe the person pictured to the class: his or her physical appearance, clothing, etc. Your classmates should try to find the picture you are describing. Use the imperfect: El sospechoso era...

C.  Describe one of your classmates as accurately as you can to the class, without naming him or her. The class should help you to give a good description by asking questions such as:

¿Cómo es la persona?

¿Qué viste/lleva/tiene puesto?

¿De qué sexo, raza, estatura, color de pelo, etcétera, es?

# 9 DANDO DIRECCIONES / Giving Directions

## I. Verbos / Verbs

| | |
|---|---|
| to follow, continue | seguir (i), continuar |
| to go back, return | regresar, volver(se) (ue) |
| to notice | notar |
| to see | ver |
| to turn | doblar, torcer (ue), girar, dar la vuelta, virar |

## II. Señales / Landmarks

**el alto/la parada**  stop sign
**la autopista/la carretera**
         freeway/highway
**la avenida**  avenue
**la calle**  street
**calle de una dirección/un sentido**
         one way street
**la carretera**  highway
**el carril / la línea**  lane
**el cruce de ferrocarril**  railroad crossing
**la curva**  curve

**la encrucijada/cruce/crucero** intersection
**la entrada a la autopista**  entrance to the
         freeway
**la manzana/cuadra**  block
**el puente**  bridge
**el río**  river

**la salida de la autopista** freeway exit
**el semáforo/las luces**  traffic lights
**el vado**  dip
**la vuelta en U**  U turn

## III. Direcciones / Directions

| | |
|---|---|
| (a la) derecha (de) | (to the) right (of) |
| (a la) izquierda (de) | (to the) left (of) |
| arriba/abajo | up/down, below |
| a un lado (de) | to one side (of) |
| encima de/debajo de | on top of/under |
| derecho, adelante | straight ahead |
| cerca (de)/lejos (de) | near (to)/far (from) |
| un poquito más | a little more, further |
| una vía corta | a shortcut |
| un pie/una milla | a foot/a mile |
| a unos (dos) kilómetros (de) | about (two) kilometers (from) |

## PRÁCTICA

A. Using the map on page 75, tell someone how to go from . . .

    1. point A to point B        3. point A to point C
    2. point B to point C        4. point A to point D

B. You are lost in the area marked X on the map, and you want to get to area Y. Working with another student, ask and answer the following questions about that situation.

    1. ¿Me puede decir cómo se llega a _____?

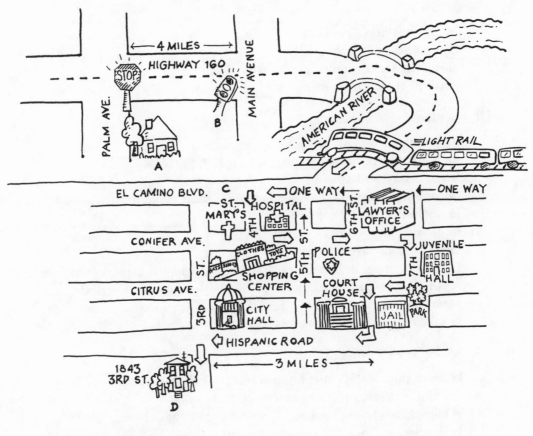

2. ¿A cuánta distancia queda _____?

3. ¿Dónde está _____?

4. ¿Me puede indicar cómo llegar a _____?

C. Make a list of places or landmarks in your city. Working with another student or in groups, write directions for getting there from your campus. Compare your directions with those of other groups. These instructions can be in the informal (tú), the formal (Ud.) or the impersonal (se___) forms.

# 10 VOCABULARIO DE CRIMINOLOGÍA / Criminal Justice Vocabulary

### I. Personal / Personnel

**el/la abogado defensor**  defense lawyer
**el/la delegado/a de organismos de patronato**  parole officer
**el/la delincuente**  delinquent
**el/la detenido/a**  detained person, person in custody
**el/la preso/a**  prisoner
**el/la recluso/a**  inmate

### II. Instituciones / Institutions

**la cárcel**  prison, jail
**la escuela de capacitación profesional**  vocational school
**el establecimiento de detención**  honor camp

la **penitenciaría**   penitentiary
el **presidio**   garrison
el **reformatorio**   reformatory, reform school
el **tribunal tutelar de menores**   juvenile court

## III. Sentencias / Sentences

**bajo fianza**   on bail
**bajo libertad condicional/provisional**   on parole
la **condena**   sentence
la **conducta honrada/buena conducta**   good behavior
la **disciplina**   discipline
la **pena**   punishment, sentence
la **pena corta/larga**   short/long sentence
la **pena de muerte/la pena capital**   death penalty, capital punishment
el **período de readaptación social**   social readjustment period
el **presidio/trabajo forzado**   hard labor
la **sanción jurídica**   judicial sanction

## IV. Miscelánea / Miscellany

la **anomalía mental**   mental instability (abnormality)
**conmutar la sentencia**   to commute a sentence
el **cumplimiento de condena**   completion of the sentence
la **deficiencia física**   physical handicap
**encarcelar**   to imprison
las **garantías/los derechos**   rights
las **leyes**   laws

la **mordida** (Mex.)   bribe
**poner en libertad**   to set free, to let out
**reformar**   to reform
la **rehabilitación social**   social rehabilitation
la **sanidad/salud**   health
el **sistema**   system

---
## PRÁCTICA
---

**A.**   Explain the following terms to someone who does not understand the judicial/penal systems of your state very well.

1. el presidio
2. el tribunal tutelar de menores
3. el reformatorio
4. el delincuente
5. el abogado defensor

6. el recluso
7. la escuela de capacitación profesional
8. la libertad condicional
9. el delegado de organismos de patronato
10. bajo fianza

**B.**   Working with another student, play the roles of a parole officer and a prisoner or ex-prisoner. The parole officer should determine as much as possible about the criminal history of the prisoner. Several sample cases are given on page 77. Use your imagination to expand the details given. The following questions will help the parole officer find out more about the prisoner.

1. ¿De qué institución se le acaba de poner en libertad?
2. ¿Cuánto tiempo pasó en _____?
3. ¿Cuándo salió de _____?
4. ¿Por qué delito se le encarceló?
5. ¿Estuvo Ud. encarcelado/a en alguna otra ocasión?
6. De joven, ¿estuvo Ud. en alguna institución para menores?
7. ¿Qué trabajo hacía en _____?
8. ¿Formaba parte de algún programa allí?
9. ¿Qué me puede contar de su trabajo nuevo?
10. ¿Cómo pasa sus horas libres después del trabajo?
11. ¿Cómo encuentra su ajuste a la sociedad?
12. ¿Qué planes tiene con su vida?
13. ¿Conoce Ud. las condiciones de su libertad condicional? ¿Cuáles son?
14. ¿Por qué no asistió a su última cita conmigo?
15. ¿Por qué cambió su lugar de residencia sin permiso?

## Case #1

Juan Pérez Martínez was cited for burglary at the age of fourteen. He was sent to Juvenile Hall but was released because it was his first offense. At fifteen he was cited for car theft and sent to Juvenile Hall for six months. When he was sixteen he committed an armed robbery and was sentenced to the State Juvenile Correctional System for three years. He was released after a year and a half for good behavior. Two years later, in a dispute in a local bar, he shot and killed another man. He was sentenced to seven years in State Prison. He served five of the seven years and is currently out on parole, looking for a job.

## Case #2

At fifteen Elena Sánchez Rodríguez was arrested for "joyriding" in a stolen car. She was sent to a girl's reformatory, where she served six months. One year later she and an accomplice were arrested for passing bad checks and for possession of stolen credit cards. She was returned to the same reformatory and served one year there. While at that facility, she participated in a vocational program and learned some secretarial skills. Now that she is out on parole, she is applying for a job through the Re-entry Job Program.

## Case #3

At twenty-one Ismael Ramírez Santiago was arrested for selling drugs to an under-cover agent. He was sentenced to three years in State Prison. While serving his sentence there, he got into a fight with another inmate, who suffered serious knife wounds. Two years were added to his sentence as a result of that incident. Six months after being released on parole, he lost contact with his parole officer and left the state. He was later arrested in New York for kidnap and forcible rape. He has served half of his ten-year sentence, and the parole board is considering his request for release on parole.

# 11 CALÓ / Slang

## I.  Las bebidas / Drinking

|  |  | *Standard Spanish* |
|---|---|---|
| to be drunk | **estar / andar cueto / bombo / jalado / pando / pedo / pisto / tomado / bebido / borracho** | estar embria- gado |
| to get drunk | **encuetarse** | embriagarse |
| to have a hangover | **curarse la cruda** | tener una resaca |
| to be a drunk | **ser pisto / pipa** | ser borracho |
| to be an alcoholic | **ser pisto / uva / waino** | ser alco- hólico |
| to drink | **pistear** | beber / tomar |
| a drink | **un trago / una copa / un cuetazo / un farolazo** | una bebida |
| beer | **una bironga, una birria, una  cheve** | una cerveza |
| a beer drinker | **un berrio** |  |
| liquor | **el pisto** | el licor |
| drunk driving test (figure four) | **hacer el cuatro** |  |

## PRÁCTICA

A.  Give standard Spanish for these expressions.

1. ser waino
2. estar pando
3. curarse la cruda

4. ser berrio
5. encuetarse

B.  Give as many slang expressions as possible for the following standard Spanish expressions.

1. andar embriagado
2. ser alcohólico

3. una bebida
4. una cerveza

C.  Express the following questions in Spanish.

1. Are you drunk?
2. Do you have a hangover?
3. Are you a drunkard?
4. How many drinks have you had?
5. How many beers have you had?

## II. Drogas / Drugs

to be under the influence of drugs   **estar endrogado**
to "kick" the drug habit   **kikear la droga**
to "push" drugs   **puchar drogas**
a person who carries drugs into prison   **el burro/caballo/mulo**
a person who gets high on aspirins   **un aspirino**
drugs in capsule (pill) form   **la cachucha**
to "pop" pills   **tomar un cachuchazo**
to make homemade pills   **encachuchar**
a pill "popper"   **un píldoro**
marijuana   **el bote/la grifa/la hierba/la juanita/la mota/el zacate/la yerba/
          la yesca**
joint, "roach"   **el leño/la cucaracha**
a marijuana user   **un grifo/moto**
to get a lid of marijuana   **apañar un bote/una lata**
to smoke dope   **tronárselas**
"reds"   **las coloradas/los colos/los diablitos/las pingas**
a person who uses "reds"   **un colorado/pingo**
to get high on "reds"   **ponerse colorado**
"whites"   **las blancas**
a person who uses "whites"   **un blanco**
to get high on "whites"   **ponerse blanco**
heroin   **la carga/la carne/el hero/el veneno**
to shoot heroin   **clavarse/componerse/chotear/filerearse/picarse con carga**
visible scars left from "shooting" heroin   **los trakes (traques)**

## PRÁCTICA

A. Explain the following slang expressions in standard Spanish.

1. grifo
2. leño
3. tomar un cachuchazo
4. clavarse con carne
5. kikear la droga

6. apañar una lata
7. ponerse blanco
8. puchar drogas
9. ponerse colorado
10. un mulo

B. Give as many slang expressions as possible for the following standard Spanish expressions and English phrases.

1. marijuana
2. heroin

3. to smoke dope
4. to shoot heroin

C. Express the following questions in Spanish.

1. Have you been taking any drugs?
2. How many "reds" have you had?
3. Have you been smoking dope?
4. Are you high on "reds" or "whites"?
5. Have you ever kicked the habit?

### III. Miscelánea / Miscellany

jail   **el bote/la pinta/el tambo**
to throw in jail   **echar en la pinta**
paddy wagon   **la julia**
police   **la ley/chota/placa/jura, los marranos/perros**
parole officer   **la cola**
a "squealer"   **un rajón/rata/soplón**
to steal   **jambar/volarse**
prostitute   **la bruja/piruja**
house of prostitution   **el congal/burdel**
pimp   **el padrote**
illegal alien   **el ilegal/alambrista/mojado**
alien registration card   **la mica**
immigration patrol   **la migra**
Anglo-American   **el/la gaba, el gabacho, la gaviota/gabacha/gabardina/
              güera**
barrio-made gun   **el fierro/cuete**
knife   **la fila/el filero**
blackjack   **la macana**

## PRÁCTICA

**A.**   Explain the following slang expressions in standard Spanish.

1. echar en la pinta          4. mica

2. cola                       5. migra

3. padrote                    6. burdel

**B.**   Give as many slang expressions as possible for the following standard Spanish expressions and English phrases.

1. la policía                 4. illegal alien

2. paddy wagon                5. Anglo woman

3. el soplón                  6. la prostituta

**C.**   Express the following questions in Spanish.

1. Are you carrying a gun or knife?

2. May I see your immigration card?

3. Do you know who stole the car?

4. Have you ever been in jail before?

# 12 EL AUTOMÓVIL / The Automobile

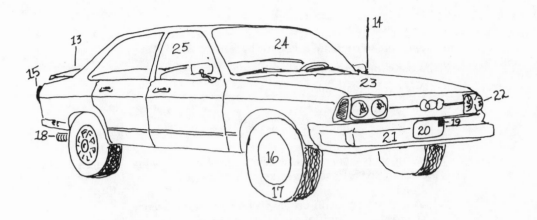

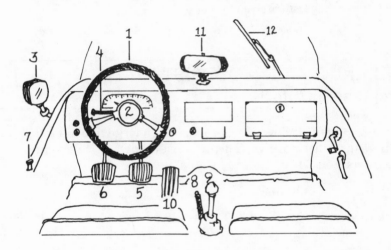

1. el volante
2. el claxon
3. el espejo lateral
4. el intermitente
5. el freno de pie
6. el embrague
7. el seguro
8. el freno de manos
9. la caja de cambios
10. el acelerador

11. el espejo retrovisor
12. el limpiaparabrisas
13. la cajuela / el porta-
    maletas
14. la antena
15. los faroles / las luces
    traseras
16. la tapa (el tapacubos)
17. la rueda / llanta, el
    neumático

18. el tubo de escape
19. la etiqueta de
    matrícula
20. la placa
21. la defensa (parachoques)
22. los faroles / las luces
    delanteras
23. el cofre
24. el parabrisas
25. la ventana, el cristal

## PRÁCTICA

**A.** Practice giving the Spanish names for the parts of a car, using the drawings above.

**B.**   Give the English equivalent of the following phrases. Pay particular attention to the use of the verbs **prender**, **poner**, and **pisar**.

1. Toque el claxon.
2. Prenda las luces delanteras.
3. Prenda las luces traseras.
4. Pise el freno.
5. Pise el acelerador.
6. Ponga el intermitente a la derecha.
7. Ponga el intermitente a la izquierda.
8. Ponga el limpiaparabrisas.
9. Ponga el freno de manos.
10. Déjeme ver su llanta de repuesto.

**C.**   Working with another student, select one of the following situations to "act out". Try to use the vocabulary and expressions from this section.

1. A highway patrol officer conducting a safety inspection.
2. A prospective buyer of a used car and a car sales person.
3. Driving lessons given by a driving instructor.

# 13 PARANDO A UN MOTORISTA / Stopping a Motorist

Practice saying the following questions. Then write two answers for each question, one negative, the other positive. Then write a follow-up statement or question for each of the answers you wrote.

|  | Question | Answers | Follow-up |
|---|---|---|---|
| *Model:* | ¿Me da su licencia de manejar? | → Sí, aquí está. <br> → No tengo licencia. | → Gracias. <br> → ¿Sabe Ud. que es contra la ley manejar sin licencia? |

1. ¿Es éste su domicilio actual?

2. ¿Tiene Ud. el documento de matrícula de su coche?

3. ¿Sabía Ud. que . . .

   a. iba a una velocidad excesiva?

   b. su matrícula no está vigente?

   c. una de sus luces no prende?

   d. sale mucho humo de su coche?

   e. seguía al otro coche muy de cerca?

   f. no paró al llegar al alto?

   g. pasó una luz roja?

|        Question        |        Answers        |        Follow-up        |
|------------------------|-----------------------|-------------------------|

4. ¿Ha sido revisado este coche
   recientemente?

5. ¿Quién es el dueño de este carro?

6. ¿Ha tomado . . .
      a. licor?     b. medicina     c. drogas

7. ¿Cómo se hizo ese abollón en el
   carro?

8. ¿Cuándo se rompió ese cristal?

9. ¿Por qué no tiene puesto su
   cinturón de seguridad?

10. ¿Me hace el favor de firmar
    aquí?

## PRÁCTICA

The following are key words that should suggest questions similar to the preceding ones. Working with another student, formulate interview questions based on the key words.

1. speed?

2. car registration expired?

3. car owner?

4. red light?

5. medicine?

6. driver's license?

7. sign here?

8. smog?

9. present address?

10. dent?

11. stop sign?

12. following close?

13. broken light?

14. liquor?

# 14 LA ADVERTENCIA MIRANDA / The Miranda Warning

Ud. tiene el derecho de permanecer callado. Lo que diga puede usarse contra Ud. en un tribunal (una corte) de justicia. Tiene el derecho de hablar a un abogado y tenerlo presente cuando Ud. sea interrogado. Si no puede pagar a un abogado, le será nombrado uno para que lo represente antes de que sea interrogado, si así lo desea.

*You have the right to remain silent. Anything you say may be used against you in a court of law. You have the right to talk to a lawyer and have him present with you while you are being questioned. If you cannot afford to hire a lawyer, one will be appointed to represent you before any questioning, if you wish one.*

## PRÁCTICA

**A.** Fill in the missing words without consulting the Spanish text.

Ud. tiene el derecho de _____ callado. Lo que diga puede _____

contra Ud. en un _____ (una _____) de justicia. Tiene el

_____ de hablar a un _____ y tenerlo presente cuando Ud. sea

_____. Si no puede _____ a un abogado, le será nombrado uno para

que lo _____ antes de que sea _____, si así lo _____.

**B.** Memorize the Miranda Warning in Spanish, and practice it with other students.

**C.** Identify the following pictures in Spanish and use the word in a sentence.

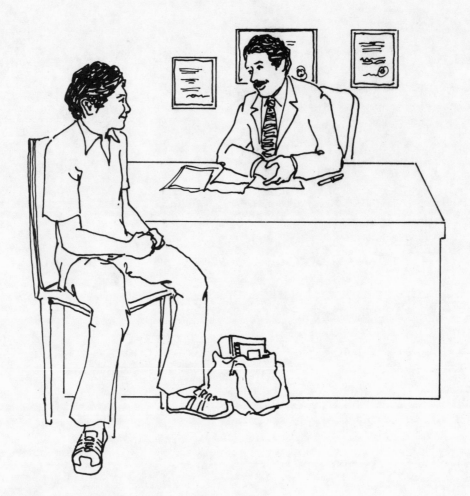

# CAPÍTULO 3

La enseñanza/
Education

# 1 DIÁLOGOS / Dialogs

## A. La matrícula

*Secretaria:* ¿Su *nombre* y *apellido*, por favor?

*Señora:* Francisca Benítez de Beltrán.

*Secretaria:* ¿Y su *hijo*?

*Señora:* Faustino Beltrán Benítez.

*Secretaria:* ¿Su *edad*?

*Señora:* ¿La mía?

*Secretaria:* No, la de su hijo Faustino.

*Señora:* Tiene once años.

*Secretaria:* Bien. ¿Nació en México?

*Señora:* Sí, señorita, en Rosarito, Baja California. Aquí está su *acta de nacimiento*.

*Secretaria:* ¿Para qué año es su *matrícula*?

*Señora:* Para el sexto *año*.

*Secretaria:* La *boleta* (*libreta*) de *calificaciones*, por favor.

*Señora:* Aquí está.

*Secretaria:* ¡Ah! Muy buenas *notas*.

*Señora:* Muy amable.

## B. El porvenir

*Consejero:* Siéntese, por favor. ¿Ud. es el *alumno* (*estudiante*) Joaquín Alemán?

*Joaquín:* Sí, señor, para servirle.

*Consejero:* Soy el señor Ignacio Godínez, su *consejero* (*asesor*) académico.

*Joaquín:* Mucho gusto.

*Consejero:* Igualmente. Quiero hablarle acerca del *examen* nacional de *capacitación* básica.

*Joaquín:* ¿Qué? ¿*Reprobé* el examen?

*Consejero:* No, al contrario. Ud. lo aprobó con una calificación de *sobresaliente*.

*Joaquín:* ¡Ah! Me da mucho gusto saber eso.

*Consejero:* Hablé con el *director* de la *escuela* y él quiere recomendarlo para una *beca* nacional de *estudios universitarios*. ¿Qué le parece?

*Joaquín:* ¡Eso sería estupendo!

*Consejero:* Ud. *se gradúa* este junio *próximo*, ¿no es así?

*Joaquín:* Con el favor de Dios.

Consejero: Bien, pues entonces *solicite* una beca del *gobierno federal.*
Nosotros le *apoyamos* su *solicitud.*

Joaquín: Muchísimas gracias. ¿Qué clase de beca *solicito*?

Consejero: Eso depende de la *vocación* que Ud. tenga. ¿Qué *profesión* le interesa? ¿Le gustaría ser *médico, abogado, profesor* de lenguas, *antropólogo*? Dígame.

Joaquín: Pues yo siempre he querido ser médico. Mis padres están de acuerdo.

Consejero: Magnífico. Aquí en esta ciudad hay una universidad con una *escuela (facultad)* de medicina de renombre. Vaya Ud. a la *rectoría* y *recoja* una solicitud para empezar los estudios preliminares. Yo le ayudo a *llenar* los *formularios.*

Joaquín: Mañana mismo lo haré. Muchas gracias, señor Godínez.

Consejero: No hay de que.

## PRÁCTICA

A.  Working with another student, practice the dialogs aloud, concentrating on pronunciation and fluency. As you become more proficient, try to vary some of the elements of the dialogs.

Model:   ¿Y su hijo? ⟶
         ¿Y su *hija*?

B.  Translate the dialogs into English. Then compare your translation with the ones given in the Appendix (pages 169–170).

C.  Translate the English text of the dialogs into Spanish, without consulting the original as you work. Then compare your translations with the Spanish version given here.

## 2 VOCABULARIO DE LOS DIÁLOGOS / Vocabulary from the Dialogs

### Vocabulario del diálogo A

**el acta (*f*) de nacimiento**   birth certificate
**el año**   year (in school)
**el apellido**   last name
**la boleta**   card
**la calificación**   grade (A, B . . .)

**la edad**   age
**el/la hijo/a**   child; son/daughter
**la libreta**   notebook; (grade) card
**la matrícula**   registration
**el nombre**   (first) name
**la nota**   grade (A, B, . . .)

### Vocabulario del diálogo B

**el/la abogado**   lawyer
**académico/a**   academic
**el/la alumno/a**   student

**el/la antropólogo/a**   anthropologist
**apoyar**   to support
**aprobar (ue)**   to pass

el/la **asesor**(a)   advisor
la **beca**   scholarship
la **capacitación**   competency
el/la **consejero/a**   advisor
el/la **director**(a)   principal
la **escuela**   school
el/la **estudiante**   student
los **estudios**   studies
el **examen**   exam
la **facultad**   school, division (of a
    university)
el **formulario**   application
el **gobierno federal**   federal government
**graduarse**   to graduate
**llenar**   to fill out

el/la **médico**   doctor, physician
el **porvenir**   future
la **profesión**   profession
el/la **profesor**(a)   teacher, professor
**próximo/a**   next
**recoger**   to pick up
la **rectoría**   administration (of a
    school)
**reprobar** (**ue**)   to fail
**sobresaliente**   outstanding
**solicitar**   to apply for
la **solicitud**   application form
la **universidad**   university
**universitario/a**   university (*adj.*)
la **vocación**   vocation

## PRÁCTICA

**A.**   Fill in the blanks with the proper form of words from the lists.

1. La persona que se gradúa de la facultad de derecho es un(a) _____.

2. Durante la _____ se escogen las clases para el año académico.

3. El que recibe una excelente calificación recibe una nota _____.

4. El documento oficial de nacimiento es el _____ _____
   _____.

5. Cuando uno termina sus estudios, se _____.

6. El sistema político de un país es el _____ _____.

7. Una persona que estudia la ciencia del hombre es un _____.

8. Ernesto recibió una _____ para hacer estudios avanzados en la
   _____.

9. Si uno solicita algo, tiene que llenar una _____. En muchos casos tiene
   que indicar su _____ completo y el _____ en que está en la
   escuela o universidad.

10. La persona que enseña idiomas es un _____ de lenguas.

11. ¿Qué _____ tiene su _____? ¿Once años?

**B.**   Give the antonym (opposite) of these words.

1. aprobar                    5. dejar

2. incapacitación             6. pasado

3. desanimar                  7. anterior

4. vaciar

C. Give a synonym (word similar in meaning) for these words.

| | |
|---|---|
| 1. calificación | 9. prueba |
| 2. estudiante | 10. estudios avanzados |
| 3. escuela | 11. nombre paterno o materno |
| 4. doctor | 12. jefe, encargado |
| 5. consejero | 13. pedir |
| 6. vocación | 14. escuela especializada |
| 7. libreta | 15. formulario |
| 8. colegio | 16. oficina del director |

# 3 VERBOS RELACIONADOS CON LA ENSEÑANZA / Verbs Related to Education

abrir  to open
aplicar  to apply
aplicarse  to apply oneself (to studies)
apoyar  to support
ausentarse  to be absent
ayudar  to help
barrer  to sweep
callarse  to be quiet
castigar  to punish
cocinar  to cook
conseguir (i)  to obtain
contestar  to answer
correr  to run
cuidar  to care for
dar (doy)  to give
devolver (ue)  to return
dividir  to divide
enfermarse  to become ill
enseñar  to teach
entregar  to turn in
escribir  to write
estudiar  to study
graduarse  to graduate
gustar  to like
hablar  to talk
hacer (hago)  to do; to make
interesar  to be interesting
ir (voy)  to go
jugar (ue)  to play

lavarse  to wash
leer  to read
levantarse  to get up
limpiar  to clean
llegar (tarde)  to arrive (late)
mandar/enviar  to send
matricularse  to enroll, register
multiplicar  to multiply
nacer (nazco)  to be born
obedecer (obedezco)  to obey
pasar lista  to take roll
pelear  to fight
perder (ie)  to lose
permitir  to permit, allow
poder (ue)  can, to be able
poner (pongo)  to put, place
preparar  to prepare
querer (ie)  to want; to like
recoger (recojo)  to pick up
restar  to subtract
romper  to break
sentarse (ie)  to sit
solicitar  to apply for
sumar  to add
supervisar  to supervise
trabajar  to work
traer (traigo)  to bring
tratar de + *infinitive*  to try to
   (do something)

## PRÁCTICA

**A.**  Working with another student, ask and answer the following questions in as many ways as possible, using verbs from the preceding list. Pay particular attention to verb tenses.

*Present:*          ¿Qué hace el estudiante?

                    *Model:*   El estudiante *abre su libro de texto.*

*Preterite:*        ¿Qué hizo el estudiante ayer?

*Imperfect:*        ¿Qué hacía la alumna cuando el profesor entró?

*Future:*           ¿Qué hará la profesora mañana?

*Present
subjunctive:*       ¿Qué quieres que haga el director?

**B.**  Fill in the blanks with the correct form of the verbs in parentheses.

Ayer Pablo _____ tarde y se _____ en su pupitre. Después de
                    (llegar)                        (sentar)

_____ lista, noté que él _____ en un papel y _____ con
   (pasar)                         (escribir)                      (hablar)

su amigo Francisco. Le pedí que me _____ el papel, pero no me
                                        (dar)

_____. Se _____ y me _____ lo que había
   (obedecer)          (levantar)            (leer)

_____. Él _____ de enseñar a Francisco a _____. Como
   (escribir)          (tratar)                                (dividir)

Ud. sabe, a Francisco no le _____ las matemáticas.
                                (gustar)

**C.**  Working with another student, ask and answer the following questions as if you were interviewing a new student.

1. ¿Eres nuevo/a en esta escuela?

2. ¿En qué escuela estudiabas antes?

3. ¿Te gusta esta escuela?

4. ¿Quién es tu consejero?

5. ¿Lees y escribes inglés?

6. ¿Te enseñaron a multiplicar y dividir?

7. ¿Adónde vas ahora?

8. ¿Qué profesión te interesa estudiar?

# 4 PERSONAL Y SITIOS ESCOLARES / Personnel and School Areas

Give the English equivalent of these words.

## I.   Personal / Personnel

el/la alumno/a, estudiante
el/la auxiliar/ayudante
el/la cocinero/a
el/la consejero/a, asesor(a)
el/la director(a)
el/la enfermero/a
el/la entrenador(a)
el estudiantado

el/la maestro/a
el/la portero/a, mozo/a
el/la profesor(a)
el profesorado
el/la rector(a)
el/la secretario/a
el/la superintendente

The word **maestro/a** is used primarily to refer to grade or high school teachers. **Profesor(a)** is more frequently used with university professors.

## II.   Sitios escolares / School Areas

el área (f) de fumar
el aula (f)/salón
el baño/excusado
la biblioteca
la cafetería
el centro estudiantil
la enfermería
la escuela de arquitectura
la escuela de bellas artes
la escuela de párvulos
el estacionamiento
el estadio
la facultad de ciencias
la facultad de derecho
la facultad de economía

la facultad de filosofía y letras
la facultad de medicina
la facultad de teología
el gimnasio
la librería
el museo
la oficina central
la oficina de consejeros
el patio de recreo
la primaria
la rectoría
la sala de los profesores
la secundaria
la universidad

## PRÁCTICA

**A.**   Working with another student, ask and answer the following questions.

1.  ¿Dónde está el/la _____?

2.  ¿Quién es ese/a señor(a)?

3.  ¿Hay un(a) _____ en esta escuela?

4.  ¿Cuántos/as _____ hay aquí?

**B.**   Describe the function of each of the persons listed in **Personal**, as if you were explaining their jobs to a newly-arrived student.

**C.** Take the same student on a tour of the school, explaining the function of each room and area.

**D.** Using personnel from the preceding list and verbs from section 3, describe the duties of four school employees, naming at least six duties per person.

*Model:* La enfermera ──→ Trabaja en la enfermería.

Pone inyecciones.

Cuida a los enfermos.

Ayuda al médico.

Manda a los estudiantes enfermos a casa.

Aplica curitas a las heridas.

# 5 MATERIALES ESCOLARES / School Materials

## I. Artículos del aula / Classroom Articles

**el aparato de proyección/proyector** projector

**el armario** closet

**la bandera** flag

**el borrador** (chalkboard) eraser

**la calculadora** calculator

**las cortinas** curtains

**la duplicadora/copiadora** copier, mimeograph machine

**el escritorio** desk

**el gis/la tiza** chalk

**la grabadora/el magnetofón** tape recorder

**el lapicero** mechanical pencil

**la máquina de escribir** typewriter

**la pantalla** screen (for movies)

**el pegamento/la pegadura** glue

**la pizarra/el pizarrón** chalkboard

**el pupitre/mesabanco** (student's) desk

**el reloj** clock, watch

**el sacapuntas** pencil sharpener

**el tablón de anuncios** bulletin board

**las tijeras** scissors

## II. Materiales del estudiante / Student's Supplies

**la bolsa de comida** lunch bag

**el borrador de goma** eraser

**el dinero para la comida** lunch money

**el lápiz** pencil

**la libreta/el cuaderno** notebook

**el libro de texto** textbook

**el maletín** book bag

**el papel/la hoja de papel** piece of paper

**el papel de color** colored paper

**las pinturas** paints

**la pluma atómica/el bolígrafo** ballpoint pen

**la pluma fuente** fountain pen

**la regla** ruler

## PRÁCTICA

**A.** Name as many of the objects in the classroom as you can without consulting the preceding lists. What other objects could be in the classroom?

**B.** Explain to a parent what materials his or her child needs to bring to school, and what objects will be supplied by the school district.

---

## 6  LOS CURSOS Y LA TAREA / Courses and Homework

**los apuntes**  notes

**el borrador**  rough draft, eraser

**el bosquejo/esquema**  outline

**la calificación/nota**  grade (A, B . . .)

**el capítulo**  chapter

**la clase**  class

**la clase de arte**  art class

**la clase de caligrafía**  penmanship

**la clase de ciencias**  science

**la clase de deletreo**  spelling

**la clase de geografía**  geography

**la clase de idioma/lengua**  language

**la clase de lectura**  reading

**la clase de matemáticas**  math

**la clase de música**  music

**el comportamiento/la conducta**
    behavior

**la composición**  composition

**el curso**  course, semester

**el deporte**  sport

**el dictado**  dictation

**el diploma**  diploma

**el ejercicio**  exercise

**la ficha**  file card, index card

**el informe**  report, term paper

**la lista**  list

**la materia/asignatura**  subject, class
**el nivel**  level
**la obra**  work (of art, of literature, . . .)
**el párrafo**  paragraph

**el permiso**  permission
**la pregunta**  question
**la prueba/el examen**  exam, test
**el recreo**  recess
**la tarea**  homework

## PRÁCTICA

A. You are a counselor giving vocational information to a new student from Colombia. Explain to him or her what the different school periods and subjects consist of, and how the school year is organized.

B. You are a teacher giving the class instructions for a homework assignment. Choose a class from the preceding list and prepare homework instructions for several meetings. For example, for a geography class you might express the following in Spanish: "O.K., class, read pages 45 to 57 in your geography text, the chapter titled 'The Geography of Mexico.' On a sheet of paper, write in pencil a rough draft of the names of all of the rivers of Mexico. This list will be turned in tomorrow. You will have an exam on pages 40 to 44 that afternoon."

C. Choose one of the school subjects given in the preceding list and prepare a list of useful vocabulary specifically for that subject area. If possible, consult grade school and high school texts for the subject.

# 7 ENFERMEDADES COMUNES DE LOS NIÑOS / Common Childhood Ailments

Give the English equivalent of these words. Consult **Capítulo 1, La medicina/Health Care**, for additional vocabulary.

I. **Enfermedades / Illnesses**

el catarro/resfriado, la gripe
el dolor de cabeza
el dolor de estómago
el dolor de garganta
el estreñimiento
el mareo
los piojos

la rubeola
el sarampión
la tos
la vacuna contra el tétano/la difteria/
   el polio
la varicela
la viruela

II. **Materiales de la enfermería / Supplies for the Infirmary**

el alcohol
el algodón
la curita / tirita (Spain)
el desinfectante
la droga
la inyección
el medicamento

el mercurio
la pastilla / píldora
la vacuna
la venda
el vendaje
el yodo
el agua oxigenada

# PRÁCTICA

A. You are the school nurse, and children with various symptoms are sent to you. Interview the students, using the following questions as a guide. What will you prescribe or recommend?

1. ¿Estás constipado/a? ¿mareado/a?

2. ¿Tienes dolor de estómago? ¿dolor de cabeza? ¿tos? ¿catarro?

3. ¿Has tenido varicela? ¿sarampión? ¿viruela? ¿rubeola?

4. ¿Te han vacunado contra el tétano? ¿el polio? ¿la difteria?

## Case #1

Juanito appears to be sluggish today. His eyes are watery, and he coughs frequently. He might even have a fever. His body aches all over.

## Case #2

Gloria appears to have a rash and a fever. She is coughing a lot, and her eyes are inflamed. She also seems to be drowsy and irritable. She didn't eat her lunch today.

## Case #3

A few days ago Víctor complained of a mild headache, loss of appetite, and fever. He was sent home. He came back to school today, but he has little red pinpoints all over his body. He scratches a lot.

## Case #4

Delia was sent home last week because of a cold (sneezing, running nose, hoarseness, mild fever). Since she did not want to miss today's field trip, she came back to school today. Her face is swollen and her eyes are watering. She seems to have a cough with a whoop, accompanied by a wheezing sound when she breathes.

B. What treatment do you recommend for the following ailments? Give as many suggestions as possible.

1. un rasguño

2. un dolor de cabeza

3. una cortadura

4. una fiebre

5. el ojo morado

6. la gripe

# 8 LA NUTRICIÓN / Nutrition

## I.  Azúcares y dulces / Sugar and Sweets

Match the Spanish words with the pictures.

1. _____ el azúcar
2. _____ el azúcar de confitería
3. _____ el azúcar moreno
4. _____ el azucarado
5. _____ el chicle
6. _____ los chocolates
7. _____ los dulces/caramelos
8. _____ el flan

9. _____ las galletas
10. _____ la jalea
11. _____ la melaza
12. _____ la mermelada
13. _____ la miel
14. _____ el pastel
15. _____ el pudín/budín

## II.  Bebidas / Drinks

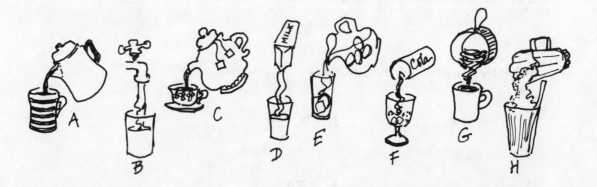

Match the Spanish words with the pictures.

1. _____ el agua (*f*)          4. _____ la leche          7. _____ un refresco /

2. _____ un café               5. _____ una limonada         una soda

3. _____ un chocolate          6. _____ la malteada       8. _____ un té

## III. Carnes / Meats

Match the Spanish words with the pictures.

1. _____ el carnero / cordero / borrego /          5. _____ el pato

     la oveja                                    6. _____ el puerco / cerdo

2. _____ el conejo / la liebre                   7. _____ la ternera / el ternero

3. _____ la gallina / el pollo                   8. _____ la vaca / la res (Mex.)

4. _____ el guajolote (Mex.) / pavo / cócono     9. _____ el venado

Give the English equivalent of the following meat products and **vísceras** (*innards*).

| | | |
|---|---|---|
| la carne picada/molida | el hígado | los riñones |
| el corazón | el jamón | el salame |
| el chorizo | el menudo/mondongo/las tripas | la salchicha |
| la chuleta | la morcilla | los sesos/la cabeza |
| la fiambre | la mortadela | el tocino |

¿Cuáles de estas víceras le gustan a Ud. y cuáles no le gustan?

## IV. Frutas / Fruits

Match the Spanish words with the pictures.

1. _____ el aguacate
2. _____ las cerezas
3. _____ las ciruelas
4. _____ las ciruelas pasas
5. _____ el chabacano/albaricoque
6. _____ el durazno/melocotón
7. _____ las frambuesas
8. _____ las fresas
9. _____ la granada
10. _____ el higo
11. _____ la lima
12. _____ el limón
13. _____ la mandarina
14. _____ el mango
15. _____ la manzana

16. _____ el melón
17. _____ el membrillo
18. _____ las moras
19. _____ la naranja
20. _____ la papaya
21. _____ las pasas
22. _____ la pera
23. _____ **el pérsimo/caqui (Spain)**
24. _____ la piña
25. _____ **el plátano/guineo/la banana**
26. _____ la sandía
27. _____ **la toronja/el pomelo (Spain)**
28. _____ las uvas
29. _____ las zarzamoras

## PRÁCTICA

Working with another student, ask and answer the following questions.

1. ¿De qué frutas es esa ensalada de fruta?

2. ¿De qué sabor es la gelatina?

3. ¿Qué jugo bebiste esta mañana?

4. ¿Te gusta el/la _____?

5. ¿Te gustan los/las _____?

6. ¿Qué frutas son citrosas?

7. ¿Qué frutas son tropicales?

## V. Nueces / Nuts

Match the Spanish words with the pictures.

1. _____ la almendra

2. _____ el anacardo

3. _____ la avellana

4. _____ el cacahuate/cacahuete/maní

5. _____ la nuez

6. _____ el piñón

7. _____ el pistacho

## VI. Grasas, aceites y aderezos / Fats, Oils, and Dressings

Match the Spanish words with the pictures.

1. _____ el aceite de cacahuete

2. _____ el aceite de girasol

3. _____ el aceite de maíz

4. _____ el aceite de oliva

5. _____ el aceite de soja

6. _____ la manteca

7. _____ la mantequilla

8. _____ la mantequilla de cacahuate

9. _____ la margarina

10. _____ la mayonesa

11. _____ la mostaza

## VII.  La leche y los productos lácteos / Milk and Dairy Products

Give the English equivalent of the following words.

la crema

la crema agria

la crema batida / la nata

**el huevo** (not a milk product)

la leche

la leche condensada

la leche cruda

**la leche evaporada**

## VIII.  Harinas y cereales / Flours and Cereals

Harina . . . **de arroz**   rice flour

**de maicena**   corn flour

**de maíz**   cornmeal

**de trigo**   wheat flour

**enriquecida (con hierro y vitamina B)**

enriched (with iron and Vitamin B) flour

Cereales . . . **el arroz**   rice

**la avena**   oats

**la cebada**   barley

**el centeno**   rye

**el salvado**   bran

**la sémola**   grits

**el trigo**   wheat

Match the Spanish words with the pictures.

1. _____ **el bizcocho**

2. _____ **la galleta de sal / soda**

3. _____ **los macarrones**

4. _____ **el pan**

5. _____ **el pan dulce**

6. _____ **el panqueque / los panquequis**

7. _____ **el pastel / «quequi»**

8. _____ **el pastel de fruta**

9. _____ **la tortilla**

## IX.  Pescados y mariscos / Fish and Shellfish

Give the English equivalent of the following words.

**las anchoas**

**el arenque (ahumado)**

**el atún**

**el bacalao**

**los calamares**

**los camarones/las gambas**

**el cangrejo**

**la langosta**

**el langostino**

**el lenguado**

**los mejillones**

**el mero**

**la ostra / el ostión**

**el salmón**

**las sardinas**

**la tortuga / caguama**

**la trucha**

## X.  Vegetales/legumbres y verduras / Vegetables and Greens

Match the Spanish words with their English equivalents.

| | | |
|---|---|---|
| _____ 1. **el ajo** | | a. peas |
| _____ 2. **la alcachofa** | | b. onion |
| _____ 3. **el apio** | | c. artichoke |
| _____ 4. **la berenjena** | | ch. beans |
| _____ 5. **el betabel/la remolacha** | | d. eggplant |
| _____ 6. **el bróculi** | | e. string beans |
| _____ 7. **el calabacín** | | f. cabbage |
| _____ 8. **la calabaza** | | g. cauliflower |
| _____ 9. **el camote** | | h. asparagus |
| _____ 10. **el camote amarillo/boniato** | | i. Brussels sprouts |
| _____ 11. **la cebolla** | | j. spinach |
| _____ 12. **la col/repollo** | | k. garlic |
| _____ 13. **la col de Bruselas** | | l. pepper |
| _____ 14. **la coliflor** | | ll. celery |
| _____ 15. **los chícharos/guisantes** | | m. pumpkin, squash |
| _____ 16. **el chile/ají** | | n. yam |
| _____ 17. **los ejotes/las judías** | | ñ. beet |
| _____ 18. **los espárragos** | | o. broccoli |
| _____ 19. **las espinacas** | | p. sweet potato |
| _____ 20. **los frijoles** | | q. zucchini |

Continue to match the Spanish words with their English equivalents.

| | | |
|---|---|---|
| _____ 1. **el garbanzo** | | a. radish |
| _____ 2. **el haba** (*f*) | | b. leek |
| _____ 3. **el hongo/champiñón/la seta** | | c. parsley |
| _____ 4. **la jícama** | | ch. potato |
| _____ 5. **la lechuga** | | d. nopal cactus, prickly pear (tuna) |
| _____ 6. **la lenteja** | | e. mustard greens |
| _____ 7. **el maíz/elote** | | f. lentil |
| _____ 8. **la mostaza** | | g. mushroom |
| _____ 9. **el nabo** | | h. lima bean |
| _____ 10. **el nopal** | | i. bell (chili) pepper |
| _____ 11. **la papa** | | j. tomato |
| _____ 12. **el pepino** | | k. chickpea |
| _____ 13. **el perejil** | | l. carrot |
| _____ 14. **el pimiento verde/rojo** | | ll. lettuce |
| _____ 15. **el puerro** | | m. corn |
| _____ 16. **el rábano** | | n. turnip |
| _____ 17. **el tomate/jitomate** | | ñ. cucumber |
| _____ 18. **la zanahoria** | | o. jicama |

## PRÁCTICA

**A.** Classify the following foods according to the general category into which they fall.

1. espinacas
2. duraznos
3. trucha
4. pepino
5. chuleta

6. almendra
7. acelga
8. manteca
9. miel
10. frambuesas

11. cerezas
12. apio
13. bizcocho
14. plátano
15. cebada

**B.** Describe in detail the ingredients found in the following dishes.

1. salad (vegetable or fruit)
2. dessert
3. sandwich
4. stew
5. casserole

**C.** Describe what you ate yesterday.

**D.** Prepare a description of a well-balanced breakfast, lunch, and dinner menu for a child. Compare your description with those of other students, and practice explaining your suggested menu as if you were speaking to a child.

**E.** Prepare a typical school cafeteria menu for one week.

**F.** You are the school nurse and are having a conference with Sergio's parents regarding his nutrition. You find him to be underweight. Express the following suggestions in Spanish, as if you were talking to Sergio's parents.

1. Sergio should see his doctor to eliminate any medical causes of his underweight condition.

2. He should have eight to ten hours rest in bed each night. A warm bath at bedtime would help him to sleep. Also, a half hour of rest before the evening meal would be a good idea.

3. While eating, he should have pleasant surroundings and avoid thinking about problems.

4. All foods should be attractively served.

5. To increase his appetite, Sergio should do mild exercise as soon as he gets up in the morning.

# 9 MANDATOS / Commands

Study the examples of how to form positive and negative **Ud.** and **tú** commands. Then complete each chart.

## I.   -Ar verbs

| infinitive | INFORMAL (tú) | | FORMAL (Ud.) | |
|---|---|---|---|---|
| | POSITIVE | NEGATIVE | POSITIVE | NEGATIVE |
| mirar | mira | no mires | mire | no mire |
| llevar | lleva | no lleves | lleve | no lleve |
| calmarse | cálmate | no te calmes | cálmese | no se calme |
| sentarse (ie) | siéntate | no te sientes | siéntese | no se siente |
| aplicarse | aplícate | no te apliques | aplíquese | no se aplique |
| apoyar | | | | |
| ausentarse | | | | |
| cocinar | | | | |
| cuidar | | | | |
| enfermarse | | | | |
| enseñar | | | | |
| jugar (ue) | | | | |
| lavarse | | | | |
| levantarse | | | | |
| comprar | | | | |
| mandar | | | | |
| matricularse | | | | |
| pasar | | | | |
| preparar | | | | |
| restar | | | | |
| solicitar | | | | |
| sumar | | | | |
| supervisar | | | | |
| trabajar | | | | |

## II.   -Er and -ir verbs

| infinitive | INFORMAL (tú) | | FORMAL (Ud.) | |
|---|---|---|---|---|
| | POSITIVE | NEGATIVE | POSITIVE | NEGATIVE |
| correr | corre | no corras | corra | no corra |
| escribir | escribe | no escribas | escriba | no escriba |
| vestirse (i) | vístete | no te vistas | vístase | no se vista |
| abrir | | | | |
| barrer | | | | |

devolver (ue) _____

dividir _____

leer _____

perder (ie) _____

beber _____

romper _____

## III.  Irregular verbs

| infinitive | INFORMAL (tú) | | FORMAL (Ud.) | |
|---|---|---|---|---|
| | POSITIVE | NEGATIVE | POSITIVE | NEGATIVE |
| poner | pon | no pongas | ponga | no ponga |
| venir | ven | no vengas | venga | no venga |
| irse | | | | |
| recoger | | | | |
| tener | | | | |
| traer | | | | |
| llegar (ue) | | | | |

## IV.  Verbs of all conjugations and kinds

| infinitive | INFORMAL (tú) | | FORMAL (Ud.) | |
|---|---|---|---|---|
| | POSITIVE | NEGATIVE | POSITIVE | NEGATIVE |
| esperar | | | | |
| ayudar | | | | |
| quitarse | | | | |
| pedir (i) | | | | |
| hacer | | | | |
| sacar | | | | |
| permitir | | | | |
| corregir (i) | | | | |
| pararse | | | | |
| buscar | | | | |
| obedecer | | | | |

## PRÁCTICA

**A.** Fill in the blanks with the appropriate command form.

1. **Permítame** su solicitud.

   _____ su solicitud.
      (dar)

   _____ su solicitud.
      (entregar)

2. **Recoja** un formulario.

   _____ un formulario.
      (llenar)

   _____ un formulario.
      (llevarse)

3. **Prepare** la lección.

   _____ la lección.
      (aprender)

   _____ la lección.
      (leer)

4. **Escriba** la tarea.

   _____ la tarea.
      (hacer)

   _____ la tarea.
      (preparar)

5. **Siéntese**, por favor.

   _____, por favor.
      (escuchar)

   _____, por favor.
      (estudiar)

6. **Cierre** la puerta.

   _____ la puerta.
      (abrir)

   _____ la puerta.
      (mirar)

**B.** Repeat exercise **A**, giving the familiar command forms.

**C.** Give the negative command forms of these positive commands.

1. Escuche (Ud.).
2. Obedezca (Ud.) al maestro.
3. Estudie (Ud.) la lección.
4. Déme (Ud.) la nota.
5. Habla (tú), por favor.
6. Devuelve (tú) el libro.
7. Pelea (tú).
8. Sal (tú).
9. Cierra (tú) la puerta.
10. Corre (tú).

**D.** Give the positive command forms of these negative commands.

1. No hable (Ud.) en clase.
2. No venga (Ud.) a la clase.
3. No leas (tú) el libro.
4. No pelee (Ud.) en clase.
5. No te sientes (tú).
6. No lo entregues (tú).

**E.** Express the following commands in Spanish. Use the **Ud.** form.

1. Do your homework.
2. Bring me the blue book.
3. Take this to the principal.
4. Read this paper to your parents.
5. Don't run in the hallways.
6. Go to the nurse's office . . . quickly!
7. Be quiet, please.

8. Speak louder, please.

9. Close the door (behind you) when you enter.

10. Pay attention to what I'm saying.

**G.** With another student taking the part of "teacher," act out with other students the roles of grade school students. Your actions should lead to commands given by the "teacher," who should use either informal or formal commands, but not mix the two.

# 10 PRONOMBRES COMPLEMENTOS / Object Pronouns

### I. Direct Object Pronouns

| SINGULAR | PLURAL |
|----------|--------|
| me | nos |
| te | |
| lo, la | los, las |

The direct object pronouns take the place of direct object nouns.

María compró **el cuaderno**.　　　Alberto aprobó **los exámenes**.

María **lo** compró.　　　Alberto **los** aprobó.

Rubén solicitó **la beca**.　　　Alicia reprobó **las pruebas**.

Rubén **la** solicitó.　　　Alicia **las** reprobó.

Direct object pronouns are placed before a conjugated verb (instead of after it, as in English). The direct object pronouns must agree in gender and number with the direct object nouns to which they refer.

### II. Indirect Object Pronouns

| SINGULAR | PLURAL |
|----------|--------|
| me | nos |
| te | |
| le | les |

Indirect object pronouns take the place of indirect object nouns. They are also placed before conjugated verbs.

Da el libro **(a mí)**.　　　Manda los lapiceros **(a nosotros)**.

Da**me** el libro.　　　Mánda**nos** los lapiceros.

Da la pluma **(a él)**.　　　Manda las tijeras **(a ellas)**.

Da**le** la pluma.　　　Mánda**les** las tijeras.

Only the third person singular and plural indirect object pronouns are different in form from the direct object pronouns: direct—**lo, la, los, las**; indirect—**le, les**. However, in some Spanish-speaking areas, especially in Mexico and the Southwestern United States, there is a tendency to substitute the indirect object pronoun when the "rules" call for the direct object pronoun.

| *Standard Form* | *Popular Usage* |
|---|---|
| **La** vi ayer en la oficina. | **Le** vi ayer en la oficina. |

## PRÁCTICA

**A.**  Replace the italicized direct objects with pronouns.

1. Ignacio compró *los libros* en la librería.
2. Magdalena abrazó *a Rubén*.
3. El vio *(a nosotros)* en el patio de recreo.
4. El portero limpió *los baños*.
5. Francisco consiguió *la beca*.
6. El profesor castigó *(a mí)*.
7. La maestra perdió *el gis*.
8. Yo leí *el libro*.
9. Yo tomé *la píldora*.
10. El director quiere recomendar *a Elena*.

**B.**  Replace the italicized indirect objects with pronouns.

1. La secretaria envió un recado *a los padres de Pablo*.
2. La cocinera preparó una sopa de fideo *para los alumnos*.
3. Ellos dieron permiso *(a nosotros)* para ir al zoológico.
4. La enfermera ayuda *a la médico*.
5. El entrenador enseña la higiene *a los alumnos*.
6. Ignacio Pérez ayudó *(a ti)* a llenar los formularios.
7. La enfermera puso *(a ellas)* una inyección para el catarro.

**C.**  Express the following sentences in Spanish.

1. The teacher gave her the report card.
2. The principal spoke to him about the scholarship.
3. The test? They passed it.
4. I filled out the application and handed it in.
5. The principal spoke to me about the scholarship.

## III. Double Object Pronouns with Commands

Reflexive and object pronouns are attached to affirmative commands, both familiar and formal. A written accent is required over the stressed vowel of the command form so as to maintain the proper stress pattern when the pronouns are added. Reflexive and object pronouns precede negative commands.

Da el libro (a mí).          Dame el libro.      Dámelo.       No me lo des.

Lava (a ti) la cara.         Lávate la cara.     Lávatela.     No te la laves.

Deja (a nosotros) el libro.  Déjanos el libro.   Déjanoslo.    No nos lo dejes.

The indirect object pronouns **le** and **les** change to **se** before **lo/los, la/las**.

Trae la libreta (a él).      Tráele la libreta.     Tráesela.

Quita (a ellos) los abrigos. Quítales los abrigos.  Quítaselos.

## PRÁCTICA

**A.** Give the negative form of these positive commands.

1. Cocínaselo.
2. Llévaselos.
3. Léenosla.
4. Escríbeselas.
5. Devuélvesela.

6. Corrígesela.
7. Termínaselo.
8. Déjamela.
9. Recógenoslos.
10. Contéstamelo.

# 11 SITUACIONES ESCOLARES / School Situations

Here are several situations and activities in which you might participate if you were a school employee, student, or interested parent. Think about each situation from the perspective of each of the persons involved. Prepare at least five statements or questions for each person. Then, working with another student or in groups, enact the situations.

### Situation #1

Teacher holds a conference with parents to discuss student's grades and progress in x grade. An overall progress report is presented to the parents, with comparisons of their child's work to that of other students in the class.

### Situation #2

Principal talks to visiting Mexican teacher. The principal explains topics such as curriculum, student government, administration-teacher relations, and special programs. The two discuss common problems.

### Situation #3

Teacher talks to students about discipline problems. The students are not attentive. There is too much talking, and some cheating on exams. Many students fail to turn in homework on time, and so on.

**Situation #4**

Nurse talks to student about health. Different types of recommended medical check-ups are explained: dental, eye, hearing, and general physical. Eating habits and proper exercise are discussed.

**Situation #5**

Coach talks to team captain. The past performance of the team is discussed, and the importance of the upcoming game with the town rival is emphasized. Recommendations are made about what the team captain should do to keep up the team spirit and improve game strategies.

**Situation #6**

Teacher explains homework assignment to class. Specific instructions are given about page numbers, questions to be answered, problems to be solved. Due date of the homework and the next exam date are given.

**Situation #7**

Teacher greets new student. The new student is introduced to the class with a brief biography. The student is given details about class procedures and is assigned to a desk. He/she receives classroom materials.

# CAPÍTULO 4

## El bienestar/
## Welfare

# 1 MONÓLOGO A / Monolog A

## Una llamada telefónica

Bueno, ¿está la señora Gutiérrez? . . . Gracias. . . . Bueno, ¿Señora Gutiérrez? . . . Soy _____, el/la *trabajador(a) social* del *Departamento de Bienestar* del *Condado*. . . . Sí, eso es. Hablé con Ud. ayer. Le llamo para contarle algunas cosas acerca de su *caso*. He hablado con el *director* del *Departamento de Seguro Social* y me ha dicho que le podemos *ayudar*. Hemos hablado con su *médico* y *nos hemos enterado* de todos los *detalles* del *accidente*. Esta mañana comenté el caso con su *jefe* y me ha dicho que Ud. *recibirá* algunos *beneficios*. Afortunadamente, su esposo es un *funcionario público* de la *ciudad* y está *cubierto* por un buen *seguro*. Me dijo el *agente de seguros* que van a hablar con los *testigos*, pues los *empleados* de la tienda vieron el accidente. Mañana pienso ir a su casa con los *formularios* necesarios. ¿A qué hora sería *conveniente* para *visitarle*? . . . Sí, a las once de la mañana es buena hora para mí. Mientras tanto, ¿le *hace falta* algo? . . . Sí, sí, ¿cómo se llama? . . . Padre Ortiz. ¿Es el *sacerdote* de Nuestra Señora de Guadalupe? . . . No, no lo conozco, pero sé quien es. Me repite el número, por favor. . . . 483 . . . 54 . . . 87 . . . Sí, con mucho gusto le llamaré para decirle que Ud. no podrá ir esta tarde. . . . No hay de que. Bueno, gusto de saludarle y hasta mañana. . . . Adiós.

## PRÁCTICA

A.  Practice the monolog aloud, concentrating on pronunciation and fluency. Then practice it with another student who will play the part of Sra. Gutiérrez and say what she must have said.

   *Model:*   ¿A qué hora sería conveniente para visitarle? . . . ⟶
   *Pues yo creo que a las once de la mañana. ¿Es buena hora para Ud.?*

B.  Translate the monolog into English. Then compare your translation with the one given in the Appendix (page 171).

C.  Translate the English text of the monolog into Spanish, without consulting the original as you work. Then compare your translation with the Spanish version given here.

## Vocabulario de bienestar de «Una llamada telefónica»

**el accidente**  accident
**el/la agente de seguros**  insurance agent

**ayudar**  to help, assist
**el beneficio**  benefit
**el caso**  case

**la ciudad**   city
**el condado**   county
**conveniente**   convenient
**cubrir (cubierto)**   to cover (covered)
**el departamento de bienestar**
    department of welfare
**el departamento de seguro social**
    department of social security
**el detalle**   detail
**el/la director(a)**   director
**el/la empleado/a**   employee
**enterarse**   to find out, be informed
**el formulario**   form

**el/la funcionario/a público/a**   public
    employee
**hacer falta**   to need
**el/la jefe**   boss, supervisor
**el/la médico**   doctor
**recibir**   to receive
**el sacerdote**   priest
**el seguro**   insurance
**el/la testigo**   witness
**el/la trabajador(a) social**   social
    worker
**visitar**   to visit

## PRÁCTICA

**A.**   Fill in the blanks with the proper form of words from the list.

1. Dos divisiones políticas de un estado son la _____

    y el _____.

2. Una persona que trabaja para el pueblo es un _____

    _____.

3. Un papel impreso para dar datos es un _____.

4. Una persona que ve algo es un _____.

5. Algo que ocurre sin planear es un _____.

6. El _____ _____ _____

    vende _____ contra accidentes.

7. El _____ social trabaja en el _____

    _____ _____.

8. En los Estados Unidos el _____ _____

    _____ _____ da a cada persona un

    número.

**B.**   Give the antonym (opposite) of these words.

1. generalidad
2. dar
3. jefe

4. inconveniente
5. paciente

**C.**   Give a synonym (word similar in meaning) for these words.

1. informarse
2. asistencia
3. trabajador
4. jefe
5. reverendo

6. tapar
7. necesitar
8. frecuentar
9. provecho
10. suceso

## 2 MONÓLOGO B / Monolog B

### Empleo y desempleo

Todos los días tengo que ir a mi *trabajo*. *Trabajo* desde las ocho de la mañana hasta las cinco de la tarde. Mi *día de descanso* es el domingo. Cada verano *me toca ir de vacaciones*. Llevo quince años con la misma *empresa*.

Tengo una familia y mi *deber* es *proveer*la del *sustento* necesario. Siempre hay muchos *gastos*, y no tengo muchos *recursos*. De mis *ingresos gasto* un veinte *por ciento* en *comida*. Para pagar algunas *deudas* es necesario ir a mis *ahorros*. Este *dinero* está reservado para mi *jubilación*.

Mis *compañeros* de trabajo *reclaman* más *días de fiesta* y un *aumento* de *sueldo* pues la vida se pone cada día más *cara*. Tenemos que tener mucho *cuidado* en el trabajo pues hay muchos *riesgos*. Uno puede sufrir un *accidente* y por una *lesión* estar *incapacitado* físicamente. Un amigo mío es *incompetente* y cree que el *patrón* le va a *despedir*. No me da pena, pues a él no le gusta trabajar en esta *fábrica*. Estoy seguro que no va a *estar sin empleo* (*desocupado*) por mucho tiempo. Él puede encontrar un empleo en un *taller* mecánico, pues me dice que esa «*chamba*» sí le gusta.

### PRÁCTICA

**A.** Practice the monolog aloud, concentrating on pronunciation and fluency. As you become more proficient, try to vary some of the elements of the monolog.

   *Model:*   Trabajo desde las ocho de la mañana hasta . . .  ⟶

   Trabajo desde las *once de la noche* hasta . . .

**B.** Restate the monolog, changing all of the verbs to the imperfect, then to the preterite.

**C.** Translate the monolog into English. Then compare your translation with the one given in the Appendix (page 171).

**D.** Translate the English text of the monolog into Spanish, without consulting the original as you work. Then compare your translation with the Spanish version given here.

### Vocabulario de bienestar de «Empleo y desempleo»

| | |
|---|---|
| **los ahorros**  savings | **la comida**  food |
| **el aumento**  raise, increase | **el/la compañero/a**  companion, friend |
| **caro/a**  expensive | **el cuidado**  care |

la **chamba**  job
el **deber**  duty, obligation
**desocupado/a**  unemployed
**despedir (i)**  to fire
la **deuda**  debt
el **día de descanso**  day off
el **día de fiesta**  holiday
el **dinero**  money
el **empleo**  job
la **empresa**  company
**estar sin empleo**  to be out of work
la **fábrica**  factory
**gastar**  to spend (money)
el **gasto**  expense
el/la **incapacitado/a**  physically handicapped person, unable to work
**incompetente**  incompetent

el **ingreso**  salary, money coming in
**ir de vacaciones**  to go on vacation
la **jubilación**  retirement
la **lesión**  injury
el/la **patrón(a)**  boss
el **por ciento**  percent
**proveer**  to provide
**reclamar**  to ask for, demand
el **recurso**  resource
el **riesgo**  risk
el **sueldo**  salary
el **sustento**  sustenance, support
el **taller**  shop
**tocarle a uno**  to be one's turn
**trabajar**  to work
el **trabajo**  job, work

## PRÁCTICA

**A.**  Fill in the blanks with the proper form of words from the list.

1. El símbolo % se escribe _____ _____ en español.

2. Unos lugares de trabajo son la _____, la _____ y el _____.

3. Algo que cuesta mucho dinero es _____.

4. La _____ es cuando uno no trabajo debido a la edad avanzada.

5. Dos días en los cuales no se trabaja son el _____ _____ _____ y el _____ _____ _____.

6. Jorge debe tener mucho _____ en el trabajo pues hay muchos _____. Es un trabajo peligroso.

**B.**  Give the antonym (opposite) of these words.

1. competente              6. pérdidas
2. estar empleado          7. capacitado
3. dar trabajo             8. ingresos
4. ahorrar                 9. peón
5. reducción               10. préstamo

**C.**  Give a synonym (word similar in meaning) for these words.

1. dar                     5. pequeña fábrica
2. pago, salario           6. lo que uno debe hacer
3. herida                  7. compañía
4. ser el turno de uno     8. moneda

9. trabajo

10. exigir

11. veranear

12. camarada

13. sustento

**D.** Working with another student, ask and answer the following questions, using vocabulary from the preceding list and supplying the appropriate information.

1. ¿En qué mes (fue, irá, iba) Ud. de vacaciones?

   Yo _____ de vacaciones el mes de _____.

2. ¿Quién le _____ a Ud.? (emplear, despedir, jubilar)

   La compañía _____ me _____.

3. ¿Tiene Ud. muchos/as (empleos, compañeros, accidentes, deberes, aumentos, ingresos, deudas, ahorros, gastos, recursos)?

   _____ tengo muchos/as _____.

4. ¿En dónde trabaja Ud.?

   Trabajo en un(a) (empresa, compañía, taller, fábrica).

5. ¿Desde qué mes está Ud. (sin empleo, desocupado/a)?

   Estoy _____ desde el mes de _____.

# 3 VERBOS RELACIONADOS CON EL BIENESTAR / Verbs Related to Welfare

**abrir**  to open

**ahorrar**  to save

**asistir**  to attend

**avisar**  to notify

**buscar**  to look for

**cambiar**  to change

**continuar**  to continue

**cubrir**  to cover

**cumplir (con)**  to meet, satisfy

**deber**  to owe; ought, must, should

**decir (digo)**  to say

**declarar**  to state

**dejar**  to leave, quit

**descansar**  to rest

**descontinuar**  to stop, discontinue

**despedir (i)**  to fire

**empezar (ie)**  to begin

**emplear**  to employ

**entrar**  to enter, to go in

**escribir**  to write

**exigir**  to demand

**ganar**  to earn, win

**hacer (hago)**  to do, make

**imprimir**  to print

**investigar**  to look into

**ir (voy)**  to go

**maltratar**  to mistreat

**morir (ue)**  to die

**pagar**  to pay

**poder (ue)**  to be able

**poner (pongo)**  to put

**programar**  to schedule

**proporcionar**  to provide

**recibir**  to receive

**reclamar**  to claim, demand

**reducir**  to reduce

**rehusar**  to refuse

**resolver (ue)**  to resolve, solve

**romper**  to tear, break

**trabajar**  to work

**ver**  to see

**volver (ue)**  to return

## PRÁCTICA

**A.** Complete the following sentences, using the indicated tenses.

*Present:*　　　El jefe _____ al trabajador. (pagar, maltratar, emplear, despedir)

*Preterite:*　　El obrero _____ al jefe. (escribir, avisar, buscar, exigir mucho trabajo, deber dinero)

*Future:*　　　La agencia _____ su caso. (abrir, ver, recibir, dejar, resolver, rehusar)

*Present subjunctive:*　Es necesario que Ud. _____. (ir, asistir, volver, descansar)

**B.** Using ten of the preceding verbs, write ten questions about welfare situations in the present, preterite, or imperfect tenses. Then write ten more questions using ten different verbs in any tense. Answer the questions of other students as they read them aloud, or ask and answer questions with a partner.

## 4 PRESENTE PERFECTO / Present Perfect

The present perfect tense consists of the auxiliary verb **haber** plus the past participle.

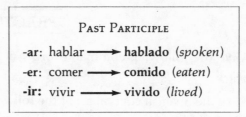

| HABER | |
|---|---|
| he | hemos |
| has | |
| ha | han |

| PAST PARTICIPLE |
|---|
| **-ar**: hablar ⟶ **hablado** (*spoken*) |
| **-er**: comer ⟶ **comido** (*eaten*) |
| **-ir**: vivir ⟶ **vivido** (*lived*) |

| PRESENT PERFECT OF **HABLAR** | | | |
|---|---|---|---|
| **he hablado** | *I have spoken* | **hemos hablado** | *we have spoken* |
| **has hablado** | *you have spoken* | | |
| **ha hablado** | *you have spoken* / *he/she has spoken* | **han hablado** | *you/they have spoken* |

## PRÁCTICA

**A.** Give the irregular past participle of the following verbs:

1. poner
2. decir
3. cubrir
4. escribir
5. romper
6. ver
7. morir
8. abrir
9. hacer
10. resolver
11. volver
12. imprimir

**B.**  Give at least five different answers for each of the following questions, using the present perfect tense of verbs in section 3.

1. ¿Qué ha hecho la agencia en este caso?
2. ¿Qué ha hecho el jefe esta mañana?
3. ¿Qué han hecho sus hijos con los ingresos?
4. ¿Qué hemos hecho que no le ha gustado nuestro servicio?
5. ¿Qué ha hecho Ud. durante su período de desempleo?

# 5  MANDATOS / Commands

The following verbs are frequently used in directions on forms and applications.

**adjuntar**  to attach
**completar**  to complete
**explicar**  to explain
**firmar**  to sign
**incluir**  to include
**indicar**  to indicate
**mandar (por correo)**  to send, mail
**marcar**  to mark, to check

**mostrar (ue)**  to show
**ponerse en contacto**  to contact
**regresar**  to return
**rellenar / llenar**  to fill out
**reportar**  to report
**señalar**  to list
**traer**  to bring (in)

## PRÁCTICA

**A.**  Give the following command forms of the preceding verbs: **Ud.** positive, **Uds.** negative, **tú** positive, **tú** negative.

**B.**  Give the Spanish equivalent of the following questions. Use the **Ud.** positive command forms.

1. Report any change . . .
2. Complete and return . . .
3. Fill out this form completely . . .
4. Sign and mail to . . .
5. List all income from . . .
6. Explain below . . .
7. Indicate the amount . . .
8. Attach a separate sheet . . .
9. Show how much . . .
10. Include information about . . .
11. Contact your social worker . . .
12. Bring in the following information . . .
13. Be sure to mark yes or no . . .
14. Return all bills . . .
15. Check the appropriate box . . .

# 6 AYUDA AL SOLICITANTE A LLENAR LOS FORMULARIOS / Assistance in Filling Out Forms

This section contains a number of questions in English that a welfare worker might ask a client while helping him/her to fill out a form or an application. Before looking at the questions, study the following vocabulary words.

## Vocabulario

**actual**  actual, present
**el apartado postal**  post office box
**el apellido de soltera**  maiden name
**la carretera**  highway
**la ciudadanía**  citizenship
**el/la ciudadano/a**  citizen
**el destino**  destination
**el domicilio**  address
**el domicilio de correspondencia**  mailing address
**el domicilio de hogar**  home address

**el estado**  state
**la inicial**  initial
**el mensaje/recado**  message
**el nombre completo**  full name
**el nombre de pila**  middle name
**el puerto**  port
**la ruta**  route
**el sobrenombre/apodo**  nickname, alias
**la vía**  way
**la zona postal**  zip code

After you have mastered the vocabulary, form Spanish questions based on the following English questions. Then compare your translations with the translations given in Appendix IV (pages 174–175).

## I.   Nombre / Name

1. What's the applicant's name?
2. What's your full name?
3. What's your last name?
4. What's your middle name?
5. What's your mother's maiden name?
6. Do you have a nickname/alias?
7. Have you ever gone by another name?
8. Do you have an initial?

## II.   Domicilio / Address

1. What's your address?
2. Where do you live?

3. Is it a street / avenue / route / highway / way?

4. What's your apartment number?

5. Is this your present address?

6. Do you have a post office box?

7. Is your home address different from your mailing address?

8. In what city do you reside?

9. In what county do you reside?

10. In what state do you reside?

11. What's your zip code?

## III. Teléfono / Telephone

1. What's your home phone number?

2. What's your work phone number?

3. Is there a number where we can leave a message?

4. What's the name of the person we can leave a message with?

5. When can a message be left at this number?

## IV. Información de inmigración / Alien Registration Information

1. What name(s) did you have upon entering this country?

2. On what date did you enter this country? (month, day, year)

3. What was your port of entry?

4. What was your destination upon entry?

5. What is your citizenship?

6. What is your alien registration number?

7. Are you an American citizen?

8. Are you a permanent resident of the United States?

9. Are you a permanent foreigner?

10. Are you a tourist?

## PRÁCTICA

**A.** Working with another student, ask and answer the questions you have prepared. The person asking the question should record the information given.

**B.** The following are key words that should suggest questions similar to the ones you have prepared. Working with another student, formulate interview questions based on the key words. Refer to the questions you have prepared if necessary.

1. work phone number?

2. message?

3. port of entry?

4. citizenship?

5. permanent resident?

6. nickname?

7. highway?

8. maiden name?

9. zip code?

10. initial?

11. post office box?

12. tourist?

# 7 ENTREVISTAS DETALLADAS / In-Depth Interviews

In each of the six parts of this section, you will be asked to formulate questions in order to conduct an in-depth interview with a client about certain aspects of his/her personal life and work situation. At the beginning of each part, there is a list of important vocabulary words. Study the list carefully, and do not attempt to write the interview questions until you have mastered the words. Then form Spanish questions based on the English questions, and compare your translations with the translations given in Appendix IV (pages 175–177).

When you are certain that the questions are correct, ask and answer them, working with another student. The person asking the question should record the information given.

After each set of English questions, there is a list of key words that should suggest questions similar to the ones you have prepared. Working with another student, formulate interview questions based on the key words. Refer to the questions you have prepared if necessary.

## I.    El empleo / Employment

### Vocabulario

**las cuotas de sindicato**  union dues
**disponible**  available
**empleado/a por sí mismo/a**  self-employed
**empleado/a temporalmente**  employed part-time
**empleado/a tiempo completo**  employed full-time
**el entrenamiento**  training

**la guardería**  child care
**el negocio**  business
**el padre sin empleo**  unemployed parent
**el pago**  payment
**el puesto**  position
**los recibos de nómina**  pay stubs
**el sueldo en bruto**  gross salary
**el sueldo neto**  net salary

### Preguntas

1. Whom do you work for?
2. Where do you work?
3. Since when have you worked there?
4. How much do they pay you per (hour, week, month, year)?
5. Are you working full-time?
6. Are you working part-time?

7. Are you self-employed?

8. How many hours do you work per day/week?

9. What is your position?

10. How often are you paid?

11. What is your gross salary?

12. What is your net pay?

13. When were you fired from there?

14. Why were you fired?

15. What was your previous job?

16. What are the dates of your employment there?

17. When was the last day you worked?

18. Are you available and actively looking for work?

19. Are you enrolled in a training program?

20. The unemployed parent, has he/ she. . .

quit a job or a training program in the last thirty days?

refused a job or a training program in the last thirty days?

21. Does the parent residing at home work less than 100 hours per month?

22. Do you have your pay stubs?

### Key Words

1. previous job?

2. training program?

3. dates of employment?

4. full-time employment?

5. fired?

6. unemployed parent?

7. job refusal?

8. part-time?

9. net pay?

10. quit job?

11. pay stubs?

12. salary per week?

13. hours per week?

14. pay?

## II.  Situación económica / Financial Situation

### Vocabulario

**A. Fuentes de ingresos, dinero o beneficios / Sources of Income, Money, or Benefits**

**las acciones**  stocks

**el acuerdo legal**  settlement

**el alojamiento gratis**  free housing

**el alquiler/la renta**  rent

**los beneficios del obrero**  worker's compensation

**los beneficios derivados de huelga** strike benefits

**los beneficios militares**  military benefits

**el bono**  bond

**la comisión**  commission

**la contribución**  contribution

**la cuenta de ahorros**  savings account

**el cupón para comida/alimentos** food stamps

**la granja/el rancho**  farm

**el pago de sostenimiento a hijos** child support

**el pago extraordinario**  bonus

**el pago por entrenamiento**  (CETA) training incentive

**la pensión**  pension

**la pensión del ferrocarril**   railroad
 pension
**el préstamo**   loan
**la propina**   tip (given to a
 waiter)
**el reembolso de impuestos**   tax
 refund
**el regalo / obsequio**   gift
**el salario / sueldo**   salary

**la seguridad del ingreso suplemental**
 **(SSI)**   supplemental security
 income
**el seguro de desempleo**   unemployment insurance
**el seguro por incapacidad**   disability insurance
**el seguro social**   social security
**la subvención**   concession, grant

## B.  Gastos / Expenses

**el agua** (*f*)   water
**el automóvil**   car
**la basura**   refuse, garbage
**la casa / vivienda**   house, housing
**la comida / los alimentos**   food
**el drenaje**   sewer
**la electricidad**   electricity
**el gas**   gas
**la herramienta**   tool
**los impuestos sobre la propiedad**
 property taxes

**el interés**   interest
**el mantenimiento**   upkeep and
 repairs
**la mensualidad**   monthly payment
**los préstamos y deudas**   loans and
 debts
**la propiedad**   property
**la ropa**   clothing
**los servicios municipales**   utilities
**la transportación**   transportation

## Preguntas

1. Did you receive _____ benefits? (military, worker's compensation)
2. Did someone in the family receive _____? (bonuses, gifts, commissions, tips)
3. When you were on strike, how much were your strike benefits?
4. How much money do you have in your savings account?
5. Have you received free housing this year?
6. How much is your grandfather receiving through social security? Is he eligible for SSI?
7. How much was your tax refund for last year?
8. Do you have rental property?
9. What is the amount you owe on loans?
10. What pensions does your grandmother have? Does she have a railroad pension?
11. What is the yearly income from your farm? (business)
12. When you were in the training program, how much was your training incentive?
13. When you were employed, did you receive any bonuses?
14. What's your daughter's salary?
15. After the accident, how much did you receive from disability insurance?
16. What expenses do you have?
17. How much do you pay for housing?
18. How much are your monthly car payments?
19. When do you receive your utility bills?
20. Have you paid your medical bill this week?

21. Do you know what expenses to indicate on this form?
22. Did your husband send all the child support payments?
23. What is the total amount of your monthly expenses?
24. Do you wish to declare any other sources of income?

## Key Words

1. rental property?
2. accident?
3. strike?
4. grandfather?
5. tax refund?
6. training incentive?
7. child support?
8. utility bills?
9. medical bills?
10. free housing?
11. daughter's salary?
12. business income?
13. bonuses?
14. disability insurance?
15. benefits?
16. car payments?
17. loans?
18. monthly expenses?
19. SSI?
20. expenses?

## III. Situación escolar / Educational Situation

### Vocabulario

**el autobús**  bus
**el carro en común**  car pool
**el carro particular**  private car
**las cuotas**  fees
**el curso de verano**  summer school
**el equipo**  equipment
**estudiantil**  student (*adj.*)
**los gastos de guardería**  child care expenses
**los gastos escolares**  school expenses
**los gastos semanales**  weekly expenses

**el laboratorio**  lab
**el libro**  book
**el material**  material
**el medio de transporte**  means of transportation
**el número de millas (ida y vuelta)**  number of miles (round trip)
**el semestre**  semester
**el transporte**  transportation
**el trimestre**  quarter

### Preguntas

1. Who at home is in school?
2. Is anyone in a training program?
3. How many hours per week does he/she attend class?
4. Does he/she have a scholarship?
5. Does he/she have a student loan?
6. How often does he/she receive this scholarship or grant?
7. Is the academic year on a semester or a quarter?
8. What school expenses does he/she have?
9. Does he/she attend school full-time? (part-time)
10. Does he/she work after school?

11. Does he/she attend summer school?

12. Are any lab fees required?

13. Has he/she looked into E.O.P. possibilities?

14. What grades are your children in?

15. When is his/her expected date of graduation?

## Key Words

1. school attendance?

2. summer school?

3. fees?

4. transportation?

5. expenses?

6. grade?

7. grant?

8. after school work?

## IV. Situación del hogar / Home Situation

### Vocabulario

**la cárcel**   jail

**la casa adoptiva**   foster home

**el centro de rehabilitación**
    rehabilitation center

**el equipo para cocinar**   cooking
    facilities

**el familiar/pariente**   relative

**el huésped/la visita**   guest

**la institución particular**   private
    institution

**la institución pública**   public
    institution

**el mayor de 65**   person older
    than 65

**el menor de edad**   minor

**el paciente interno**   inpatient

**el paciente no interno**   outpatient

**la pareja casada**   married couple

**la parte separada de la casa**
    separate quarters

**el reformatorio**   juvenile hall

**sin parentesco**   unrelated

**el aborto**   abortion

### Preguntas

1. How many persons live with you?

2. How many are minors?

3. Is anyone under eighteen living here?

4. Is anyone over sixty-five living here?

5. Are they your relatives?

6. Are they guests?

7. Are they sick or handicapped?

8. Who pays for room, board, or both?

9. Do they live in separate quarters of the house?

10. Do you have cooking facilities where you live?

11. Are you or your spouse unable to prepare foods for health reasons?

12. Where do you eat your meals?

13. Are you, or is anyone in the household, a member of a rehabilitation center?

14. Are you an inpatient or outpatient?

15. Have you entered or left a public institution (foster home, juvenile hall, jail) or a private institution?

16. Is an unrelated adult male living here?

17. Are you a married couple?

### Key Words

| | |
|---|---|
| 1. inpatient? | 6. rehabilitation center? |
| 2. meals eaten? | 7. guests? |
| 3. room and board? | 8. separate quarters? |
| 4. minors? | 9. unrelated adult male? |
| 5. public institution? | 10. relatives? |

## V. Citas / Appointments

### Vocabulario

**el aviso**  notification
**la cita**  appointment
**con antelación**  in advance
**la entrevista**  interview
**la información**  information

**el intérprete**  interpreter
**el material**  item, material
**programado/a**  scheduled
**siguiente**  following

### Preguntas

1. Did you receive notice of the appointment?
2. Please have the items listed below ready for the scheduled interview.
3. Would you like an interpreter?
4. Please have an interpreter with you.
5. Are you unable to obtain an interpreter?
6. Do you want us to provide an interpreter for you?
7. Let us know one day in advance if you cannot make your appointment.
8. Can you provide us with the following information?
9. It is absolutely essential that you keep this appointment.

### Key Words

| | |
|---|---|
| 1. interpreter? | 4. scheduled interview? |
| 2. information? | 5. keeping the appointment? |
| 3. notice of appointment? | 6. not making the appointment? |

## VI. Elegibilidad / Eligibility

### Vocabulario

**el aspecto**  aspect
**la audiencia**  hearing

**la cantidad**  amount
**imparcial**  impartial

## Preguntas

1. Do you think this grant should not be changed?

2. Why do you think the amount of this grant should not be reduced?

3. How many children are included in the grant?

4. Do you know when the decision is going to affect your grant?

5. Is your grant going to be discontinued?

6. Do you know that your aid will continue until the impartial hearing reaches a decision?

7. Do you know that you can state why you are not satisfied with the amount of the grant?

8. Are you applying for a grant that will help you pay for the child care center?

9. Why shouldn't your grant be discontinued?

10. What aspect of your grant do you want to talk about?

## Key Words

1. children in grant?

2. impartial hearing?

3. child care center?

4. satisfied with amount?

5. grant discontinuation?

---

# 8 BENEFICIOS MÉDICOS / Medical Coverage

**la agencia de salud doméstica** home health agency

**el aparato ortopédico** orthopedic device

**el aparato prótesis** prosthetic apparatus

**el audífono** hearing aid

**la audiología** audiology

**el cuidado** care

**el cuidado de pie** podiatry

**el cuidado en el hospital** hospital care

**el cuidado en los asilos** care in a nursing home

**dar a luz** to give birth

**la droga prescrita** prescribed drug

**embarazarse** to get pregnant

**el embarazo terminado** terminated pregnancy

**los miembros y abrazaduras artificiales** assistive devices

**la óptica (lentes, ojos artificiales)** optical needs (lenses, artificial eyes)

**el optómetro** optometrist

**la planificación de la familia** family planning

**los rayos equis/las radiografías** x-rays

**el reconocimiento médico** physical examination

**los servicios de psiquiatría** clinical psychology

**los servicios dentales** dental treatment

**los servicios quiroprácticos** chiropractic treatment

**la terapia** therapy

**la terapia del habla** speech therapy

**la terapia ocupacional** occupational therapy

**la transportación médica** medical transportation

## PRÁCTICA

**A.** A welfare recipient has come to your office to have his/her medical coverage explained. Give a simple explanation—in lay terms—of the preceding vocabulary, listing the benefits to which the recipient is entitled.

**B.** Compare your explanations with those of other students in the class.

## 9 PEQUEÑO GUIÓN / Short Skit

Working with two other students, practice the following dialog aloud, concentrating on pronunciation and fluency. Alternate roles until all of you have played all three parts.

### Un matrimonio en crisis

*Consejero:* Por favor, siéntense. Me alegro que Ud., señor Pérez, y Ud., señora Pérez, me hayan llamado para que hablemos de sus problemas matrimoniales. Eso me demuestra que Uds. no quieren que su matrimonio se vaya a pique.*

*Señor:* Bueno, la verdad es que el juez nos exigió que viniéramos a verle, porque si fuera por mí, yo no estaría aquí.

*Señora:* Ya ve, señor Miranda, ésa es su actitud, siempre de mal humor.

*Consejero:* Bueno, bueno. ¿Por qué no empezamos desde un principio? Así llegaremos a la raíz del problema.

*Señor:* La raíz del problema empezó cuando yo me casé.

*Señora:* . . . y yo cuando te conocí.

*Consejero:* Por favor, les pido que guarden sus comentarios si éstos van a ser satíricos. Según el informe que tengo, Ud., señor Pérez, ha estado sin empleo por año y medio. Esto ha causado que la señora tenga que buscar empleo como recamarera en un hotel. Por lo visto, Ud. ha empezado a beber y, en una ocasión, intentó maltratar a su mujer.

---

\* **se vaya a pique** *to break up*

*Señor:* Sí, es verdad, pero ella me echa en cara mi mala suerte y constantemente me humilla, llamándome «flojo» y «vago». Gracias a cuando trabajaba que tenemos la casa que ahora tenemos.

*Señora:* Pero Ud. cree que en un año y medio no pueda encontrar un empleo, pues aunque sea de lavaplatos.

*Señor:* ¡De lavaplatos! Quizá yo sea un poco orgulloso, pero antes yo era gerente de un pequeño negocio hasta que murió el dueño. Por eso se cerró el negocio . . . ¡Y ahora quiere que yo sea un lavaplatos!

*Consejero:* Por lo que veo, ha habido un cambio importante en sus vidas. Antes Ud. era el que ganaba el sustento de la familia, y ahora lo gana su señora. En cambio, Ud., señora, se ha visto obligada a trabajar y esto le ha traído nuevas tensiones: pagar las cuentas, preparar la casa, mandar los niños a la escuela . . .

*Señora:* Así es. Todos los días tengo que madrugar y paso todo el día haciendo una cosa y haciendo otra. No pasa día sin que me acueste muy tarde. Y él, con amigos y con mujeres.

*Señor:* ¡Eso no es verdad! Paso horas fuera de casa pero haciendo cola en la oficina de empleo; de un lado para otro, buscando empleo y nada. Nunca le he sido infiel, ni hay otra mujer en mi vida. Ella es celosa. Eso sí, a veces mis amigos me invitan a ir a tomar una copa . . .

*Señora:* Casi todas las noches . . .

*Consejero:* Bueno, es obvio que ambos tienen que ver los nuevos cambios en su matrimonio desde una nueva perspectiva. Deben tomar en cuenta que lo más probable es que su situación sea momentánea. Quiero hacerles unas preguntas y, por favor, contéstenme sinceramente. ¿Está Ud., señor Pérez, contento sin empleo?

*Señor:* ¡Claro que no! Yo quisiera estar trabajando en este momento.

*Consejero:* Y Ud., señora, ¿está Ud. contenta?

*Señora:* Yo preferiría estar en casa con los niños, pues ellos son muy pequeños y me necesitan.

*Consejero:* Y otra pregunta: ¿Verdaderamente quieren divorciarse?

*Señor y señora:* (a la vez) ¡NO!

*Señora:* No, no me quiero divorciar, pero es que vivimos como perros y gatos.

*Señor:* Es que me ha tocado una racha de mala suerte. Antes de pasar todo esto, éramos muy felices . . . pero eso ha cambiado.

*Consejero:* Señor, ha cambiado, pero por el momento. Les vuelvo a repetir que ha habido graves cambios en su vida y Uds. no los aceptan. En esto veo la clave de todo. Deben comprender que todo puede volver a la normalidad si mutuamente se comprenden.

*Señor:* Pues, tal vez. Es que yo me crié en un ambiente en el cual el hombre gana el pan, y . . .

*Señora:* Y yo, a no tener que trabajar.

*Consejero:* Precisamente. Y ahora es cuando más falta les hace la comprensión. Si quieren que prospere el matrimonio, ambos tienen que hacer un esfuerzo por aceptar la situación como pasajera.

*Señora:* Bueno, reconozco que a veces le reprocho mucho su mala suerte y . . .

*Señor:* Y que yo tengo mucho orgullo y no acepto la situación.

*Consejero:* Bien, veo que ya van comprendiendo su problema. Con esta actitud, estoy seguro que tendrán más tolerancia.

## PRÁCTICA

**A.** After you are familiar with all of the parts as written, vary the dialog by changing or adding the following elements:

1. The wife insists on getting a divorce.

2. The husband gets fired or quits jobs on a regular basis.

3. The wife's grandparents are living with them and are a source of financial and emotional friction.

4. The husband has come home drunk on several occasions.

**B.** Working with several students, create a dialog of a similar format about one of the following topics, and present it to the class.

1. A woman comes to the welfare office after her husband has left her. She has three small children.

2. A handicapped man has just lost his wife and needs assistance.

3. A migrant worker couple and their family are in need of assistance and financial advice in general.

# 10 CASOS DE BIENESTAR / Welfare Case Histories

Working with another student, ask and answer questions, playing the roles of welfare client and social worker, based on the case histories suggested here. The case worker should compile a complete "file" on the case. Then compare your "files" with those of other students in the class to see the different directions the interviews have taken.

### Case #1

Mrs. Hernandez has visited at least ten social service agencies in the past ten years. She has been married twice and has eight children, not all of them by her two former husbands. Her first husband, a farm worker, died in an automobile accident, leaving her with three children. She lived with her second husband for two years before they got married. They had a violent relationship, and after a year of marriage, he abandoned her and has not been heard from since. He left just before he was to appear before a judge on charges of wife beating. She had two children with him.

For the past five years she has been living on welfare and has shown signs of mental instability. Mrs. Hernández has been referred to an alcoholics anonymous center for her drinking problem. The County Welfare Office has threatened to take away her children because of child neglect. On various occasions the county has withdrawn aid from her because an adult male was found living with her.

### Case #2

Mrs. Sandoval is a seventy-three-year-old widow who is in good health, considering her advanced age. Her mind is alert, but she presently has a broken leg due to a fall in the shower. Her husband died a month ago; he did not leave her a pension, nor did the two of them have a savings account. When he was alive, she depended on him for everything from grocery shopping to filing her annual alien registration card in January. She does not speak English and is going to need a number of social services as well as help in doing some long-overdue paper work. She has no children and cannot drive a car. She will also need someone to help her with domestic chores, at least until her cast is removed.

# CAPÍTULO 5

## El comercio/
## Business

# 1 DIÁLOGO / Dialog

## Ayudando a un cliente

*Dependiente:* Buenas tardes, señora. *¿Le puedo ayudar?*

*Señora:* Buenas tardes, señorita. Busco algo para *regalar* a mi sobrina para su cumpleaños.

*Dependiente:* *¿Le interesa* alguna *prenda* de *ropa?*

*Señora:* Sí, creo que una *falda* le gustaría. Ella es muy particular y debo tener cuidado de lo que le *compro.*

*Dependiente:* ¿Sabe Ud. su *talla?*

*Señora:* Sí, yo diría que es un cinco. Me interesa una falda *larga,* como la que Ud. *lleva puesta.*

*Dependiente:* Bien, aquí tenemos estas faldas. No son exactamente como la que *tengo puesta* pues ya *se nos acabaron.* Tuvimos una *venta de rebajas* la semana pasada y *se agotaron.* Éstas son muy *parecidas. ¿De qué color* le interesa? ¿Qué tal esta roja?

*Señora:* No, ése es muy *chillón.* Me interesa más bien un verde . . . algo semejante a este *tono* pero un poco más *ligero.*

*Dependiente:* Creo que la que busca es ésta. La tenemos en dos *estilos,* con *pliegues* o *lisa.* ¿Cuál *prefiere?*

*Señora:* Prefiero la falda lisa pero sin *cinturón.*

*Dependiente:* El cinturón *viene incluído* pero si Ud. o su sobrina no lo quieren, no importa, pues esta falda puede *lucirse* sin el cinturón.

*Señora:* Excelente. *Me la llevo.*

*Dependiente:* Por favor, *sígame* a la *caja.* ¿Es *al contado* o en la *cuenta?*

*Señora:* *Póngamela en la cuenta.* Aquí está mi *tarjeta de crédito.* Además, ¿me puede decir dónde *envuelven regalos?*

*Dependiente:* Sí, eso está en el tercer piso cerca de la *oficina de pagos.* Puede tomar el *ascensor* que está a la izquierda o la *escalera movediza* que está a la derecha.

*Señora:* Gracias.

*Dependiente:* No hay de que. Bueno, aquí está su *compra.* El *recibo* está dentro de la *bolsa. Vuelva otra vez. (Gusto en servirle.)*

## PRÁCTICA

**A.** Working with another student, practice the dialog aloud, concentrating on pronunciation and fluency. As you become more proficient, try to vary some of the elements of the dialog.

*Model:* Sí, creo que una falda le gustaría . . . ⟶

Sí, creo que *un suéter* le gustaría.

**B.** Translate the dialog into English. Then compare your translation with the one given in the Appendix (page 172).

**C.** Translate the English text of the dialog into Spanish, without consulting the original as you work. Then compare your translation with the Spanish version given here.

## 2 VOCABULARIO COMERCIAL DEL DIÁLOGO / Business Vocabulary from the Dialog

**al contado** cash
**el ascensor** elevator
**la bolsa** bag; purse
**la caja** cash register
**el cinturón** belt
**la compra** purchase
**comprar** to buy
**la cuenta** account
**chillón(a)** loud (of colors)
**el/la dependiente** clerk
**envolver (ue)** to wrap
**la escalera movediza** escalator
**el estilo** style
**la falda** skirt
**largo/a** long
**ligero/a** light (in shade)
**liso/a** plain
**lucir(se) (luzco)** to wear; to be worn

**llevar** to wear
**llevar puesto/a** to have on
**la oficina de pagos** credit (payments) office
**parecido/a** similar
**el pliegue** pleat
**preferir (ie)** to prefer
**la prenda** garment, article of clothing
**el recibo** receipt
**regalar** to give as a gift
**el regalo** gift
**la ropa** clothing
**la talla** size
**la tarjeta de crédito** credit card
**el tono** shade
**venir (ie) incluído/a** to be included
**la venta de rebajas** discount sale

### Expresiones del diálogo / Expressions from the Dialog

**¿De qué color?** What color?
**Gusto en servirle.** It's a pleasure to serve you.
**¿Le interesa?** Are you interested?
**¿Le puedo ayudar?** May I help you?
**Me la llevo.** I'll take it (buy it). I'll take it with me.
**Póngamelo/a en la cuenta.** Put it on my account.
**Se nos acabaron/agotaron.** We are all out (of them). We ran out (of them).
**Sígame.** Follow me.
**Vuelva otra vez.** Come back again.

## PRÁCTICA

**A.** Fill in the blanks with the proper form of words from the lists.

1. Para ir al quinto piso de un edificio, se puede subir en un _____ o en una

_____  _____

2. Las palabras _____, _____ y _____ tienen que ver con colores.

3. Lo que se pone en torno a la cintura es un _____.

4. Un objeto de plástico que se usa en vez de dinero es una _____ _____ _____.

5. El papelito que uno recibe al concluir una compra es un _____.

6. La mujer se acerca a la _____ y busca dentro de su _____ el dinero para pagar el balance de su _____.

7. Si una falda está doblada sistemáticamente, tiene _____.

8. Se paga una cuenta en la _____ _____ _____.

9. ¿Qué color _____ Ud., el verde o el azul?

**B.** Give the antonym (opposite) of these words.

1. recibir
2. compra
3. corto
4. oscuro

5. vender
6. pantalón
7. desenvolver
8. con pliegues

**C.** Give a synonym (word similar in meaning) for these words.

1. llevar puesto
2. dinero en efectivo
3. elevador
4. color fuerte
5. venga conmigo
6. semejante

7. prenda
8. vuelva otra vez
9. se nos acabaron
10. ¿necesita ayuda?
11. ¿le gusta?
12. tamaño

# 3 EXPRESIONES DE CORTESÍA / Expressions of Courtesy

## I. Saludos / Greetings

**Buenos días.** Good morning. (until 12:00 noon)
**Buenas tardes.** Good afternoon. (until 6:00 p.m. or until dark)
**Buenas noches.** Good evening/night. (after 6:00 or 7:00)
**Adiós.** Goodbye.
**¡Que le vaya bien!** Good luck! Have a good time!

## II. Títulos / Titles

**señor (Sr.)** Mr.: **Sr. Sánchez**
**señora (Sra.)** Mrs.: **Sra. Pérez**
**señorita (Srta.)** Miss/Ms.: **Srta. Díaz**
**don** title of respect, with no English equivalent: **don Pablo**
**doña** title of respect, with no English equivalent: **doña Elvira**

## III. Pedidos / Requests

**quiero** + *infinitive:*   **Quiero ver los trajes.**
*I want to see the suits.*

**me permite** + *infinitive:*   **¿Me permite probar el vestido?**
*May I try on the dress?*

In Spanish, the use of the conditional or the past subjunctive softens the harshness of a direct command, as in the following examples.

**quisiera** + *infinitive:*   **Quisiera ver los trajes.**
*I would like to see the suits.*

**podría** + *infinitive:*   **¿Podría probarme el vestido?**
*Might I try on the dress?*

**tendría la bondad de** + *infinitive:*   **¿Tendría la bondad de indicarme . . .?**
*Would you be so kind as to show me . . .?*

**sería tan amable de** + *infinitive:*   **¿Sería tan amable de decirme dónde . . .?**
*Would you be so kind as to tell me where . . .?*

**querría** + *infinitive:*   **¿Querría decirle al gerente . . .?**
*Would you like to tell the manager . . .?*

Direct commands can be softened by using **por favor**, and the present tense can be used instead of a command.

**Por favor, . . .**     **déjeme ver . . .**  } *Please let me see . . .*
            **me deja ver . . .**

            **dígame . . .** } *Please tell me . . .*
            **me dice . . .**

## IV. Otras expresiones / Other Expressions

**Cómo no.**   Of course.
**Con mucho gusto.**   Gladly.
**Gracias.**   Thanks. Thank you.
**Muchas gracias.**   Many thanks. Thank you very much.
**Mil gracias.**   A thousand thanks.
**Un millón de gracias.**   A million thanks.
**De nada.**   You're welcome.
**No hay de que.**   You're welcome. Think nothing of it.
**Disculpe(me). Dispense. Perdone(me).**   Excuse me.
**Con permiso.**   Excuse me. (used to pass by someone, to enter, or to leave)
**Ud. es muy amable.**   You're very kind.
**Pase adelante. Entre.**   Come in.
**Siéntese.**   Have a seat. Be seated.
**Sírvase.**   Help yourself.

## PRÁCTICA

**A.** How would you respond if . . .

1. the store had just opened in the morning, and a customer approached you.
2. two customers were talking in an aisle, and you had to pass by them.
3. you would like to see a customer's driver's license.
4. a customer said goodbye to you.
5. a customer thanked you profusely.

**B.** Give an appropriate response to these statements or questions.

1. ¿Me puede ayudar?

2. ¿Puedo pasar?

3. Buenas noches.

4. Ud. es muy amable.

5. ¡Que le vaya bien!

**C.** Working with another student or students, write and present to the class a short skit involving a customer and a sales clerk. Use as many of the preceding expressions as possible.

## 4 PREGUNTAS Y EXPRESIONES DE LA TIENDA / Questions and Expressions Related to Shopping

## PRÁCTICA

**A.** Practice reading the following questions aloud.

**B.** Answer all of the following questions. Listen to the answers that other students in the class give.

**C.** Working with another student, ask and answer the questions.

**I. Preguntas que hace un dependiente / Questions Asked by a Clerk**

1. ¿Le puedo ayudar?

   No, sólo estoy mirando.

   Sí, busco _____ (una camisa, el departamento de niños).

   *May I help you?*

   *No, I'm only looking.*

   *Yes, I'm looking for _____ (a shirt, the children's department).*

2. ¿Es esto lo que buscaba?

   _____ eso es lo que buscaba.

   *Is this what you were looking for?*

3. ¿Es éste el (color, tamaño, estilo, tono, precio, peso) que buscaba?

   _____ es el _____ que busco.

   *Is this the (color, size, style, shade, price, weight) you were looking for?*

4. ¿Cómo le parece esto?

   Me parece muy (grande, pequeño, corriente, caro).

   *How do you like this?*

   *It seems to be a little too (big, small, ordinary, expensive).*

5. Ésta es de mejor calidad, ¿no le parece?

   Sí, me gusta más que la otra.

   No, tampoco me gusta.

   *This is of a better quality, don't you think?*

6. ¿Qué tamaño usa?

   Uso el tamaño _____.

   *What size do you wear?*

7. Esto le sale más barato.

   ¿Está de venta o tiene algún defecto?

   *This is less expensive.*

   *Is it on sale or is something wrong with it?*

8. ¿Hay otra cosa?

   No, eso es todo.

   *Will there be anything else?*

9. ¿Es al contado o a crédito?

   Es al contado.

   *Is this cash or charge?*

10. ¿Tiene Ud. tarjeta de crédito de nuestra tienda?

    _____ tengo.

    *Do you have a charge account (credit card) with our store?*

11. ¿Gusta llenar estos formularios para solicitar nuestra tarjeta de crédito?

    Sí, con mucho gusto.

    No, ahora tengo prisa.

    *Would you like to fill out these forms to get our credit card?*

12. ¿Me permite ver su (tarjeta de crédito, licencia de manejar, tarjeta de identificación, recibo)?

    Aquí está.

    Aquí lo/la tiene Ud.

    *May I see your (credit card, driver's license, I.D. card, receipt)?*

## II.  Preguntas que hace un cliente / Questions Asked by a Client

13. ¿Dónde está(n) el/los _____?

    Allí está(n).

    En la (cuarta, quinta) planta.

    Está(n) en el departamento de

    _____.

    *Where is/are the _____?*

    *On the (fourth, fifth) floor.*

14. ¿Está en venta?

    Sí, en venta de fin de mes.

    *Is it on sale?*

    *Yes, an end-of-the-month sale.*

15. ¿Cuál es más barato/a?                     *Which is cheaper?*

    Éste/a es más barato/a.

16. ¿Puedo devolver/cambiar esto?              *Can I return/exchange this?*

    Cómo no. ¿Tiene el recibo?

17. ¿Cuánto cuesta _____?                    *How much does _____ cost?*

    Cuesta _____ dólares.

    ¿Cuál es el precio de _____?             *What's the price of _____?*

    El precio es de _____.

    ¿Cuánto vale _____?                      *How much is _____ worth?*

    Vale _____.

18. ¿Tiene uno más (bonito, pequeño,           *Do you have a (prettier, smaller,*
    sencillo)?                                 *plainer) one?*

    ¿Puede mostrarme uno más                   *Could you show me a _____ one?*

    _____?

    ¿Qué le parece éste?

19. ¿Cuándo me lo podrían llevar a mi          *When could you deliver it to my*
    casa?                                      *house?*

    Se lo podríamos llevar el _____.

20. ¿A cuánto saldrían los pagos a             *How much would the monthly pay-*
    plazos cada mes?                           *ments be?*

    Le saldrían a _____ por mes.

21. ¿Lo puedo devolver si no le gusta?         *Can I return it if he/she doesn't like it?*

    Sí, pero traiga el recibo.

22. ¿Me dio el recibo?                          *Did you give me the receipt?*

    Sí, lo metí en la bolsa.

## PRÁCTICA

Here is a list of key words that should suggest questions similar to the preceding ones. Working with another student, formulate questions and answers based on the key words. Refer to the preceding list of questions and answers if necessary.

1. ¿tamaño?                                    6. ¿buscar?

2. ¿calidad?                                   7. ¿contado?

3. ¿recibo?                                    8. ¿a plazos?

4. ¿devolver?                                  9. ¿venta?

5. ¿barato?                                    10. ¿crédito?

# 5 DEPARTAMENTOS DE UNA TIENDA / Departments of a Store

**Planta primera**

fotografía
música
libros
caballeros
licor

**Planta segunda**

señoras
peletería
niños
adolescentes
perfumería

**Planta tercera**

electrodomésticos
zapatería
papelería
ferretería
automóvil

**Planta cuarta**

deportes
jardinería
**loza y cristal**
muebles
cortinas

**Planta quinta**

cafetería
oficina de pagos
baños

## PRÁCTICA

Working with another student, ask and answer the following question, using the preceding vocabulary and the items listed below.

*Model:*　¿Dónde están *las camisas de hombre*? ⟶
　　　　　Están en *la primera planta*.

1. la película
2. los discos
3. los televisores
4. las plumas fuentes
5. los abrigos de mujer

6. los balones de fútbol
7. los zapatos
8. las vajillas
9. la crema para la cara
10. los trajes de señor

11. el vino
12. los sofás
13. la cafetería
14. las llantas
15. las lavadoras

## 6　TIENDECITAS / TIENDITAS
## Specialty Shops

The names of small shops that specialize in certain merchandise or services end with the suffix **-ería**: **zapato** ⟶ **zapatería**. Complete the following chart with the appropriate names of shops.

| Product | Shop Name | Product | Shop Name |
|---|---|---|---|
| 1. carne | carnicería | 7. pan | panad_____ |
| 2. fruta | frutería | 8. pastel | pastel_____ |
| 3. juguete | juguet_____ | 9. perfume | perfum_____ |
| 4. lavar | lavand_____ | 10. pescado | pescad_____ |
| 5. leche | lech_____ | 11. sombrero | sombrer_____ |
| 6. mueble | muebl_____ | 12. tortilla | tortill_____ |

The name of some specialty shops is totally different from that of the product sold: **dulce** ⟶ **confitería**; **salchicha** ⟶ **charcutería**; **limpiar** ⟶ **tintorería**.

## PRÁCTICA

Working with another student, ask and answer the following question, using the preceding vocabulary and the items listed below.

*Model:* ¿Dónde puedo comprar

_____?

Váyase a la _____.
Allí se vende.

| | |
|---|---|
| 1. calamares | 8. perfume |
| 2. juguetes | 9. dulces |
| 3. tortillas | 10. leche |
| 4. bananas | 11. una gorra |
| 5. salchichas | 12. un sillón |
| 6. pasteles | 13. crema |
| 7. pan | 14. chuletas |

## 7 PERSONAL DEL BANCO / Bank Personnel

**el/la ayudante**  helper, aide
**el/la banquero**  banker
**el/la cajero/a**  cashier
**el/la cajero/a para automovilistas**  drive-in teller
**el/la cliente del banco**  bank client
**el/la contador(a)**  accountant
**el/la dependiente**  clerk
**el/la depositor(a)**  depositor
**el/la ejecutivo/a del banco**  bank executive
**el/la empleado/a de ventanilla**  bank teller

**el/la gerente**  manager
**el hombre/la mujer de negocios**  business man/woman
**el/la mecanógrafo/a**  typist
**el/la notario público**  notary public
**el/la oficial de préstamos**  loan officer
**el/la presidente/a del banco**  bank president
**el/la representante**  representative
**el/la secretario/a**  secretary
**el/la tenedor(a) de libros**  bookkeeper
**el/la vicepresidente/a**  vice-president

### PRÁCTICA

Working with another student, ask and answer the following questions.

1. ¿Puedo hablar con el/la _____ del banco?

   El/la _____ está ocupado/a de momento.

2. ¿Quién es el/la _____ del banco?

   El Sr./Sra./Srta. Sánchez es el/la _____ del banco.

3. ¿Le está ayudando el/la _____?

   No, no he visto al/a la _____ todavía.

4. ¿Quién firmó el documento?

   Me lo firmó el/la _____.

# 8 VOCABULARIO GENERAL DEL BANCO / General Banking Vocabulary

**anual**  annual
**aprobado/a**  approved
**atrasado/a**  delinquent
**el balance/saldo**  balance
**el balance de la cuenta**  account balance
**la bancarrota/quiebra**  bankruptcy
**el billete**  bill (*money*)
**la caja de ahorros**  savings and loan office
**la caja fuerte de banco**  bank vault
**el cambio**  change
**la cantidad**  quantity, amount
**la cantidad financiada**  amount financed
**la casa matriz**  main branch
**el Club de Navidad**  Christmas club
**las comisiones bancarias**  bank charges
**la contabilidad**  accounting
**el contrato**  contract
**el crédito**  credit
**la cuenta**  account
**la cuenta congelada**  blocked/frozen account
**la cuenta corriente**  checking account
**el cheque cancelado**  cancelled check
**el cheque certificado**  certified check
**el cheque de viajero**  traveler's check
**el cheque posdatado**  postdated check
**el depósito**  deposit

**el dinero en efectivo**  cash
**la dirección**  address
**el endorso**  endorsement
**la factura/cuenta/letra, el giro/billete**  bill
**el financiamiento de auto**  new car loan
**el índice de crédito**  credit rating
**insolvente/quebrado/a**  bankrupt
**el interés compuesto**  compound interest
**la letra bancaria/el billete de banco**  bank note/bill
**la libreta de cheques**  checkbook
**la libreta de depósito**  bankbook
**el libro de cuenta**  account book
**la moneda**  currency, coin
**el número de la cuenta**  account number
**el papel para depósito**  deposit slip
**el prestador/prestamista**  lender
**el préstamo bancario**  bank loan
**el prestatario**  borrower
**el/la que pide prestado**  borrower
**la seguridad colateral**  collateral
**la solicitud**  application
**la sucursal**  branch (of a bank)
**el sumario/resumen/extracto**  abstract
**la tasa bancaria**  bank rate
**el tipo de cambio**  rate of exchange
**los valores**  assets

## PRÁCTICA

**A.** Fill in the blanks with the proper form of words from the list.

1. El dinero en el banco se guarda dentro de la _____ _____

   _____ _____ .

2. Cuando no hay dinero para pagar las deudas se está en _____ .

3. El banco principal se llama _____ _____ .

4. Los bancos que no son principales son _____ .

5. Un cheque que regresan al dueño después de pagar la cantidad indicada es un cheque

   _____.

6. Un documento legal que sirve como acuerdo a un negocio es un _____.

7. Un documento que indica lo que se ha pagado es un(a) _____.

8. Cuando uno lleva dinero al banco hace un _____.

9. La persona que presta dinero es un _____.

10. Una institución como un banco es una _____ _____

    _____.

11. Si uno quiere cambiar dólares a pesos, debe saber el _____ _____

    _____.

12. Se indica la cantidad depositada en el _____ _____

    _____.

13. Si uno busca _____ _____ auto, tiene que tener un buen

    _____ _____ _____.

**B.** Give the antonym (opposite) of these words.

   1. negado                    2. prestatario

**C.** Give a synonym (word similar in meaning) for these words.

   1. quiebra                6. bienes
   2. billete de banco        7. billete
   3. resumen                 8. cambio
   4. giro                    9. cantidad financiada
   5. saldo

**D.** Define the following terms as if you were explaining them to a customer.

   1. Club de Navidad          9. contabilidad
   2. cuenta corriente        10. cheque certificado
   3. interés compuesto       11. balance de la cuenta
   4. cheque de viajero       12. libreta de cheques
   5. cheque posdatado        13. libreta de depósito
   6. endorso                 14. talón de cheques
   7. seguridad               15. comisiones ban-
   8. cuenta congelada            carias

**E.** Write ten questions that a customer might ask a bank employee and ten questions that an employee might ask a customer. Working with another student, ask and answer the questions you have prepared.

**F.** Describe the last transaction you had with your bank, giving as many details as possible.

# 9 VOCABULARIO GENERAL DE COMERCIO / General Business Vocabulary

Match the Spanish words with their English equivalents.

| | | | |
|---|---|---|---|
| 1. _____ to amortize | a. la comisión |
| 2. _____ analyst | b. el/la analista |
| 3. _____ auction | c. predecir (i) |
| 4. _____ audit | ch. consolidado/a |
| 5. _____ budget | d. la deuda |
| 6. _____ business | e. la depreciación |
| 7. _____ business hours | f. los dividendos |
| 8. _____ capital | g. la empresa |
| 9. _____ commission | h. amortizar |
| 10. _____ company | i. la subasta/el remate |
| 11. _____ consolidated | j. las horas de negocio/hábiles |
| 12. _____ construction | k. el capital |
| 13. _____ contract | l. la construcción |
| 14. _____ cost | ll. la economía |
| 15. _____ customer | m. la auditoría |
| 16. _____ debt | n. el contrato |
| 17. _____ deed | ñ. los gastos |
| 18. _____ depreciation | o. el presupuesto |
| 19. _____ dividends | p. el costo |
| 20. _____ earnings/gain | q. las ganancias |
| 21. _____ economy | r. el/la cliente |
| 22. _____ enterprise | rr. la fábrica |
| 23. _____ equity | s. la compañía |
| 24. _____ expenses | t. la firma |
| 25. _____ factory | u. la pérdida |
| 26. _____ financial | v. el negocio |
| 27. _____ firm | w. financiero/a |
| 28. _____ to forecast | x. la escritura/el título de propiedad |
| 29. _____ foreign currency | y. la diferencia entre el valor y la hipoteca |
| 30. _____ loss | z. la moneda extranjera |

Continue to match the Spanish words with their English equivalents.

| | |
|---|---|
| 1. _____ income | a. la valuación |
| 2. _____ industry | b. el/la corredor(a) de la bolsa |
| 3. _____ insurance | c. la diferencia de precio |

| | | |
|---|---|---|
| 4. _____ inventory | | ch. los ingresos/la renta/las entradas |
| 5. _____ to lease, rent | | d. el riesgo |
| 6. _____ liabilities | | e. las ganancias |
| 7. _____ license | | f. el valor actual |
| 8. _____ lot (land) | | g. el inventario |
| 9. _____ market | | h. **la provisión/oferta** |
| 10. _____ owner | | i. la transacción |
| 11. _____ payroll | | j. la fuente |
| 12. _____ present value | | k. la licencia/el permiso |
| 13. _____ price spread | | l. el mercado |
| 14. _____ profit | | ll. la cantidad |
| 15. _____ quantity | | m. la industria |
| 16. _____ renting | | n. el seguro |
| 17. _____ risk | | ñ. el/la accionista |
| 18. _____ sales | | o. el/la administrador(a) |
| 19. _____ source | | p. el solar/la parcela |
| 20. _____ stocks | | q. el arrendamiento |
| 21. _____ stockbroker | | r. el/la dueño/a, el/la propietario/a |
| 22. _____ stockholder | | rr. arrendar (ie) |
| 23. _____ stock market | | s. las acciones |
| 24. _____ supply | | t. las ventas |
| 25. _____ tax | | u. el comercio |
| 26. _____ trade | | v. las deudas/obligaciones |
| 27. _____ transaction | | w. los días laborales |
| 28. _____ trustor | | x. la bolsa |
| 29. _____ valuation | | y. el impuesto |
| 30. _____ workdays | | z. la nómina |

# 10 VERBOS RELACIONADOS CON EL COMERCIO / Verbs Related to Business

**ahorrar dinero**  to save money
**alcanzar**  to reach
**añadir/sumar**  to add
**aprobar (ue)/autorizar/sancionar**  to approve
**aumentar/incrementar**  to increase
**calcular interés compuesto**  to compound interest
**cambiar**  to exchange

**cancelar**  to cancel
**cobrar**  to charge
**comprar**  to buy, purchase
**deducir (deduzco)**  to deduct
**descontar (ue)**  to discount
**endosar**  to endorse
**enviar por correo**  to mail
**esperar**  to wait
**exportar**  to export

financiar   to finance
firmar   to sign
importar   to import
incurrir   to incur
ordenar   to order
pagar   to pay
pasar un cheque   to cash/clear a check
pedir prestado   to borrow

prestar   to lend
reembolsar   to refund
registrar   to record
solicitar/pedir (i)   to apply for
suponer (supongo)   to imply
totalizar   to total
volver (ue), devolver (ue), regresar
    to return

## PRÁCTICA

**A.** Fill in the blanks with the proper form of the verbs in parenthesis, in the indicated tense.

*Present:*   Yo nunca _____ prestado a mis amigos.   (pedir)

*Preterite:*   Todos los días _____ algunos cheques sin firmar.   (devolver)

*Present Perfect:*   Sí, yo _____ todas las cuentas del mes pasado.   (pagar)

*Present:*   ¿Desde cuándo _____ Ud. pedidos sin firma?   (aprobar)

*Preterite:*   ¿Por qué _____ Ud. sólo el cinco por ciento?   (deducir)

**B.** Fill in the blanks with the proper form of verbs from the preceding list. Try to complete the paragraph without using any verb more than once.

Ayer yo _____ los papeles para _____ un carro nuevo. El otro día había _____ crédito de la caja de ahorros y hoy ellos me _____ la solicitud. Tendré que _____ el carro en veinticuatro plazos a $100 la mensualidad. Me van a _____ los pagos de mi sueldo y así no corro el riesgo de tener pagos atrasados. Para _____ mi compra, la caja de aho-rros pidió que yo _____ un cheque mío de $500 a la agencia de carros como entrada. En la caja de ahorros

sólo tuve que _____ unos quince minutos para que se _____ la emisión del cheque por el resto.

En la agencia de carros me trataron muy bien. Por mi carro viejo me _____ $300 y _____ los gastos de transporte del nuevo. Esto se debe a que el carro es del Japón y al no tener mi modelo en existencia tienen que _____ el mío. Mientras tanto, y sin que me _____ por ello, me _____ un carro de la agencia.

**C.** Make a list of ten more verbs related to business, and write a question related to business with each one in any tense. Working with another student, ask and answer the questions you have prepared.

# 11 VOCABULARIO ESPECIFICO DE CIERTOS COMERCIOS
## UN REPASO

### A. MAS VOCABULARIO MISCELANEO
Match the vocabulary from Column A with its English equivalent in Column B.

| *A* | *B* |
|---|---|
| 1. **vigente** | import |
| 2. **al portador** | for sale |
| 3. **maquiladora** | export |
| 4. **cotizar** | North American Free Trade Agreement |
| 5. **Fdo.** | market |
| 6. **cheque cobrado** | loose change |
| 7. **importar** | P.S. (postscript) |
| 8. **el / la inversionista** | (fiscal) year |
| 9. **deducir, restar** | net income |
| 10. **exportar** | per share |
| 11. **cifra** | the strike |
| 12. **el impuesto** | to quote a price |
| 13. **la inflación** | to deduct |
| 14. **la huelga** | tax |
| 15. **aranceles de aduana** | abbreviation for "signed" |
| 16. **P.D. (posdata)** | inflation |
| 17. **el ejercicio** | investor |
| 18. **cambio, feria, suelto, vuelto** | assembly plant |
| 19. **el mercado** | cleared check |
| 20. **NAFTA** | figure (numerical) |
| 21. **por acción** | custom's duties |
| 22. **sacar, retirar** | the fluctuation |
| 23. **la renta neta** | to withdraw |
| 24. **se vende** | to the bearer (cash) |
| 25. **el alza y la baja** | effective, in force |

B. Consultando las listas de vocabulario anteriores, escriba una nueva lista de palabras para los siguientes comercios indicados. Algunas palabras tal vez se repitan.

1. LA BOLSA

2. LOS COMERCIOS

3. LA INMOBILIARIA (BIENES Y RAICES)

4. FINANCIAMIENTO

C. Fill in the blanks with the proper form of words from the list.

1. Productos que entran a un país son _____ mientras que los que salen para venderse son _____.

2. Con el acuerdo de _____, las _____ de México no tendrán que pagar los _____ ____ _____ que antes pagaban.

3. A los cheques sin nombre de persona se le pone _____ _____.

4. El _____ de este año refleja el _____ y la _____ de los precios del _____ global.

5. En la bolsa el _____ está atento al precio _____ _____.

6. Esta es una _____ muy alta y no está _____ hoy día.

7. Los obreros empezaron la _____ para protestar las malas condiciones de trabajo.

8. Si uno quiere vender algo tiene que poner un letrero que diga ____ _____.

9. Casi nadie se salva de pagar _____ que cobra el gobierno.

10. Dar un presupuesto de precio es _____ su valor.

# 12 CORRESPONDENCIA COMERCIAL / Business Letters

## I. Encabezamientos/comienzos de cartas / Greetings

**Sr. Dn.** Mr.
**Sra. Dña.** Mrs.
**Srta.** Miss, Ms.
**Señores** Gentlemen
**Señora** Madam
**Respetable señora** Dear Madam
**Mi amigo/a** My friend
**Mi buen(a) amigo/a** My good friend
**Mi querido/a amigo/a** My dear friend
**Mi muy querido/a _____** My dearest _____
**Muy señor mío** My dear sir
**Muy señores míos** My dear sirs
**Muy señor nuestro** Our dear sir
**Muy señores nuestros** Our dear sirs
**Estimado señor** Esteemed sir
**Estimados señores** Esteemed sirs
**Muy estimada doctora Herrera** Highly esteemed Dr. Herrera

II. Finales/pies de cartas / Closing Words

**Reciba Ud. mis afectos**   Receive my affection
**Le saluda . . .**   . . . greets you
**Salúdolo afectuosamente S.S.S.**   I greet you affectionately
**S.S.S. Su seguro servidor**   Your faithful servant
**Le saluda S.S.S.**   Greetings from your faithful servant
**Saludos de S.S.S.**   Greetings from your faithful servant
**Saludos cordiales de . . .**   Cordial greetings from . . .
**Reciba el afecto cariñoso de . . .**   Receive affection from . . .
**Saludos cariñosos de . . .**   Affectionate greetings from . . .
**Te saluda cariñosamente . . .**   . . . greets you affectionately
**Aprecios sinceros de . . .**   Sincere appreciation from . . .
**Afectos de su . . .**   Affection from your . . .
**Sin otro particular le saluda atentamente . . .**   That's all for the moment, and
   greetings from . . .
**De usted muy atentamente, . . .**   I take leave of you, . . .
**Sinceramente**   Sincerely
**Anexo**   Enclosure
**Anexos (4)**   Four Enclosures

III. Expresiones útiles / Useful Expressions

**Acuso recibo de . . .**   I acknowledge receipt of . . .
**Me es grato comunicarle . . .**   It is my pleasure to inform you . . .
**Lamento no poderle . . .**   I regret not being able to . . .
**Le ruego . . .**   I kindly ask you . . .
**Si tiene a bien . . .**   If you see fit to . . .
**Les anticipamos las gracias . . .**   We thank you in advance . . .
**A quien corresponda . . .**   To whom it may concern . . .
**Sírvase enviarme . . .**   Please send me . . .
**En espera de sus gratas . . .**   We look forward to . . .
**Agradeceré su confirmación . . .**   Your confirmation will be appreciated . . .

## PRÁCTICA

A. Fill in the blanks with expressions from the preceding list.

Sr. _____ José Pérez
Librería La Paz
Avda. Reforma, 839
México, D.F. 3

_____

_____ _____ _____ su pedido de quince ejemplares del
libro *Español correcto* que con fecha de hoy ha llegado.

_____ _____ _____ _____ que sin demora

alguna despachamos su pedido hoy mismo por correo aéreo. _____

_____ acuse recibo de nuestro envío.

Si tiene a bien _____ _____ un catálogo de la distribución de

libros que Uds. publican.

_____ _____ _____ _____ _____ _____

noticias.

Le saluda _____ _____ _____,

A. Martínez,
Gerente

**B.** Write a business letter about one of the following situations.

1. The shipment of goods requested is on its way. It was sent today via airmail. The shipment of goods is insured and registered. The invoice is enclosed. Please pay for the merchandise in U.S. dollars.

2. Receipt of invoice number x is acknowledged. Said invoice quotes the merchandise at a higher price than specified in a recent company catalog. A corrected invoice is requested. The order is to be cancelled if the old price is not in effect. Merchandise will be returned immediately if that is the case.

3. Interest in a product is expressed, with a request for a price quotation. The quotation is requested per unit or — if the product is less expensive that way — by the dozen.

**C.** Translate the following additional vocabulary:

1. Le adjunto
2. Le envío
3. Su pedido
4. menudeo
5. mayoreo
6. Sírvase enviarme
7. vía aérea/por correo aéreo/por avión

# APÉNDICE I

Selected Bibliography of Spanish-English/
Inglés-Español Dictionaries and Specialized
Materials

Ballesteros. *Diccionario técnico de electromecánica*. Mexico City: Editorial Limusa, 1976.

Bimse, Marguerite D., and Julián H. Alfaro. *Practical Spanish for Medical and Hospital Personnel*. New York: Pergamon Press, 1973.

Black, Henry C. *Black's Law Dictionary*. 4th ed. St. Paul, Minn.: West Publishing Co., 1968.

Caldero de Walters, Luz. *Compendio de Términos y Palabras Legales y de Contabilidad de Español al Inglés*. Mexico City: Herrero Hnos., 1962.

California, State of. *California Driver's Handbook (in Spanish)*. Sacramento: Department of Motor Vehicles, 2415 1st Avenue.

———. *English/Spanish Glossary of Cosmetology Terms*. Sacramento: Department of Consumer Affairs, 1020 N Street.

———. *English-Spanish Glossary for Health Aides*. Sacramento: Department of Health, Publications Division, 714 P Street.

———. *A Spanish Glossary Supplement to the State Hearings Handbook for Interpreters — Un glosario suplementario a la guía para intérpretes en las audiencias estatales*. Sacramento: Health and Welfare Agency, Department of Benefit Payments, 1976.

Carbajo, Antonio. *American Slang (interpreted into Spanish)*. Miami Springs: Language Research Press, P.O. Box 546, Florida 33166.

———. *Idiomatic Expressions*.

———. *Spanish for Airlines and Travel Agents*.

———. *Spanish for Banks and Savings and Loan Institutions*.

———. *Spanish for Doctors, Dentists, Oculists/Optometrists, and Nurses*.

———. *Spanish for Homemakers*.

———. *Spanish for Hotels and Motels*.

———. *Spanish for Restaurants*.

———. *Spanish for Retail Selling*.

*Conference Terminology: A Manual for Conference Members and Interpreters in English, French, Spanish, Russian, Italian, German*. 2d ed. New York: Elsevier.

Crowson, Ben F., Jr., ed. *Spanish English List of Automobile Terms*. Washington, D.C.: Topical Spanish Word Lists, P.O. Box 6188.

———. *Spanish English List of Banking Terms*.

———. *Spanish English List of Christmas Toys and Gifts*.

———. *Spanish English List of Dental Terms*.

———. *Spanish English List of Diplomatic and International Terms*.

———. *Spanish English List of Feminine Terms*.

———. *Spanish English List of General Merchandise Terms*.

———. *Spanish English List of Hotel Terms*.

———. *Spanish English List of Journalism Terms*.

———. *Spanish English List of Library and Literary Terms*.

———. *Spanish English List of Night Club Terms*.

———. *Spanish English List of Police and Crime Terms*.

———. *Spanish English List of Post Office Terms*.

———. *Spanish English List of Restaurant Terms*.

———. *Spanish English List of Sports Terms*.

*Dictionary of Chemistry and Chemical Technology, in Six Languages: English, German, Spanish, French, Polish, Russian*. Rev. ed. New York: Pergamon Press, 1966.

Dolz, Mario A. *Special Spanish Course for Hospital and Clinic Personnel*. 3506 W. 11th St., Inglewood, Calif., 1974.

Dorian, A. F., ed. *Six-Language Dictionary of Electronics, Automation, and Scientific Instruments: A Comprehensive Dictionary in English, French,*

*German, Italian, Spanish, and Russian*. London: Iliffe Books; Englewood Cliffs, N.J.: Prentice-Hall, 1962.

*Duden español: Diccionario por la imagen*. 2d ed. Mannheim: Bibliographisches Institut, 1963.

*Elsevier's Dictionary of Automation, Computers, Control, and Measuring in Six Languages: English/American, French, Spanish, Italian, Dutch, and German*. New York: Elsevier, 1961.

*Elsevier's Dictionary of Cinema, Sound, and Music in Six Languages: English/ American, French, Spanish, Italian, Dutch, and German*. New York: Elsevier, 1956.

*Elsevier's Dictionary of Criminal Science in Eight Languages: English/American, French, Italian, Spanish, Portuguese, Dutch, Swedish, German*. New York: Elsevier, 1960.

*Elsevier's Dictionary of Industrial Chemistry in Six Languages: English/American, French, Spanish, Italian, Dutch, and German*. New York: Elsevier, 1967.

*Elsevier's Dictionary of Library Science, Information, and Documentation in Six Languages: English/American, French, Spanish, Italian, Dutch, and German*. New York: Elsevier, 1973.

*Elsevier's Dictionary of Nuclear Science and Technology in Six Languages: English/American, French, Spanish, Italian, Dutch, and German*. New York: Elsevier, 1958.

*Elsevier's Lexicon of Detergents, Cosmetics, and Toiletries, in English, French, Spanish, Italian, German, Portuguese, Swedish, and Dutch*. New York: Elsevier, 1958.

*Elsevier's Lexicon of International and National Units: English/American, German, Spanish, French, Italian, Japanese, Dutch, Portuguese, Polish, Russian*. Amsterdam: Elsevier, 1969.

*Elsevier's Wood Dictionary in Seven Languages: English/American, French, Spanish, Italian, Swedish, Dutch, and German*. New York: Elsevier, 1968.

Finch, Bernard Ephraim. *Multilingual Guide for Medical Personnel, in English, French, Italian, German, Spanish, and Russian*. Flushing, N.Y.: Medical Examination Publishing Co., 1963.

Flynn, Gerard. *Spanish for Urban Workers*. Boulder, Colo.: Pruett Publishing Co., 1975.

Freeman, Roger L. *English-Spanish, Spanish-English Dictionary of Communications and Electronic Terms*. London: Cambridge University Press, 1972.

Frías-Sucre Giraud, Alejandro. *Novísimo diccionario comercial "El secretario" . . . española-inglesa, inglesa-española*. Madrid: Editorial Juventud, 1965.

Galván, Roberto A., and Richard Teschner. *El diccionario del español chicano*. Silver Spring, Md.: Institute of Modern Languages, 1977.

Garza Bores, Jaime. *Diccionario técnico de terminología comercial, contable, y bancaria*. Mexico City: Editorial Diana, 1971.

Gaynor, Frank. *International Business Dictionary in Five Languages: English, German, French, Spanish, Italian*. New York: Philosophical Library, 1946.

George, Wilma. *Eating in Eight Languages (in English, French, Italian, German, Spanish, Portuguese, Greek, and Serbo-Croatian)*. New York: Stein & Day, 1968.

Gómez-Vidal, Oscar, and Harry Walter Kock. *Communicating with the Spanish Speaking (for people in government, business, and the professions)*. San Francisco: Ken Books, 1976.

———. *Spanish for the Law-Enforcement Profession*. San Francisco: Ken Books, 1976.

Guinle, R. L. *A Modern Spanish-English and English-Spanish Technical and Engineering Dictionary.* New York: E. P. Dutton, 1950.

Haensch, Gunther. *Dictionary of International Relations and Politics: Systematic and Alphabetical in Four Languages: German, English/American, French, Spanish.* New York: Elsevier, 1965.

Hirschhorn, Howard H. *Spanish-English, English-Spanish Medical Guide.* New York: Regents Publishing Co., 1968.

Horn, Stefan. *Glossary of Financial Terms in English/American, French, Spanish, German.* New York: Elsevier, 1965.

Horten, Hans Ernest. *Woodworking Machines in Four Languages, in English, German, French and Spanish.* London: C. R. Brooks, 1968.

Huerta Peredo, José María de Jesús. *Correspondencia Mercantil.* 5th ed. Mexico City: Editorial Herrero, 1974.

*International Dictionary of Applied Mathematics, in English, French, German, Russian, Spanish.* Princeton, N.J.: Van Nostrand, 1960.

*International Dictionary of Physics and Electronics, in French, English, German, Spanish, and Russian.* 2d ed. Princeton, N.J.: Van Nostrand, 1961.

*International Encyclopedia of Chemical Science.* Princeton, N.J.: Van Nostrand, 1964.

James, Glenn. *Mathematics Dictionary, in French, German, English, Russian, and Spanish.* 3d ed. Princeton, N.J.: Van Nostrand, 1968.

Labarre, E. J. *Dictionary and Encyclopedia of Paper and Paper Making with Equivalents of the Technical Terms in French, German, Dutch, Italian, Spanish, and Swedish.* 2d ed. Amsterdam: Swets & Seitlinger, 1969.

Laidler, F. F. *A Glossary in English, French, German, Spanish of Terms Used in Home Economics Education.* London: Constable, 1963.

Lana, Gabriella. *Glossary of Geographical Names in Six Languages: English, French, Italian, Spanish, German, and Dutch.* New York: Elsevier, 1967.

Massa Gil, Beatriz. *Diccionario Técnico de Biblioteconomia español-inglés. Technical Dictionary of Librarianship. English-Spanish.* Mexico City: Editorial F. Trillas, 1964.

Misch, Robert Jay. *Foreign Dining Dictionary, in French, German, Italian, Portuguese, and Spanish.* Garden City, N.Y.: Doubleday, 1955.

Mortiz, Heinrich, ed. *Technical Dictionary of Spectroscopy and Spectral Analysis: English, French, German, Russian, with a supplement in Spanish.* New York: Pergamon Press, 1971.

Navarro Dagnino, Juan. *Vocabulario marítimo inglés-español y español-inglés.* 3d ed. Barcelona: G. Gili, 1957.

Nevada, State of. *Spanish Manual for Court Interpreters and a Guide for Competent Court Interpreting.* Las Vegas.

Newmark, Maxim. *Dictionary of Science and Technology in English-French-German-Spanish.* New York: Philosophical Library, 1934.

North Atlantic Treaty Organization, Advisory Group for Aeronautical Research and Development. *AGARD Aeronautical Multilingual Dictionary.* New York: Pergamon Press, 1960.

Nova González, Emilio. *Terminología usual en la ciencia y en la técnica de la telecomunicación* [in Spanish, French, and English]. Madrid: Paraninfo, 1965.

Oran, Daniel. *Law Dictionary for Non-Lawyers.* St. Paul, Minn.: West Publishing Co., 1975.

Paenson, Isaac. *Systematic Glossary English/French/Spanish/Russian of Selected Economic and Social Terms.* New York: Pergamon Press, 1963.

Pei, Mario Andrew. *Liberal Arts Dictionary in English, French, German, Spanish.* New York: Philosophical Library, 1952.

Pérez Guerrero, Jorge. *Glosario Español-Inglés de Términos Médicos.* Oaxaca: Universidad Benito Juárez.

Pipics, Zoltan. *Dictionarium Bibliotecarii practicum . . . : The Librarian's Practical Dictionary in Twenty Languages.* 3d ed. Munich: Verlag Dokumentation, 1969.

Rae, Kenneth. *An International Vocabulary of Technical Theater Terms, in Eight Languages: American, Dutch, English, French, German, Italian, Spanish, Swedish.* New York: Theater Arts Books, 1960.

Reyes Orozco, Carlos. *Spanish-English/English-Spanish Commercial Dictionary.* New York: Pergamon Press, 1969.

Robayo, Luis Alfredo. *Spanish-English, English-Spanish Technical, Legal, and Commercial Dictionary.* Montreal: Dictionary Publishing Co., 1952.

Robb, Louis Adams. *Diccionario para ingenieros.* New York: Connwilep & Sons, 1955.

____. *Diccionario para ingenieros. (Español-Inglés/Inglés-Español).* Mexico City: Editorial Continental, 1977.

____. *Dictionary of Business Terms: Spanish-English and English-Spanish.* New York: John Wiley, 1950.

____. *Dictionary of Legal Terms (Spanish-English and English-Spanish).* New York: John Wiley, 1955; Mexico City: Editorial Limusa, 1975.

Ruiz Torres, Francisco. *Diccionario inglés-español y español-inglés de medicina.* 3d ed. Madrid: Editorial Alhambra, 1965.

Sears, Roebuck & Co. *Se Habla Consumerism.* Alhambra, Calif.

Simeon, Rikard. *Enciklopedijski rjecnik lingvistickih nziva: na 8 jedikz, hrvatskosrpski, latinski, ruski, njemacki, engleski, francuski, talijanski, spajoslski.* [Encyclopedic Dictionary of Linguistics in Eight Languages: Serbo-Croatian, Latin, Russian, German, English, French, Italian, Spanish]. Zagreb: Matica Hrvatska, 1969.

Steel de Maeza, Barbara. *Manual de Correspondencia Comercial, Español/Inglés-Inglés/Español.* New York: Regents Publishing Co., 1973.

*Systematic Glossary of Terminology of Statistical Methods: English-French-Spanish-Russian.* New York: Published for Intercentre by Pergamon Press, 1970.

Thompson, Anthony. *Vocabularium bibliothecarii: English, French, German, Spanish, Russian.* 2d ed. Paris: UNESCO, 1962.

Tweney, C. F., and L. E. C. Hughes, eds. *Chambers diccionario tecnológico: Español-Inglés, Inglés-Español.* Barcelona: Ediciones Omega, 1952.

U.S. Department of the Treasury. *English-Spanish Glossary of Words and Phrases Used in Publications by the IRS.* Washington, D.C.: Government Printing Office.

University of California, Davis. *Layman's Glossary of Selected Criminal Law Terms.* Vol. 8. Davis.

Varela Colmeneiro, Guillermo. *Diccionario comercial y económico moderno.* Madrid: Editorial Interciencia, 1964.

Vásquez, Máximo L. *Diccionario de correspondencia comercial.* New York: Latin American Institute Press, 1953.

Weck, Johannes. *Dictionary of Forestry in Five Languages: German, English, French, Spanish, Russian.* New York: Elsevier, 1966.

Wittfoht, Annemarie. *Plastics Lexicon: Processing and Machinery, in Six Languages: German, English, French, Spanish, Italian, Dutch.* New York: Elsevier, 1963.

World Meteorological Organization. *International Meteorological Vocabulary, in English, French, Russian, and Spanish.* Geneva, 1966.

Zazueta, Fernando R. *Attorney's Guide to the Use of Court Interpreters with an English and Spanish Glossary of Criminal Law Terms.* Vol. 8. Davis: University of California, 1975.

# APÉNDICE II

La conjugación del verbo

**A.   REGULAR VERBS:** see pages 9–14, **Capítulo preliminar.**

**B.   RADICAL-CHANGING VERBS**

*Class 1:* **-ar** and **-er** verbs, such as **cerrar, contar, entender, volver**

e ⟶ ie and o ⟶ ue when stem vowel is accented in the present indicative and present subjunctive

*Pres. ind.*   cierro, cierras, cierra, cerramos, cerráis, cierran
*Pres. subj.*  cierre, cierres, cierre, cerremos, cerréis, cierren

*Pres. ind.*   cuento, cuentas, cuenta, contamos, contáis, cuentan
*Pres. subj.*  cuente, cuentes, cuente, contemos, contéis, cuenten

*Pres. ind.*   entiendo, entiendes, entiende, entendemos, entendéis, entienden
*Pres. subj.*  entienda, entiendas, entienda, entendamos, entendáis, entiendan

*Pres. ind.*   vuelvo, vuelves, vuelve, volvemos, volvéis, vuelven
*Pres. subj.*  vuelva, vuelvas, vuelva, volvamos, volváis, vuelvan

Other Class 1 radical-changing verbs include **acordar(se), acostar(se), atravesar, comenzar, despertar(se), empezar, encontrar, jugar, mostrar, negar, pensar, probar, recordar, sentar(se); defender, encender, llover, mover**

*Class 2:* **-ir** verbs only, such as **preferir, dormir**

e ⟶ ie and o ⟶ ue when stem vowel is accented in the present indicative and present subjunctive

e ⟶ i and o ⟶ u when stem vowel is unaccented in the present participle, first and second persons plural of the present subjunctive, third person singular and plural of the preterite, and all forms of the imperfect subjunctive

*Pres. part.*  prefiriendo
*Pres. ind.*   prefiero, prefieres, prefiere, preferimos, preferís, prefieren
*Pres. subj.*  prefiera, prefieras, prefiera, prefiramos, prefiráis, prefieran
*Pret.*        preferí, preferiste, prefirió, preferimos, preferisteis, prefirieron
*Imp. subj.*   prefiriera, prefirieras, prefiriera, prefiriéramos, prefirierais, prefirieran

*Pres. part.*  durmiendo
*Pres. ind.*   duermo, duermes, duerme, dormimos, dormís, duermen
*Pres. subj.*  duerma, duermas, duerma, durmamos, durmáis, duerman
*Pret.*        dormí, dormiste, durmió, dormimos, dormisteis, durmieron
*Imp. subj.*   durmiera, durmieras, durmiera, durmiéramos, durmierais, durmieran

Other Class 2 radical-changing verbs include **advertir(se), consentir, convertir, divertir(se), mentir, morir, sentir(se)**

*Class 3:* **-ir** verbs only, such as **servir**

e ⟶ i when changes occur in Class 2 radical-changing verbs

*Pres. part.*  sirviendo
*Pres. ind.*   sirvo, sirves, sirve, servimos, servís, sirven
*Pres. subj.*  sirva, sirvas, sirva, sirvamos, sirváis, sirvan
*Pret.*        serví, serviste, sirvió, servimos, servisteis, sirvieron
*Imp. subj.*   sirviera, sirvieras, sirviera, sirviéramos, sirvierais, sirvieran

Other Class 3 radical-changing verbs include **concebir, corregir, elegir, pedir, reír, repetir, seguir, vestir(se)**

## C.  ORTHOGRAPHIC CHANGES

-car:          c ⟶ qu before e, é:  buscar: **busque, busqué**

-cer, -cir:    c ⟶ z before o, a:  conocer: **conozco, conozca**

-gar:          g ⟶ gu before e, é:  pagar: **pague, pagué**

-ger, -gir:    g ⟶ j before o, a:  escoger: **escojo, escoja**

-guar:         gu ⟶ gü before e, é:  averiguar: **averigüe, averigüé**

-guir:         gu ⟶ g before o, a:  conseguir: **consigo, consiga**

-zar:          z ⟶ c before e, é:  almorzar: **almuerce, almorcé**

Unaccented i ⟶ y between vowels:  creer: **creyó, creyeron**

Note: A number of -iar and -uar verbs require a written accent on the i or u in all persons of the singular and the third person plural of the present indicative and subjunctive:

guiar: guío, guías, guía, guiamos, guiáis, guían

guíe, guíes, guíe, guiemos, guiéis, guíen

## D.  IRREGULAR VERBS

Irregular forms are most generally found in the first person singular of the present indicative, preterite, present subjunctive, imperfect subjunctive, future, and conditional. Only tenses with irregular forms are given; other tenses follow the rules for the formation of tenses of regular verbs. Compounds of irregular verbs follow the same pattern of conjugation as regular verbs.

1.  **dar:** *to give*

   *Pres.:*          doy, das, da, damos, dais, dan
   *Pres. subj.:*    dé, des, dé, demos, deis, den
   *Pret.:*          di, diste, dio, dimos, disteis, dieron
   *Imp. subj.:*     diera, dieras, diera, diéramos, dierais, dieran
   *Imperatives:* da, dad, dé Ud., den Uds.

2.  **decir:** *to say, to tell*

   *Pres. part.:*   diciendo          *Past part.* dicho
   *Pres.:*          digo, dices, dice, decimos, decís, dicen
   *Pres. subj.:*    diga, digas, diga, digamos, digáis, digan
   *Fut.:*           diré, dirás, dirá, diremos, diréis, dirán
   *Cond.:*          diría, dirías, diría, diríamos, diríais, dirían
   *Pret.:*          dije, dijiste, dijo, dijimos, dijisteis, dijeron
   *Imp. subj.:*     dijera, dijeras, dijera, dijéramos, dijerais, dijeran
   *Imperatives:* di, decid, diga Ud., digan Uds.

3.  **estar:** *to be*

   *Pres.:*          estoy, estás, está, estamos, estáis, están
   *Pres. subj.:*    esté, estés, esté, estemos, estéis, estén
   *Pret.:*          estuve, estuviste, estuvo, estuvimos, estuvisteis, estuvieron
   *Imp. subj.:*     estuviera, estuvieras, estuviera, estuviéramos, estuvierais, estuvieran
   *Imperatives:* está, estad, esté Ud., estén Uds.

4.  **haber:** *to have* (auxiliary verb)

   *Pres.:*          he, has, ha, hemos, habéis, han
   *Pres. subj.:*    haya, hayas, haya, hayamos, hayáis, hayan
   *Fut.:*           habré, habrás, habrá, habremos, habréis, habrán
   *Cond.:*          habría, habrías, habría, habríamos, habríais, habrían

*Pret.:*      hube, hubiste, hubo, hubimos, hubisteis, hubieron
*Imp. subj.:*   hubiera, hubieras, hubiera, hubiéramos, hubierais, hubieran

5. **hacer:** *to do, to make*

  *Past part.:*   hecho
  *Pres.:*       hago, haces, hace, hacemos, hacéis, hacen
  *Pres. subj.:*  haga, hagas, haga, hagamos, hagáis, hagan
  *Fut.:*        haré, harás, hará, haremos, haréis, harán
  *Cond.:*      haría, harías, haría, haríamos, haríais, harían
  *Pret.:*       hice, hiciste, hizo, hicimos, hicisteis, hicieron
  *Imp. subj.:*  hiciera, hicieras, hiciera, hiciéramos, hicierais, hicieran
  *Imperatives:* haz, haced, haga Ud., hagan Uds.

6. **ir:** *to go*

  *Pres. part.:*  yendo
  *Pres.:*       voy, vas, va, vamos, vais, van
  *Pres. subj.:*  vaya, vayas, vaya, vayamos, vayáis, vayan
  *Imperf.:*    iba, ibas, iba, íbamos, ibais, iban
  *Pret.:*       fui, fuiste, fue, fuimos, fuisteis, fueron
  *Imp. subj.:*  fuera, fueras, fuera, fuéramos, fuerais, fueran
  *Imperatives:* ve, id, vaya Ud., vayan Uds.

7. **oír:** *to hear*

  *Pres. part.:*  oyendo
  *Pres.*        oigo, oyes, oye, oímos, oís, oyen
  *Pres. subj.:*  oiga, oigas, oiga, oigamos, oigáis, oigan
  *Pret.:*       oí, **oíste**, oyó, oímos, oísteis, oyeron
  *Imp. subj.:*  oyera, oyeras, oyera, oyéramos, oyerais, oyeran
  *Imperatives:* oye, oíd, oiga Ud., oigan Uds.

8. **poder:** *to be able*

  *Pres. part.:*  pudiendo
  *Pres.:*       puedo, puedes, puede, podemos, podéis, pueden
  *Pres. subj.:*  pueda, puedas, pueda, podamos, podáis, puedan
  *Fut.:*        podré, podrás, podrá, podremos, podréis, podrán
  *Cond.:*      podría, podrías, podría, podríamos, podríais, podrían
  *Pret.:*       pude, pudiste, pudo, pudimos, pudisteis, pudieron
  *Imp. subj.:*  pudiera, pudieras, pudiera, pudiéramos, pudierais, pudieran

9. **poner:** *to put, to place*

  *Past. part.:*  puesto
  *Pres.:*       pongo, pones, pone, ponemos, ponéis, ponen
  *Pres. subj.:*  ponga, pongas, ponga, pongamos, pongáis, pongan
  *Fut.:*        pondré, pondrás, pondrá, pondremos, pondréis, pondrán
  *Cond.:*      pondría, pondrías, pondría, pondríamos, pondríais, pondrían
  *Pret.:*       puse, pusiste, puso, pusimos, pusisteis, pusieron
  *Imp. subj.:*  pusiera, pusieras, pusiera, pusiéramos, pusierais, pusieran
  *Imperatives:* pon, poned, ponga Ud., pongan Uds.

10. **querer:** *to want, to wish*

  *Pres.:*       quiero, quieres, quiere, queremos, queréis, quieren
  *Pres. subj.:*  quiera, quieras, quiera, queramos, queráis, quieran
  *Fut.:*        querré, querrás, querrá, querremos, querréis, querrán

*Cond.:*       querría, querrías, querría, querríamos, querríais, querrían
*Pret.:*        quise, quisiste, quiso, quisimos, quisisteis, quisieron
*Imp. subj.:*  quisiera, quisieras, quisiera, quisiéramos, quisierais, quisieran

11.   **saber:** *to know*

*Pres.:*        sé, sabes, sabe, sabemos, sabéis, saben
*Pres. subj.:*  sepa, sepas, sepa, sepamos, sepáis, sepan
*Fut.:*        sabré, sabrás, sabrá, sabremos, sabréis, sabrán
*Cond.:*       sabría, sabrías, sabría, sabríamos, sabríais, sabrían
*Pret.:*        supe, supiste, supo, supimos, supisteis, supieron
*Imp. subj.:*  supiera, supieras, supiera, supiéramos, supierais, supieran
*Imperatives:* sabe, sabed, sepa Ud., sepan Uds.

12.   **salir:** *to leave, to go out*

*Pres.:*        salgo, sales, sale, salimos, salís, salen
*Pres. subj.:*  salga, salgas, salga, salgamos, salgáis, salgan
*Fut.:*        saldré, saldrás, saldrá, saldremos, saldréis, saldrán
*Cond.:*       saldría, saldrías, saldría, saldríamos, saldríais, saldrían
*Imperatives:* sal, salid, salga Ud., salgan Uds.

13.   **ser:** *to be*

*Pres.:*        soy, eres, es, somos, sois, son
*Pres. subj.:*  sea, seas, sea, seamos, seáis, sean
*Imperf.:*     era, eras, era, éramos, erais, eran
*Pref.:*        fui, fuiste, fue, fuimos, fuisteis, fueron
*Imp. subj.:*  fuera, fueras, fuera, fuéramos, fuerais, fueran
*Imperatives:* sé, sed, sea Ud., sean Uds.

14.   **tener:** *to have*

*Pres.:*        tengo, tienes, tiene, tenemos, tenéis, tienen
*Pres. subj.:*  tenga, tengas, tenga, tengamos, tengáis, tengan
*Fut.:*        tendré, tendrás, tendrá, tendremos, tendréis, tendrán
*Cond.:*       tendría, tendrías, tendría, tendríamos, tendríais, tendrían
*Pret.:*        tuve, tuviste, tuvo, tuvimos, tuvisteis, tuvieron
*Imp. subj.:*  tuviera, tuvieras, tuviera, tuviéramos, tuvierais, tuvieran
*Imperatives:* ten, tened, tenga Ud., tengan Uds.

15.   **traer:** *to bring*

*Pres. part.:*  trayendo
*Pres.:*        traigo, traes, trae, traemos, traéis, traen
*Pres. subj.:*  traiga, traigas, traiga, traigamos, traigáis, traigan
*Pret.:*        traje, trajiste, trajo, trajimos, trajisteis, trajeron
*Imp. subj.:*  trajera, trajeras, trajera, trajéramos, trajerais, trajeran
*Imperatives:* trae, traed, traiga Ud., traigan Uds.

16.   **valer:** *to be worth*

*Pres.:*        valgo, vales, vale, valemos, valéis, valen
*Pres. subj.:*  valga, valgas, valga, valgamos, valgáis, valgan
*Fut.:*        valdré, valdrás, valdrá, valdremos, valdréis, valdrán
*Cond.:*       valdría, valdrías, valdría, valdríamos, valdríais, valdrían
*Imperatives:* val (vale), valed, valga Ud., valgan Uds.

17.   **venir:** *to come*

*Pres. part.:*  viniendo

| *Pres.:* | vengo, vienes, viene, venimos, venís, vienen |
|---|---|
| *Pres. subj.:* | venga, vengas, venga, vengamos, vengáis, vengan |
| *Fut.:* | vendré, vendrás, vendrá, vendremos, vendréis, vendrán |
| *Cond.:* | vendrían, vendrías, vendría, vendríamos, vendríais, vendrían |
| *Pret.:* | vine, viniste, vino, vinimos, vinisteis, vinieron |
| *Imp. subj.:* | viniera, vinieras, viniera, viniéramos, vinierais, vinieran |
| *Imperatives:* | ven, venid, venga Ud., vengan Uds. |

18. **ver:** *to see*

| *Past part.:* | visto |
|---|---|
| *Pres.:* | veo, ves, ve, vemos, veis, ven |
| *Pres. subj.:* | vea, veas, vea, veamos, veáis, vean |
| *Imperf.:* | veía, veías, veía, veíamos, veíais, veían |

# APÉNDICE III

## English Translations of Spanish Dialogs

## CAPÍTULO 1

### An Emergency in the Street

*Nurse:* Here, Doctor, come quickly. There's been an accident. A young lady is lying on her back on the street. I think she's injured—there's a lot of blood.

*Doctor:* A young lady? What's the matter with her? Has she fallen or has someone run over her? (They go out into the street.) Ohhh, what a bloody mess, and yet the young lady isn't complaining. Don't move, Miss, we're going to help you.

*Dolores:* Ohhh, ohhh. Where am I? What's this? Blood! My blood! I'm going to die. How I hurt! Help me!

*Nurse:* (very calm) Calm down, Miss. Here's Doctor Jiménez to help you. Don't worry. It's nothing serious. Tell me, what happened?

*Doctor:* (to the nurse) Shh, don't bother the patient. What a pity, poor thing, how she's suffering. Nurse, bring me my bag. It's an emergency! (The nurse leaves.)

*Dolores:* Doctor, help me! Look at all the blood. I'm in pain. I'm going to die. Please help me, Doctor!

*Doctor:* Calm down, calm down. You're not going to die. We have to examine a few things first. Where do you feel the pain? Does your foot hurt? Perhaps it's your toes? Is it your ankle? Your leg isn't broken.

*Dolores:* Ohhh, I'm afraid! I can't stand the sight of blood. How I hurt! I'm going to die.

*Nurse:* Doctor, here's your bag. How's the patient?

*Doctor:* I don't know yet. We'll see. Please, Miss, try to move your legs . . . yes, everything seems to be OK.

*Dolores:* Ohhh, no, Doctor, not there, higher up. It hurts further up.

*Doctor:* Further up? Can it be the spinal column?

*Nurse:* Doctor, I think that . . .

*Doctor:* (interrupting her) Shhh, I think the pain is in her hand. Does your wrist hurt? . . . or the elbow? Maybe your arm?

*Dolores:* No, Doctor, my back hurts. It's a sharp pain.

*Nurse:* Your back? No wonder. Look, Doctor, she's fallen (and landed) on a bag of groceries. It's not blood. A bottle of tomato catsup has broken.

## CAPÍTULO 2

### Reporting a Car Theft

*Mr. Sandoval:* Pardon me, are you Officer Ramírez? I've been told that I can report a car theft here.

*Officer Ramírez:* Yes, I'm the person in charge of taking down the necessary information. Let's see . . . could you give me your complete name and address?

*Mr. Sandoval:* Yes, I'm Manuel Sandoval Gutiérrez. I live at 1483 El Cerrito Street, in this city.

*Officer Ramírez:* Are you the owner of the car?

*Mr. Sandoval:* Yes, I am.

*Officer Ramírez:* Have you brought proof of ownership (with you)?

*Mr. Sandoval:* No, I left it at home, and the registration (paper) is in the glove compartment of the car.

*Officer Ramírez:* Well, that's not important. Where was your car stolen?

*Mr. Sandoval:* It was parked on El Monte Street, at the corner of Madera Street (and El Monte). It must have been stolen between eleven and twelve in the morning.

*Officer Ramírez:* What make and year is your car?

*Mr. Sandoval:* It's a 1975 Ford.

*Officer Ramírez:* Do you remember the license number?

*Mr. Sandoval:* Yes, it's 083 MTZ, from this state.

*Officer Ramírez:* What's its value?

*Mr. Sandoval:* It's worth about $5,500, since it has some valuable accessories.

*Officer Ramírez:* What accessories does it have?

*Mr. Sandoval:* It has a radio and cassette with an antenna on the front right side. Oh, it also has some new tires on special rims. They are the wide racing type.

*Officer Ramírez:* What color is your car?

*Mr. Sandoval:* It's a two-tone. The main color is light yellow with a dark brown roof. It also has a luggage rack on top.

*Officer Ramírez:* How many doors does it have?

*Mr. Sandoval:* It's a two door, and the right door has a dent.

*Officer Ramírez:* Was it locked?

*Mr. Sandoval:* No. I left the windows open and carelessly left the keys in place (in the ignition).

*Officer Ramírez:* Is your car insured?

*Mr. Sandoval:* Yes, it's insured with the American Auto Insurance Company.

*Officer Ramírez:* Are there any other details or marks that might help us locate your car?

*Mr. Sandoval:* No. Well . . . now that I think about it, one of the front lights is broken.

# CAPÍTULO 3

## A.   Registration

*Secretary:* Your first and last name, please?

*Woman:* Francisca Benítez de Beltrán.

*Secretary:* And your son's name?

*Woman:* Faustino Beltrán Benítez.

*Secretary:* Age?

*Woman:* Mine?

*Secretary:* No, your son Faustino's (age).

*Woman:* He's eleven years old.

*Secretary:* Fine. Was he born in Mexico?

*Woman:* Yes, Miss, in Rosarito, Baja California. Here's his birth certificate.

*Secretary:* What grade is he enrolling in?

*Woman:* In the sixth grade.

*Secretary:* His grade card, please.

*Woman:* Here it is.

*Secretary:* Ah! (These are) Good grades.

*Woman:* It's nice of you to say that.

## B.   The Future

*Advisor:* Please be seated. You're Joaquín Alemán?

*Joaquín:* Yes, sir, at your service.

*Advisor:* I'm Mr. Ignacio Godínez, your academic advisor.

*Joaquín:* It's a pleasure to meet you.

*Advisor:* Likewise. I want to speak to you about the national basic competency exam.

*Joaquín:* What? Did I fail the exam?

*Advisor:* No, to the contrary. You passed it with an excellent grade.

*Joaquín:* Ah! I'm really glad to hear that.

*Advisor:* I spoke with the school principal, and he wants to recommend you for a national scholarship for university studies. What do you think?

*Joaquín:* That would be great!

*Advisor:* You graduate this coming June, right?

*Joaquín:* God willing.

*Advisor:* Well then, apply for a federal government scholarship. We will support your application.

*Joaquín:* Thanks a lot. What type of scholarship should I apply for?

*Advisor:* That depends on your vocational interests. What profession interests you? Would you like to be a doctor, a lawyer, a language teacher, an anthropologist? Tell me.

*Joaquín:* Well, I've always wanted to be a doctor. My parents agree.

*Advisor:* Magnificent. Here in this city there's a university with a famous medical school. Go to the administration (building) and pick up an application (blank) for premed studies. I'll help you fill out the forms.

*Joaquín:* I'll do it tomorrow. Thanks a lot, Mr. Godínez.

*Advisor:* You're welcome.

# CAPÍTULO 4

## Monólogo A

### A Telephone Call

Hello, is Mrs. Gutiérrez in? . . . Thank you. . . . Hello, Mrs. Gutiérrez? . . . I'm _____, the social worker from the County Welfare Department. . . . Yes, that's right. I spoke with you yesterday. I'm calling to let you know a few things about your case. I've spoken with the director of the Social Security Department, and he has told me that we can help you. We've spoken with your doctor, and we've found out about all the details of your accident. This morning I mentioned the case to your boss, and he told me that you will receive some benefits. Fortunately, your husband is a city employee, and he is covered by a good insurance policy. The insurance agent told me that they are going to speak with the witnesses, since the store employees saw the accident. I'm planning to go to your house tomorrow with the necessary forms. What time would be convenient (for me) to visit you? . . . Yes, eleven in the morning is a good time for me. Meanwhile, do you need anything? . . . Yes, yes, what's his name? . . . Father Ortiz. Is he the priest of Our Lady of Guadalupe? . . . No, I don't know him, but I know who he is. . . . Could you repeat the number, please? . . . 483 . . . 54 . . . 87 . . . Yes, I'll be glad to call him to tell him that you will not be able to go this afternoon. . . . You're welcome. Well, it's been nice talking with you. See you tomorrow. . . . Goodbye.

## Monólogo B

### Employment and Unemployment

I have to go to my job every day. I work from eight in the morning until five in the afternoon. My day off is Sunday. Every summer I go (it's my turn to go) on vacation. I've been with the same company for fifteen years.

I have a family and my duty is to provide for them (provide them with the necessary sustenance). There are always many expenses, and I don't have many resources. I spend twenty percent of my income on food. In order to pay some debts, I have to (it's necessary to) go to my savings. This money is reserved for my retirement.

My fellow workers demand more holidays and an increase in salary, since life becomes more expensive every day. We have to be very careful in our job, for there are many risks. You can have an accident and become physically handicapped because of an injury. A friend of mine is incompetent and thinks that the boss is going to fire him. I don't feel sorry for him, since he doesn't like working in this factory. I'm sure he won't be unemployed for long. He can find a job in a mechanic's shop, since he says he likes that kind of work (job.)

# CAPÍTULO 5

## Helping a Client

*Sales Clerk:* Good afternoon, madam. Can I help you?

*Lady:* Good afternoon, Miss. I'm looking for something to give my niece as a birthday present.

*Sales Clerk:* Are you interested in (an article of) clothing?

*Lady:* Yes, I think she would like a skirt. She's very particular, and I have to be careful about what I buy her.

*Sales Clerk:* Do you know her size?

*Lady:* Yes, I would say a five. I'm interested in a long skirt, like the one you have on.

*Sales Clerk:* Well, here are these skirts. They're not exactly like the one I have on, since we're out of those. We had a sale last week and ran out of them. These are very similar. What color are you interested in? How about this red one?

*Lady:* No, that (color) is too loud. I'm more interested in a green . . . something similar to this shade but a little lighter.

*Sales Clerk:* I think that the one you're looking for is this one. We have it in two styles, with pleats or plain. Which do you prefer?

*Lady:* I prefer the plain skirt but without a belt.

*Sales Clerk:* The belt is included, but if you or your niece don't want it, it doesn't matter, since this skirt can be worn without the belt.

*Lady:* Good. I'll take it.

*Sales Clerk:* Follow me to the cash register, please. Is this cash or charge (credit)?

*Lady:* Put it on my account. Here's my credit card. Also, can you tell me where gift wrapping is done?

*Sales Clerk:* Yes, that's on the third floor, near the credit office. You can take the elevator (that's) to the left or the escalator (that's) to the right.

*Lady:* Thanks.

*Sales Clerk:* You're welcome. Well, here's your purchase. The receipt is in the bag. Come again. (It's a pleasure to serve you.)

# APÉNDICE IV

Spanish Translations of Welfare Questions

CAPÍTULO 4

## 6 AYUDA AL SOLICITANTE A LLENAR LOS FORMULARIOS

### I. Nombre / Name

1. ¿Cómo se llama el solicitante/el que solicita ayuda?
2. ¿Cuál es su nombre completo?
3. ¿Cuál es su apellido?
4. ¿Cuál es su nombre de pila?
5. ¿Cuál es el apellido de soltera de su madre?
6. ¿Tiene Ud. un apodo/sobrenombre?
7. ¿Ha usado Ud. otro nombre?
8. ¿Tiene Ud. inicial?

### II. Domicilio / Address

1. ¿Cuál es su domicilio?
2. ¿Dónde vive Ud.?
3. ¿Es una calle/avenida/ruta/carretera/vía?
4. ¿Cuál es el número de su apartamento?
5. ¿Es éste su domicilio actual?
6. ¿Tiene Ud. apartado postal?
7. ¿Es su domicilio de hogar distinto al de su correspondencia?
8. ¿En qué ciudad vive Ud.?
9. ¿En qué condado vive Ud.?
10. ¿En qué estado vive Ud.?
11. ¿Cuál es su zona postal?

### III. Teléfono / Telephone

1. ¿Cuál es el número de teléfono de su casa?
2. ¿Cuál es el número de teléfono de su empleo?
3. ¿Hay un número donde se puede dejar un mensaje/recado?
4. ¿Cómo se llama la persona a quien se le puede dejar el recado?
5. ¿Cuándo (¿a qué hora) se puede dejar un mensaje?

### IV. Información de inmigración / Alien Registration Information

1. ¿Qué nombre(s) tenía al entrar a este país?
2. ¿En qué fecha entró a este país? (mes, día, año)
3. ¿Por cuál puerto entró?
4. ¿Qué destino tenía al entrar?
5. ¿De qué país es ciudadano/a?
6. ¿Cuál es el número de su mica/tarjeta de inmigración?

7. ¿Es Ud. ciudadano/a americano/a?

8. ¿Es Ud. residente permanente de los Estados Unidos?

9. ¿Es Ud. extranjero/a permanente?

10. ¿Es Ud. turista?

# 7 ENTREVISTAS DETALLADAS

## I.  El empleo / Employment

1. ¿Para quién trabaja?

2. ¿Dónde trabaja?

3. ¿Desde cuándo trabaja allí?

4. ¿Cuánto le pagan por (hora, semana, mes, año)?

5. ¿Está Ud. empleado/a tiempo completo?

6. ¿Está Ud. empleado/a temporalmente?

7. ¿Está Ud. empleado/a por sí mismo/a?

8. ¿Cuántas horas trabaja por día/semana?

9. ¿Qué puesto tiene Ud.?

10. ¿Cada cuándo le pagan?

11. ¿Cuánto es su sueldo en bruto?

12. ¿Cuánto es su sueldo neto?

13. ¿Cuándo le despidieron de allí?

14. ¿Por qué le despidieron?

15. ¿Qué trabajo tenía antes?

16. ¿De qué fecha a qué fecha trabajó allí?

17. ¿Cuál fue el último día que trabajó?

18. ¿Está Ud. disponible y activamente busca empleo?

19. ¿Está Ud. en algún programa de entrenamiento?

20. El padre sin empleo, ¿ha . . .
     dejado algún empleo o entrenamiento en los últimos treinta días?
     rehusado algún empleo o entrenamiento en los últimos treinta días?

21. El padre que vive en casa, ¿trabaja él/ella menos de 100 horas por mes?

22. ¿Tiene Ud. los recibos de nómina?

## II.  Situación económica / Financial Situation

1. ¿Recibió Ud. _____ beneficios? (militares, del obrero)

2. ¿Recibió algún miembro de la familia _____? (pagos extraordinarios, regalos, comisiones, propinas)

3. Cuando estuvo de huelga, ¿cuánto eran sus beneficios derivados de huelga?

4. ¿Cuánto dinero tiene Ud. en su cuenta de ahorros?

5. ¿Ha recibido alojamiento gratis este año?

6. ¿Cuánto recibe su abuelo a través del seguro social?
     ¿Cumple él con los requisitos de la seguridad del ingreso suplemental?

7. ¿Cuánto fue su reembolso de impuestos del año pasado?

8. ¿Tiene Ud. propiedad en alquiler?

9. ¿Cuánto debe Ud. de préstamos?

10. ¿Qué pensiones tiene su abuela? ¿Tiene pensión del ferrocarril?

11. ¿Cuánto son los ingresos de su granja? (negocio)

12. Cuando Ud. estuvo en el programa de entrenamiento, ¿cuánto eran sus pagos por entrenamiento?

13. Cuando Ud. estuvo empleado/a, ¿recibió algún pago extraordinario?

14. ¿Cuánto es el salario de su hija?

15. Después del accidente, ¿cuánto recibió del seguro por incapacidad?

16. ¿Qué gastos tiene Ud.?

17. ¿Cuánto paga Ud. por vivienda?

18. ¿Cuánto son sus mensualidades de carro?

19. ¿Cuándo recibe sus cuentas de servicios municipales?

20. ¿Ha pagado su cuenta de médico esta semana?

21. ¿Sabe Ud. qué gastos debe indicar en este formulario?

22. ¿Mandó su esposo todos los pagos de sostenimiento a hijos?

23. ¿Cuál es el total de los gastos mensuales?

24. ¿Quiere declarar otras fuentes de ingresos?

## III. Situación escolar / Educational Situation

1. ¿Quién en su casa está en la escuela?

2. ¿Hay alguien que esté en un programa de entrenamiento?

3. ¿Cuántas horas por semana asiste a clase?

4. ¿Recibe alguna beca?

5. ¿Tiene él/ella un préstamo estudiantil?

6. ¿Cada cuándo recibe esta beca o préstamo?

7. ¿Es el año académico semestre o trimestre?

8. ¿Qué gastos escolares tiene?

9. ¿Asiste a la escuela tiempo completo o menos del tiempo completo? ¿temporalmente?

10. ¿Trabaja después de la escuela?

11. ¿Asiste a los cursos de verano?

12. ¿Hay cuotas de laboratorio?

13. ¿Ha investigado las posibilidades del E.O.P.?

14. ¿En qué año van sus hijos?

15. ¿Para cuándo piensa graduarse él/ella?

## IV. Situación del hogar / Home Situation

1. ¿Cuántas personas viven con Ud.?

2. ¿Cuántos son menores de edad?

3. ¿Viven menores de dieciocho años aquí?

4. ¿Viven mayores de sesenta y cinco años aquí?

5. ¿Son familiares suyos?

6. ¿Son huéspedes (visita)?

7. ¿Están enfermos o incapacitados?

8. ¿Quiénes pagan por cuarto, comidas o ambas cosas?

9. ¿Viven en una parte separada de la casa?

10. ¿Hay equipo para cocinar donde vive Ud.?

11. ¿No puede Ud. o su esposo/a preparar comidas por razones de salud?

12. ¿Dónde recibe Ud. sus comidas?

13. ¿Es Ud. o cualquiera de la casa miembro de un centro de rehabilitación?

14. ¿Está Ud. como paciente interno o no interno?

15. ¿Ha ingresado o salido de una institución pública (casa adoptiva, reformatorio, cárcel) o de una institución particular?

16. ¿Vive aquí un varón adulto sin parentesco?

17. ¿Son Uds. una pareja casada?

## V. Citas / Appointments

1. ¿Recibió un aviso de la cita?

2. Por favor, prepare lo siguiente/los materiales siguientes para la entrevista que se le ha programado.

3. ¿Querría un intérprete?

4. Por favor, traiga un intérprete consigo.

5. ¿No puede conseguir un intérprete?

6. ¿Quiere que nosotros le consigamos un intérprete?

7. Déjenos saber con un día de antelación.

8. ¿Nos puede proporcionar la siguiente información?

9. Es absolutamente necesario que Ud. cumpla con esta cita.

## VI. Elegibilidad / Eligibility

1. ¿Cree Ud. que esta subvención no debe cambiarse?

2. ¿Por qué cree que no se debe reducir la cantidad de esta subvención?

3. ¿Cuántos niños están incluídos en la concesión?

4. ¿Sabe Ud. cuándo la decisión va a afectar su subvención?

5. ¿Se va a descontinuar su subvención?

6. ¿Sabe Ud. que su ayuda continuará hasta que la audiencia imparcial llegue a una decisión?

7. ¿Sabe Ud. que puede declarar el por qué no está satisfecho/a con la cantidad de la subvención?

8. ¿Solicita una subvención que le ayude a pagar la guardería?

9. ¿Por qué no se debe descontinuar su concesión?

10. ¿Sobre qué aspecto de su subvención quiere hablar?

# VOCABULARIO

This vocabulary gives only meanings that correspond to the text use. Spanish words that are exact or nearly exact cognates of English words are not included when meaning and gender are clear. Also excluded are most specialized slang words; names of countries that are close or exact cognates of their English names; personal pronouns; definite and indefinite articles; possessive adjectives and pronouns; demonstrative adjectives and pronouns; diminutive and superlative forms of nouns and adjectives; conjugated verb forms and regular participles; and numbers. Adverbs ending in **-mente** are not listed if the adjectives from which they are derived are included.

The gender of nouns is listed except for masculine nouns ending in **-o** and feminine nouns ending in **-a**, **-dad**, **-tad**, **-tud**, or **-ión**. If a verb has a radical change, it is indicated in parentheses.

## Abbreviations

| | | | |
|---|---|---|---|
| *ab* | abbreviation | *m* | masculine |
| *adj* | adjective | *Mex* | Mexico (Mexican usage) |
| *adv* | adverb | *n* | noun |
| *coll* | colloquial | *pl* | plural |
| *conj* | conjunction | *prep* | preposition |
| *f* | feminine | *sing* | singular |
| *inf* | infinitive | *v* | verb |

# A

a   to, at

a través de   from, through, via

abajo   down, below

abierto   open

ablandar   to soften

abogado/a   lawyer; __ defensor   defense lawyer

abogar   to defend

abollón m   dent

abrazadura   brace

abrazar   to hug, embrace

abrigo   coat

abril   April

abrir   to open; __ con llave   to unlock

abuela   grandmother

abuelo   grandfather

acabar   to finish; -sele a uno   to run out of

académico   academic

accesorio   accessory

accidentado   hurt, injured

accidente m   accident

acción   action; stock; __ en circulación   outstanding share

accionista m + f   shareholder, stockholder

aceite m   oil

acelerador m   accelerator

acelga   chard

aceptar   to accept

acerca (de)   about

acercarse   to approach, draw near

acne m   acne

acordar (ue)   to agree, to remind; -se   to remember

acostarse (ue)   to lie down; to go to bed

acta de nacimiento   birth certificate

actitud   attitude

actividad   activity

actual   present, current

acuerdo n   agreement, accord; settlement; estar de __   to be in agreement

acusación   accusation

acusado/a   accused (person)

acusar   to accuse; to acknowledge

adelante   forward; come in

además   moreover, likewise, further, in addition

aderezo   (salad) dressing

adiós m sing   goodbye

adjuntar   to attach

adjunto   enclosed (with this letter), attached

administrador(a)   administrator

adolescente m + f   adolescent

adolorido   painful, aching

adoptivo   adopted, adoptive

adverso   adverse

aéreo adj   air

afectado   affected

afecto   affection; concern

afeitar(se)   to shave (oneself)

aflojar   to loosen

afortunadamente   luckily, fortunately

afuera   outside

agencia   agency

agente m + f   agent, officer; __ de policía   police officer; __ de tránsito   traffic officer

agitación   agitation, turbulence

agosto   August

agotarse   to run out; to become exhausted

agradecer   to acknowledge a favor; to thank

agravar   to aggravate, to complicate

agrio   sour

agua   water; __ oxigenada   hydrogen peroxide

aguacate m   avocado

aguantar   to bear, to endure

agudo   sharp

ahora   now

ahorcar   to hang

ahorrar   to save

ahorro   savings

ahumado   smoked

aire m   air

ajedrezado   checkered

ají m   chili

ajuste m   adjustment, settlement

al contado   cash

albañil m + f   mason, bricklayer

albaricoque m   apricot

alcachofa   artichoke

alcalde/alcadesa   mayor

alcaldía   office of the mayor

alcance m   reach

alcanzar   to reach
alcohol *m*   alcohol
alcohólico *adj*   alcoholic
alcoholismo   alcoholism
alegrarse   to be happy, become happy
alegre   merry, joyful
alergia   allergy
alérgico   allergic
algo   something
algodón *m*   cotton
alguacil *m + f*   sheriff, constable, peace
   officer
alguno *n*   someone; *adj* some, several
aliento   breath
alimento   nourishment, food
aliviar   to relieve; to get well
allí   there
almendra   almond
almohada   pillow
alojamiento   lodging
alquiler *m*   wages or hire; rent
alto *adj*   tall; *n* halt, stop sign
alucinógeno   hallucinogenic drug
aluminio   aluminum
alumno/a   pupil, student
amable   kind
amarillo   yellow
ambiente *m*   atmosphere, environment
ambos *adj*   both, the two
ambulancia   ambulance
amigdalitis *f sing*   tonsilitis
amigo/a   friend
amortizar   to amortize; to write off
ampolla   blister; vial, flask
anacardo   cashew nut
analista *m + f*   analyst
anaranjado   orange-colored
anatomía   anatomy
anciano/a   old man/woman
ancho   broad; large
anchoa   anchovy
andar   to walk; to be
anestesista *m + f*   anesthetist
anexo   enclosure
anillo   ring
ano   anus
anoche   last night
anomalía   anomaly
anormal   abnormal

anteayer, antier (*coll*), antes de ayer   day
   before yesterday
antecedente *m*   antecedent
antelación   precedence in order of time;
   con __   in advance
antena   antenna
anteojos *pl*   glasses
anterior   former, previous
antes *adv*   before; __ de   *prep* before;
   __ de que   *conj* before
anticipar   to anticipate
antropólogo/a   anthropologist
anual   annual
anuncio   advertisement
añadir   to add
año   year; tener . . . años   to be . . .
   years old
apagar   to quench; to turn off (a light, an
   appliance, and so on)
aparato   apparatus, machine
aparquear (*coll*)   to park
apartado postal   post office box
apartamento   apartment
apellido   last name; __ de soltera   maiden
   name
apéndice *m*   appendix
apendicitis *f sing*   appendicitis
apetito   appetite
apio   celery
aplicar   to apply; to study or devote
   oneself (to a thing)
apodo   nickname
apoyar   to favor, support
aprecio   appreciation
aprobado   approved, passed (an
   examination)
aprobar (ue)   to approve, pass
aproximar   to approximate, to approach
apunte *m*   note
aquí   here
arañazo   long, deep scratch
área   area
arenque *m*   herring
arete *m*   earring
argentino/a   Argentine
armario   shelf; closet, cabinet
arquitectura   architecture
arreglarse   to be arranged or settled; to
   dress up

arrendamiento   act of renting
arrendar (ie)   to rent
arrestar   to arrest
arriba   above, over, up, high
arriesgar   to risk, jeopardize
arte *f*   art; **belles artes**   fine arts
arteria   artery
articulación   joint
artritis *f sing*   arthritis
arzobispo   archbishop
asadura   chitterlings
asaltador(a)   assailant
asaltante *m + f*   assailant
asaltar   to assault
asalto   assault
asar   to roast
ascensor *m*   elevator
asegurar   to secure; to insure
asesinar   to assassinate; to murder
asesinato   assassination, murder
asesino/a   assassin
asesor(a)   counselor, adviser
así   so, thus
asignatura   course or class at a university
asilo   asylum
asimismo   exactly so, likewise
asistencia   assistance, help
asistir   to be present, to attend
asma   asthma
aspecto   aspect
aspirina   aspirin
ataque   attack; __ **cardíaco**   heart attack;
   __ **cerebral**   stroke
atentamente   respectfully
aterrar   to terrorize
atestiguar   to witness
atleta *m*   athlete
atracador(a)   bank robber
atracar   to hold up a bank
atraco   bank holdup
atrasado   delinquent (of an account)
atrasar   to leave (another) behind
atropellar   to run over
atún *m*   tuna fish
audiencia   hearing (in a court)
audífono   hearing aid
audiología   audiology
auditoría   audit, auditing
aula   classroom

aumentar   to augment, to increase; to gain
aumento   increase
aunque   although, notwithstanding
ausentarse   to be absent
ausente   absent
auto   car, automobile
autobús *m sing*   bus
automóvil *m*   automobile
autopista   freeway
autorizar   to authorize
auxiliar *m + f*   aide, assistant
avanzar   to advance
avellana   hazelnut
avena   oats
avenida   avenue
avisar   to inform, to give notice
aviso   notification
axila   armpit
ayer   yesterday
ayuda *n*   help, aid
ayudante *m + f*   aide, assistant
ayudar   to help, aid
azar *m*   unforeseen disaster, disappointment
azúcar *m*   sugar; __ **de confitería**
   confectioner's sugar; __ **morena**
   brown sugar
azucarado   cake frosting
azul   blue

# B

baca   (car) luggage rack
bacalao   cod
baile *m*   dance
bajarse (de)   to get down (from, off of)
bajo   under, below; __ **fianza**   on bail;
   __ **libertad condicional/provisional**
   on parole
balance *m*   balance
balón *m*   large football
bancarrota   bankruptcy
banco   bank; bench
bandera   flag
banquero *m + f*   banker
baño   bathroom, bath
barato   inexpensive, cheap
barba   beard; **sin** __   clean shaven
barbilla   chin

**barbitúrico** barbiturate
**barbudo** bearded
**barrer** to sweep
**barrio** neighborhood
**báscula** scale
**básico** basic
**basura** sweepings; filth; trash
**batido** whipped
**bazo** spleen
**beber** to drink
**bebida** *n* drink
**bebido** *adj* drunk, tipsy
**beca** scholarship
**bello** beautiful
**beneficio** benefit; **beneficios derivados de huelga** strike benefits
**berenjena** eggplant
**betabel** *m* beet
**biblioteca** library
**bicicleta** bicycle
**bien** *adv* well, fine
**bienes** *n m pl* property; goods, possessions
**bienestar** *m* welfare
**bígamo/a** bigamist
**biliario** *adj* biliary, of the gallbladder
**billete** *m* bill; ticket
**bizcocho** biscuit
**blanco** white
**blusa** blouse
**boca** mouth; __ **abajo** face down; __ **arriba** face up
**bocio** goiter
**boleta** (grade) card
**boliviano/a** Bolivian
**bolsa** bag; exchange; stock market; __ **de comida** lunch bag
**bolsillo** purse; pocket
**bolso** purse
**bondad** kindness
**boniato** sweet potato
**bonito** pretty
**bono** bond; certificate
**borracho/a** drunk
**borrador** *m* (chalkboard) eraser; rough draft; __ **de goma** eraser
**borrego** lamb
**bosquejo** outline
**bostezar** to yawn
**botella** bottle
**brasileño/a** Brazilian

**brazo** arm
**bróculi** *m* broccoli
**bronquitis** *f sing* bronchitis
**bruto** coarse, unpolished
**budín** *m* pudding
**bueno** *adj* good; *adv* well
**bufete** *m* lawyer's office
**bulto** bulk; tumor, swelling
**bursitis** *f sing* bursitis
**buscar** to search, to seek

# C

**caballero** gentleman
**cabello** hair of the head
**cabeza** head
**cabezón** *m* having a large head
**cabo** end, extremity
**cacahuate** *m* peanut (*Mex*)
**cacahuete** *m* peanut
**cachete** *m* cheek
**cachucha** cap
**cada** *adj* each, every
**cadáver** *m* cadaver, corpse
**cadera** hip
**caer(se)** to fall (down)
**café** *n m* coffee; *adj* brown
**cafetería** cafeteria
**caguama** tortoise, turtle
**caja** cash register; box; __ **de ahorros** savings and loan office; __ **de cambios** gearbox; __ **fuerte** strongbox; bank vault
**cajero/a** teller, cashier; __ **para automovilistas** drive-in teller
**cajuela** trunk (of a car)
**calabacín** *m* zucchini (*Mex*)
**calabaza** pumpkin, squash
**calabozo** jail
**calamar** *m* squid
**calambre** *m* cramp; muscle spasm
**calcetín** *m* sock
**calculadora** calculator
**calcular** to calculate
**cálculo** calculation; gallstone
**calentura** fever
**calidad** quality
**caliente** hot, warm
**calificación** grade

californiano/a   Californian
caligrafía   penmanship
calmado   calm
calmarse   to calm oneself
calor *m*   heat; **tener __** to be warm, hot
calvo   bald
callar   to silence; **-se** to be silent
calle *f*   street
cama   bed
camarada *m*   mate, pal
camarón *m*   shrimp
cambiar   to change
cambio   exchange; change; **__ de vida**
   change of life
caminar   to walk
camisa   shirt
camiseta   undershirt, T-shirt
camote *m*   yam; **__ amarillo** sweet potato
campesino/a   farmworker
campo   country, field; area (of study)
canal *(coll) m*   ovarian tube
cancelar   to cancel or annul (a policy,
   check, and so on)
cáncer *m*   cancer
cangrejo   crawfish, crab
cantidad   amount
capacidad   capacity, capability; mental
   ability
capacitación   competency
capital *m*   sum of money, capital; *f* capital
   (city)
capítulo   chapter
cápsula   capsule
capturar   to capture
caqui *m*   khaki; persimmon
cara   face
caramelo   (sugar) candy
cárcel *f*   jail
cardíaco   cardiac, related to the heart
cardiólogo *m + f*   cardiologist
cariñoso   affectionate
carne *f*   meat; **__ picada** ground meat
carnero   sheep, mutton
carnicería   meat market
carrera   career; race
carretera   highway
carro   car; **__ en común** car pool
carta   letter
casa   house; **__ adoptiva** foster home;
   **__ matriz** main branch

casado   married
casarse   to get married
caso   case
cassette *m*   cassette
castaño   hazel
castigar   to punish
catálogo   catalog
catarro   (head) cold
cauce *m*   (river) bed
causa   cause; **a __ de** because of
caza   hunt
cebada   barley
cebolla   onion
ceja   eyebrow
celda   (jail) cell
celoso   jealous
centeno   rye
centro   center; downtown; **__ estudiantil**
   student union
cepillar(se)   to brush (oneself)
cerca *adv*   near; *prep* **__ de** close to
cercar   to enclose, fence in
cerdo   pork
cereal *m*   cereal
cerebro   brain
cereza   cherry
cerrar (ie)   to close; **__ con llave** to lock
certificado   certificate
cerveza   beer
cerviz *f*   cervix; nape of the neck
cesta   basket
cicatriz *f*   scar
ciencia   science
cierre del ejercicio *m*   fiscal year's end
cifra   arithmetical mark, figure
cigarro   cigarette
cinta   tape; ribbon
cintura   waist
cinturón *m*   belt
circulatorio   circulatory
ciruela   plum
ciruela pasa   prune
cirugía   surgery
cirujano *m + f*   surgeon
cita   appointment; date
citar   to make an appointment
citroso   citric
ciudad   city
ciudadanía   citizenship
ciudadano/a   citizen

clase *f*  class

clave *f*  code, key

clavícula  clavicle

claxon *m*  auto horn (*Mex*)

cliente *m* + *f*  customer

clínica  clinic

coágulo  clot; __ de sangre  blood clot

cobrar  to collect; to charge

cobro  collection; charge

cocinar  to cook

cocinero/a *n*  cook

cócono  turkey (*Mex*)

coche *m*  car

codo  elbow

cofre *m*  chest, trunk; hood (of a car)

cohete *m*  firecracker

cojear  to limp

cojo *adj*  crippled

col *f*  cabbage; __ de Bruselas  Brussels
  sprouts

cola  tail; line; hacer __  to stand in line

colegio  college; school

colesterol *m*  cholesterol

colgar (ue)  to hang (up)

cólico  colic

coliflor *f*  cauliflower

colombiano/a  Colombian

color *n m*  color

color de rosa *adj*  pink

collar *m*  necklace

comandancia  command; police station
  (*Mex*)

comentar  to comment on, to talk about

comer  to eat

comerciante *m* + *f*  business person,
  merchant

comercio  commerce, business dealings

cometer  to commit

comida  food

comisión  trust; commission

como  as, like; cómo no  of course

¿cómo?  how?

compañero/a  companion, friend

compañía  company

comparativo  comparative

comparecer  to appear before a judge

completamente  completely; perfectly

completar  to complete; to perfect

comportamiento  behavior

composición  composition

compra *n*  purchase

comprar  to buy

compuesto  composed; compound

común  common

comunicar  to communicate, inform

concluir  to conclude; to end

concusionario/a  embezzler, extortioner

condado  county

condena  sentence

condensado  condensed

conducir  to drive

conducta  conduct, behavior

conductor(a)  driver

conejo  rabbit

confiscar  to confiscate

confitería  candy store

congelar  to freeze

congestionar  to congest; __ se  to
  become congested

conmigo  with me, with myself

conmutar  to commute (a sentence)

consecuencia  consequence

consecutivo  consecutive

conseguir (i)  to obtain, to get

consejero/a  advisor, counselor

consigo  with you/him/her/them

consolidar  to consolidate

conspiración  conspiracy, plot

conspirador(a)  conspirator

conspirar  to conspire, plot

constante *adj*  constant, firm

constipar  to constipate

constituir  to constitute

consulta  doctor's office

consultorio  doctor's office

consumir  to consume, use

contabilidad  bookkeeping, accounting

contador(a)  bookkeeper, accountant

contagioso  contagious

contar (ue)  to count; to tell

contento  glad, pleased

contestar  to answer

continuar  to continue

contra  against, contrary to

contrabandista *m* + *f*  smuggler, dealer in
  contraband

contrabando  contraband

contrario  contrary, opposite

contrato  contract

conveniente  useful, advantageous

convenir (ie)  to agree

copa  drink (alcoholic)

copiadora  copier

corazón *m*  heart

corbata  necktie

cordero  lamb

coronilla  crown, top of head

correccional *m*  reformatory

corredor *m*  corridor

corredor(a)  runner; __ de la bolsa stockbroker

corregir (i)  to correct

correo  mail; post office; __ aéreo  air mail

correr  to run; __ el riesgo  to run the risk

corresponder  to return a favor; to correspond

corriente *adj*  current; plain, ordinary

cortadura  cut, incision

cortar  to cut

cortesía  courtesy

cortina  curtain

corto  short

cosa  thing

costado  side; rib cage

costar (ue)  to cost

costilla  rib

costo  cost, price

cráneo  skull, cranium

crecer  to grow; to increase

crecimiento  growth

crédito  credit

creer  to believe

crema  cream; __ agria  sour cream; __ batida  whipped cream

criado/a  servant

criar  to rear; to breed; -se  to be brought up

crimen *m*  crime

criminal *m + f*  criminal, felon

criminología  criminology

cristal *m*  crystal, glass

crónico  chronic

cruce *m*  crossing, crossroads; __ de ferrocarril  railroad crossing

crudo  raw; crude

cuaderno  notebook

cuadra  block (of houses)

¿cuál?  what? which?

cualquier(a)  any

¿cuándo?  when?

¿cuánto?  how much? how many?

cuarto  room; quarter

cubano/a  Cuban

cubierto *adj*  covered

cubo  cube

cubrir  to cover

cucharada  spoonful

cucharita  teaspoon

cuello  neck

cuenta  bill; account; __ corriente  checking account; __ de ahorros  savings account; tomar en __  to keep in mind

cuidado  care; __ intensivo  intensive care

cuidar  to take care of, care for

cumpleaños *m sing*  birthday

cumplimiento  completion, fulfillment

cumplir  to fulfill, meet, satisfy

cuñado  brother-in-law

cuota  quota, fee; dues

cupón *m*  coupon; __ para comida/ alimentos  food stamps

cura *m*  priest; *f* cure

curar  to cure

curita  band-aid

curso  course; academic year; __ de verano  summer school

curva  curve

# CH

chabacano  apricot

chaleco  vest

chamba (*coll*)  work, employment

champiñon *m*  mushroom

chantaje *n m*  blackmail

chantajear *v*  (*coll*) to blackmail

chantajista *m + f*  blackmailer

chapa  license plate

chaqueta  jacket

charcutería  pork and sausage store

cheque *m*  check; __ del banco  bank draft; __ de viajero  traveler's check

cherif (*coll*) *m + f*  sheriff

chicle *m*  chewing gum

chícharos *pl*  peas (*Mex*)

chichón *m*  lump

chile *m*  pepper

**chileno/a** Chilean
**chillón** loud (of a color); shrill, shrieking
**chocado** dented
**chocar** to crash, bump
**chocolate** *m* chocolate
**chofer** *m* chauffeur
**chorizo** (pork) sausage
**chuleta** chop, cutlet

# D

**dar** to give; __ **de alta** to release; __ **la vuelta** to turn; __ **a luz** to give birth
**dato** data, information
**debajo** *adv* under, underneath, below; __ **de** *prep* under
**deber** *v* to owe; must, should, ought to; *n m* obligation
**débil** weak
**décimo** tenth
**decir (i)** to say
**declarar** to declare; to witness
**dedo** finger; __ **del pie** toe; __ **índice** index finger
**deducir** to deduce, to infer; to deduct
**defecto** defect
**defender (ie)** to defend
**defensa** defense; bumper (of a car)
**defensor(a)** defender, defense lawyer
**deficiencia** deficiency, imperfection; handicap
**degollar (ue)** to behead; to slash someone's throat
**dejar** to let, to permit; __ **de** + *inf* to stop (doing something); __ **en paz** to leave in peace
**delantero** *adj* front
**delatar** to inform; to denounce
**delegación** delegation; __ **de policía** police station
**delegado/a de organismos de patronato** parole officer
**deletreo** *n* spelling
**delgado** thin, slender
**delincuente** *m* + *f* delinquent, offender
**delito** crime; delinquency
**demanda** demand; lawsuit
**demandado/a** defendant

**demandar** to sue
**demora** delay
**demostrar (ue)** to show, demonstrate
**dentista** *m* + *f* dentist
**dentro (de)** within, inside (of)
**denunciar** to denounce
**departamento** department; __ **de tránsito** traffic control department
**depender** to depend
**dependiente** *m* + *f* dependent; clerk
**deponer** to depose; to vomit
**deporte** *m* sport
**depositar** to deposit
**depósito** that which is deposited
**depositor(a)** depositor
**depreciación** depreciation, decrease in price
**derecha** right (direction)
**derecho** *n* law; *adj* right; *adv* straight ahead
**derivar** to derive
**dermatólogo** *m* + *f* dermatologist
**desanimar** to dishearten
**desarrollo** development
**descansar** to rest
**descanso** rest; **día de** __ day off
**descontar (ue)** to discount
**descontinuar (ue)** to discontinue
**descuidar** to neglect
**descuido** carelessness
**desde** from, since, after
**desear** to desire, to wish
**desempleo** unemployment
**desenvolver (ue)** to unfold; to unroll
**desinfectante** *m* disinfectant
**desnutrición** malnutrition
**desocupado** unemployed
**desocupar** to evacuate; to empty
**despachar** to dispatch, to expedite
**despedir (i)** to emit; to dismiss from office
**después** *adv* after, afterward; __ **de** *prep* after
**destino** destiny
**desvestir (i)** to undress; **-se** to get undressed
**detalle** *m* detail
**detective** *m* + *f* detective
**detención** detention
**detener (ie)** to detain
**detenido/a** person in custody, detained person

deuda debt

devolver (ue) to return, to refund; to vomit

día *m* day; __ de descanso day off; __ de fiesta holiday; __ laboral work day

diabetes *f sing* diabetes

diagnosticar to diagnose, give a diagnosis

diálogo dialog

diario *adj* daily

diarrea diarrhea

diciembre December

dictado dictation

diente *m* tooth

dieta diet; de __ on a diet

difamación *n* libel

difamador(a) defamer, libeler

difamar *v* to libel

diferencia difference

difteria diphtheria

digerir (ie) to digest

dinero money; __ en efectivo cash

Dios *m sing* God

diploma *m* diploma

dirección direction; address

director(a) director; principal

disciplina discipline

disco disk; record

disculpa *n* apology; excuse

disculpar to pardon

diseño design

disparar to shoot

dispensar to dispense; to excuse

disponer to arrange; to get ready, prepare

distancia distance

distrofia muscular *f* muscular dystrophy

dividendo dividend

dividir to divide

divorciado divorced

divorciarse to get a divorce

doblar to bend; to turn

doctor(a) doctor; __ de cabecera family doctor

documento document

dólar *m* dollar

doler (ue) to pain, to hurt

dolor *n m* pain, hurt

doméstico *adj* domestic

domicilio address; residence; __ de correspondencia mailing address; __ de hogar home address

domingo Sunday

dominicano/a Dominican

don, doña titles of respect

¿dónde? where?

dotado gifted; bien dotada buxom

drenaje *m* sewer; drainage

droga drug; tener drogas to be in debt (*Mex*)

drogadicto/a drug addict

dueño/a owner

dulce *n m* sweet, candy; *adj* sweet-tasting

duplicadora copier

durante during

durazno peach

# E

ebrio/a drunk, inebriate

economía economy

económico economical

ecuatoriano/a Ecuadorian

eczema *m* eczema

echar to cast; to throw; -se to lie down; -se aires to pass wind

edad age

edificio building

efectivo effective; true; en __ cash

eje *m* axle

ejecutar to execute, to perform

ejecutivo/a executive

ejemplar *n m* pattern, model, copy (of a book, etc.); *adj* exemplary

ejemplo example, model

ejercicio exercise; fiscal year

ejotes *m pl* string beans (*Mex*)

electricidad electricity

electrocutar to electrocute

electrodomésticos *pl* electrical housewares

elegibilidad eligibility

elevador *m* elevator

elote *m* tender ear of corn (*Mex*)

ello that (*pronoun*)

embarazarse to get pregnant

embarazo pregnancy; __ terminado terminated pregnancy

emborracharse to get drunk

embrague *m* clutch

embriagarse to get drunk

embriaguez *f* drunkenness

**emisión** emission; issuing
**emocional** emotional
**empacador(a)** packer, cannery worker
**empeine** *m* instep; ringworm
**empezar (ie)** to begin
**empleado/a** employee; __ de la ventanilla bank teller
**emplear** to employ
**empleo** job; sin __ unemployed
**empresa** enterprise, company
**en** in, on; __ efectivo in cash
**enano/a** *n* dwarf; *adj* midget, little
**encarcelar** to imprison
**encargado** person in charge, agent
**encender (ie)** to light; to set on fire
**encía** gum (of the mouth)
**encima** *adv* above, over; *prep* __ de on top of
**encontrar (ue)** to find, to encounter
**encrucijada** crossway, crossroads, intersection
**endorso** endorsement
**endosar** to endorse
**endrogar** to drug; to get into debt (*Mex*); -se to take drugs
**enero** January
**enfermar(se)** to become ill
**enfermedad** illness; __ venérea venereal disease
**enfermería** infirmary
**enfermero/a** nurse
**enfermizo** infirm, sickly
**enfermo** sick
**enfisema** *m* emphysema
**enfrente (de)** in front (of)
**engordar** to fatten; -se to gain weight
**enjuagar** to rinse the mouth and teeth
**enojado** angry
**enorme** enormous
**enriquecer** to enrich
**ensalada** salad
**enseñanza** teaching, education
**enseñar** to teach
**enterar** to inform thoroughly, to acquaint; -se de to find out about
**entonces** well, then
**entrada** entrance; entry; down payment; *pl* income
**entrar** to enter
**entregar** to hand in; to deliver

**entrenador(a)** trainer, coach
**entrenamiento** training
**entrenar** to train
**entrevista** interview
**envenenamiento** poisoning
**enviar** to send; __ por correo to mail
**envío** *n* remittance; shipment
**envolver (ue)** to wrap up, to wrap around
**enyesar** to plaster, to put on a cast
**epígrafe** epigraph, title; __ de operaciones de títulos securities transactions
**epilepsia** epilepsy
**equipo** team; equipment; __ para cocinar cooking facilities
**equis** *f* letter *x*
**equivalente** *m* equivalent
**esbelto** slender
**escalera** staircase, stair; ladder; __ movediza escalator
**escalofrío** *n* chill
**escápula** shoulder blade
**escocés** Scotch; con tipo __ plaid
**escoger** to choose, to select
**escolar** *n m + f* student; *adj* scholastic
**escribir** to write
**escritorio** desk
**escritura** deed, legal paper
**escuela** school; __ de capacitación professional vocational school
**esfuerzo** courage, spirit; effort
**esófago** esophagus
**espalda** upper part of the back
**español(a)** *adj* Spanish; *n* Spaniard
**espárrago** asparagus
**especialista** *m + f* specialist
**especializar** to specialize
**espejo** looking glass, mirror; __ lateral side mirror; __ retrovisor rear-view mirror
**espera** *n* waiting; wait (period of time)
**esperanza** *n* hope
**esperar** to hope; to wait
**espina dorsal** spinal column
**espinaca** spinach
**espinilla** pimple; shin bone
**esposo/a** husband/wife
**esquema** *m* plan, sketch; outline
**esquina** (street) corner
**esquizofrenia** schizophrenia
**establecimiento** establishment; __ de detención honor camp

estacionamiento   parking lot

estacionar   to station; to park

estadio   stadium

estado   state

estadounidense *m + f*   person from the
    United States

estafa   fraud, swindle

estafador(a)   swindler, embezzler

estafar   to embezzle, swindle

estampilla   stamp; **estampillas para comida**
    food stamps

estándar *adj*   standard

estar   to be; __ **boca arriba**   to be face up

estatura   height; **de __ mediana**   medium
    height

esterilizador *m*   sterilizer

esterilizar   to sterilize

estilo   style

estimado   dear

estimar   to estimate, to value

estomacal   pertaining to the stomach

estómago   stomach

estreñimiento   obstruction; constipation

estreñir   to bind, to constipate

estudiantado   student body

estudiante *m + f*   student, pupil

estudiantil *adj*   scholastic, pertaining to a
    student

estudiar   to study

estudio   study, application to books and
    learning

estupefaciente *n m*   narcotic; hallucinogenic
    drug

estupendo   stupendous, wonderful

etiqueta de matrícula   car registration
    sticker, decal

evitar   to avoid

exactamente   exactly

examen *m*   examination

examinar   to examine

excelente   excellent

excesivo   excessive

excremento   excrement

excusado *n*   bathroom

exigir   to demand, to require

explicar   to explain

exportar   to export

expresión   expression, saying

extenderse (ie)   to spread, get bigger

exteriormente   externally, outwardly

externo   external, visible

extorsión   extortion

extorsionar   to extort

extorsionista   extortionist

extracto   extract

extranjero *n*   stranger, foreigner, alien;
    abroad; foreign land; *adj* strange,
    foreign, alien

extraordinario   extraordinary

# F

fábrica   factory

fabricación   manufacture, construction

factura   bill of sale

facultad   specialized school of a university

falda   skirt

falsificación   forgery

falsificador(a)   falsifier, counterfeiter,
    forger

falsificar   to falsify, to counterfeit

faltar   to be deficient, to be wanting

fallar(se)   to fail, not to work properly

familia   family

familiar *adj*   familiar, well known; of the
    family; *n m* relative

fantasma *m*   ghost

farmacia   pharmacy

farol *m*   light (on a car)

favor *m*   favor; help; **por __**   please

febrero   February

fecha   date

feliz   happy, fortunate

femenino   feminine

ferretería   hardware store or department

ferrocarril *m*   railroad

fiador(a)   bondsperson, guarantor

fiambre *f*   cold meat; cold cuts

fianza   guarantee, bond, bail

fiar   to bail; to trust

ficha   file card; token

fichar   to book for suspicion of a crime

fideos *pl*   vermicelli; noodles

fiebre *f*   fever; __ **de heno**   hay fever; __
    **escarlatina**   scarlet fever; __ **reumática**
    rheumatic fever

fiesta   party; entertainment

filosofía   philosophy

fin *m* end
financiamiento financing
financiar to finance
financiero financial
firma signature; business and its commercial name
firmar to sign
fiscal *m* + *f* district attorney
fiscalía office of the district attorney
fiscalizar to investigate
física physics
flaco skinny
flan *m* custard
flebitis *f sing* phlebitis
flojo lax, lazy; loose
flor *f* flower
forma manner, method
formular to formulate
formulario form, application blank
forzar (ue) to force
fotografía photography
fracaso downfall, failure
fractura *n* break, fracture
fracturar to fracture, to break
frambuesa raspberry
franja stripe
frecuentar to frequent, to visit often
frecuente *adj* frequent, often
freno brake; __ de manos hand brake; __ de pie foot brake
frente *f* forehead; front
fresa strawberry
frijol *m* bean (*Mex*)
frío *n* cold; tener __ to be cold
frotar to rub against
fruta fruit
frutería fruit store
fuente *f* source; fountain
fuera (de) outside (of), out (of)
fumar to smoke
funcionar to function
funcionario/a public official
fútbol *m* soccer; football

# G

gabardina gabardine; raincoat
gafas *pl* spectacles; __ oscuras sunglasses

galleta cracker; cookie; __ de sal/soda soda cracker
gallina hen
gamba prawn, shrimp
gana desire; tener ganas de + *inf* to feel like (doing something)
ganancia gain, profit
ganar to earn; to win
garantía right, guarantee
garbanzo chickpea
garganta throat
gas *m sing* gas
gasa gauze
gasolina gasoline
gastar to expend; to waste
gasto expense; __ de explotación operation expense
gato cat
gelatina gelatin
generalidad generality
geografía geography
gerente *m* + *f* manager, director
gestionar to gesture; to negotiate
gimnasio gymnasium
ginebra gin
ginecólogo *m* + *f* gynecologist
girar to girate, to turn
girasol *m* sunflower
giro money order
gis *m sing* chalk
gitano/a gypsy
glándula gland
glaucoma *m* glaucoma
gobierno government
golpe *m* blow, bump
golpear to hit; to beat
goma gum, rubber; eraser
gonorrea gonorrhea
gordo fat
gorra cap
gorro cap
gota drop; small quantity of any liquid; gout
grabadora tape recorder
gracias thanks
grado grade (in school); level
graduarse to graduate
gragea sugar-coated pill
granada pomegranate
grande great; large

granito   granite; pimple

granja   farm

grano   grain; pimple

grasa   fat, grease

gratis   free (of charge)

grato   pleasing

grave   weighty, serious; grave

gripa   influenza, flu (*Mex*)

gripe *f*   influenza, flu

gris   grey

grueso   fat

guajolote *m*   turkey (*Mex*)

guantera   glove compartment

guapo   attractive, handsome, cute, good-
   looking

guardar   to keep; to save; __ **cama**   to
   stay in bed

guardería   (day) nursery; child care

guardia *m* + *f*   guard

guatemalteco/a   Guatemalan

guineo   variety of banana

guión *m*   hyphen; skit

guisantes *m pl*   peas

¿Gusta de + *inf*?   Would you like to (do
   something)?

gustar   to please; to like

gusto   pleasure; task; **mucho** __   pleased
   to meet you; __ **de/en** + *inf*   (it is/
   was) a pleasure to (do something); **con**
   **mucho** __   gladly


# H

haba   lima bean

haber   to have (auxiliary verb)

hábil   capable

hablar   to speak, to talk

hacer   to do; to make; to form; __ **falta**
   to need

hambre *f*   hunger; **tener** __   to be hungry

hampón *m* + *f*   gangster

harina   flour

hay   there is, there are; **no** __ **de que**
   you're welcome

hembra   woman; female

hemorragia   hemorrhage

hepatitis *f sing*   hepatitis

hereditario   hereditary

herida *n*   wound

herir (i)   to wound

hermano/a   brother/sister

heroina   heroin

herramienta   tool

hielo   ice

hierro   iron (mineral)

hígado   liver

higiene *f*   hygiene

higo   fig

hijo/a   son/daughter

hijos *pl*   children

hinchar   to swell

hinchazón *m*   swelling

hipoteca   mortgage

historia   story; history

hogar *m*   home

hoja   leaf; __ **de papel**   sheet of paper

hombre *m*   man

hombro   shoulder

homicida *n*   *m* + *f* murderer; *adj*
   homicidal

homicidio *n*   murder, homicide

hongo   mushroom; fungus

honrado   honest, honorable

hora   hour; **horas de negocio/hábiles**
   business hours

hormona   hormone

hospicio   charitable institution; __ **para**
   **ancianos**   nursing home

hospital *m*   hospital

hospitalizar   to hospitalize

hoy   today

huelga   strike (labor); **estar de** __   to be
   on strike

huella   track, print

hueso   bone

huésped(a) *m* + *f*   guest

huir   to flee; to escape

hule *m*   rubber

humillar   to humble; to lower

humo   smoke

humor *m*   humor

hurtar   to steal, rob

hurto   theft


# I

ictericia   jaundice

ida y vuelta   round trip

**identificación** identification
**identificar** to identify
**idioma** *m* language
**igual** identical, equal
**igualmente** equally; the same here
**imparcial** impartial
**impermeable** *m* raincoat
**importar** to import; to be important, to matter
**impreso** printed
**imprimir** to print; to stamp
**impuesto** *n* tax, duty
**incapacidad** incapacity, inability
**incapacitación** incompetency
**incapacitar** to incapacitate
**incendiar** to kindle; to set on fire
**incendiario/a** firebug, incendiary, arsonist
**incendio** fire; __ **provocado** arson
**incluir** to include
**incompetente** incompetent
**inconsciente** unconscious
**incrementar** to increase, to intensify
**incremento** increment, increase
**incubación** incubation
**incurrir** to incur
**indicar** to indicate, to show
**índice** *m* index; __ **de crédito** credit rating; __ **precio/utilidades** price/earnings ratio
**indicio** sign, indication
**indiferente** indifferent
**industria** industry
**infarto** infarct, heart attack
**infección** infection
**infiel** unfaithful
**inflación** inflation
**inflamación** inflammation
**inflamar** to inflame
**influenza** flu, influenza
**información** information
**informar** to inform; **-se** to find out
**informe** *m* report; (legal) brief
**infracción** violation, infraction
**infringir** to infringe (the law)
**ingle** *f* groin
**inglés** *m sing* English (language)
**ingreso** income; __ **de explotación** operating income
**inicial** *n f* initial
**inmigración** immigration

**inocencia** innocence
**inocente** *m + f* innocent (person)
**insolvente** insolvent
**insomnio** insomnia
**inspeccionar** to inspect, to examine
**inspector(a)** detective, inspector
**institución** institution
**insulina** insulin
**intensivo** intense, intensive
**intentar** to try
**interés** *m sing* interest, concern; __ **compuesto** compound interest
**interesar** to be interesting; **-se** to be concerned or interested in
**intermitente** *n m* turn signal
**internar** to intern; to put into a hospital
**internista** *m + f* internist
**interno** interior, internal
**interpretar** to interpret
**interrogar** to question, to interrogate
**intestino** intestine
**inventar** to invent
**inversionista** *m + f* investor
**investigar** to investigate
**invierno** winter
**involucrar** to be implicated
**inyección** injection
**inyectar** to inject
**ir** to go; __ **de vacaciones** to go on vacation
**irritar** to irritate, to make angry
**izquierda** left (direction)

# J

**jalea** jelly
**jamón** *m* ham
**Japón** *m* Japan
**japonés/japonesa** *m + f* Japanese
**jaqueca** migraine headache
**jarabe** *m* (cough) syrup
**jardinería** gardening
**jardinero/a** gardener
**jefatura de policía** police station
**jefe** *m + f* boss, chief; __ **de policía** police chief
**jícama** edible root (*Mex*)
**jinete** *m* horseman, jockey
**jirafa** giraffe

jitomate *m* tomato (*Mex*)

joven *n m + f* youth, young person; *adj* young, youthful

juanete *m* bunion

jubilación retirement

jubilar to pension off, to retire

judía bean; string bean

jueves *m sing* Thursday

juez *m + f* judge

jugar (ue) to play (a sport)

jugo juice

juguete *m* toy

juguetería toy store or department

julia paddy wagon (*Mex*)

julio July

junio June

jurado jury

jurídico judicial

juzgado tribunal, court of justice

juzgar to judge

# K

kilómetro kilometer

# L

labio lip

laboral *adj* work, pertaining to work

laboratorio laboratory

lácteo milky

lado side; a un __ (de) to one side (of)

ladrón/ladrona thief, robber, burglar

lamentar to regret

lana wool

langosta lobster

langostino prawn

lapicero mechanical pencil

lápiz *m* pencil

largo long

laringitis *f sing* laryngitis

lastimar to hurt, to wound

lateral *adj* side, pertaining to the side

latino/a Latin

lavadora washer; dishwasher

lavaplatos *m sing* dishwasher

lavar to wash; __ se to wash oneself

laxante *m* laxative

lectura reading

leche *f* milk

lechuga lettuce

leer to read

lejos *adj* distant, remote; *prep* __ de far from

lengua tongue; language

lenguado sole, flounder

lente *m* lens; *pl* eyeglasses; __ de contacto contact lens

lenteja lentil

lentilla contact lens

lesbiana lesbian

lesión hurt, damage, wound

letra letter (of the alphabet); bill of exchange

leucemia leukemia

levantar to raise, to lift; -se to get up

ley *f* law

libertad liberty

libra pound (weight)

libre free

librería bookstore

libreta booklet; grade card; notebook; __ de cheques checkbook; __ de depósito bankbook

libro book; __ de texto textbook

licencia license

licenciado/a lawyer; person with a master's degree

licor *m* liquor

liebre *f* hare

ligero *adj* light

lima lime

limón *m* lemon

limonada lemonade

limpiaparabrisas *m sing* windshield wiper

limpiar to clean; to scour; -se to clean oneself

liso plain, even, flat

lista slip of paper; list; (class) roll

lo que what, that which

localizar to locate, to find

lógica logic

loza square stone used for pavement; dishware (*Mex*)

lucir to dress well; -se to be dressed to one's advantage

lugar *m* place

**lunar** *m* mole; beauty mark; polka dot
**lunes** *m sing* Monday
**luz** *f* light; **luces delanteras** headlights;
    **luces traseras** rear lights

## LL

**llaga** wound; sore
**llamada** (telephone) call
**llamar** to call; **-se** to be named, called
**llanta** tire
**llave** *f* key
**llegar** to arrive
**llenar** to fill (up); to fill out
**llevar** to carry; to take; to have
    accumulated (time)
**llover** (ue) to rain
**lluvia** rain

## M

**macarrón** *m* macaroni
**madera** wood
**madrastra** stepmother
**madre** *f* mother
**madrugar** to rise early
**maestro/a** teacher
**mafioso/a** gangster
**magnetofón** tape recorder
**maicena** corn flour; corn starch
**maíz** *m* corn
**mal** *adv* badly; *n m* evil; **__ de mar**
    seasickness
**mala práctica** malpractice
**maletín** *m* satchel; doctor's bag; book bag
**malignidad** malignancy; malice
**malo** bad, evil
**malteada** malted milk
**maltratar** to mistreat
**mamá** mother, mom
**mandar** to command; to send
**mandarina** tangerine
**mandato** command
**manejar** to drive
**manga** sleeve
**maní** *m* peanut (*Cuba, Peru, Chile*)
**mano** *f* hand
**manteca** lard

**mantener(se)** (ie) to support (oneself)
**mantenimiento** maintenance; sustenance;
    upkeep and repairs (on property)
**mantequilla** butter; **__ de cacahuate**
    peanut butter
**manzana** apple
**mañana** tomorrow
**máquina** machine; **__ de escribir** typewriter
**mar** *m* sea
**marca** mark; model
**marcar** to mark
**marco** frame
**marearse** to become dizzy
**mareo** dizziness; nausea
**margarina** margarine
**marihuana** marijuana
**marisco** shellfish
**martes** *m sing* Tuesday
**marzo** March
**más** more
**masculino** masculine
**masticar** to chew
**matar** to kill
**materia** matter; subject
**material** *m* material
**maternidad** maternity; childbirth
**materno** maternal
**matrícula** registration; matriculation fee
**matricular(se)** to matriculate, to register
**matrimonio** matrimony
**mayo** May
**mayonesa** mayonnaise
**mayor** greater, larger
**mayordomo** *m + f* bailiff
**mecánico/a** mechanic
**mecanógrafo/a** typist
**mediano** medium
**medicamento** medicine
**medicina** medicine
**médico** *adj* medical; *n m + f* physician,
    doctor; **__ forense** coroner
**medio** half, in part
**medir** (i) to measure
**mejilla** cheek
**mejillón** *m* mussel
**mejor** better
**mejorar(se)** to get better
**melaza** molasses
**melenudo** long-haired (of a person);
    "hippie"

melocotón *m* peach

melón *m* melon

membrillo quince

meningitis *f sing* meningitis

menor *adj* minor; younger; *adv* less; *n m*
    minor

menospreciar to underrate; to despise

mensaje *m* message, errand

mensualidad monthly payment

mentiroso lying, dishonest

menudo tripe

mercado market

mercurio mercury

mermelada marmalade

mero bass

mes *m sing* month

mesabanco (student's) desk

mesero/a waiter/waitress

metal *m* metal

meter to place; to put in

mexicano/a Mexican

mezclilla denim

mezcla mixture

mica (*coll*) alien registration card

miedo fear; **tener** __ to be afraid

miel *f* honey

miembro member (of a family, club,
    etc.); limb of the body

mientras in the meantime, meanwhile,
    while

miércoles *m sing* Wednesday

militar *adj* military

milla mile

mimar to caress; to indulge, spoil

minuto *n* minute

mirar to look (at); to watch

misceláneo miscellaneous

mismo same, similar, equal

modelo model

molestar(se) to bother, to trouble

molesto upset, bothered

molleja gizzard

momentáneo momentary; temporary

momento moment

mondongo tripe

montaña mountain

mora blackberry, mulberry

morado purple

mordedura bite

morder (ue) to bite

moreno brown, blackish brown, brunette

morirse (ue) to die

mortadela bologna

mostaza mustard; mustard greens

mostrar (ue) to show, demonstrate

motocicleta motorcycle

motorista *m + f* driver

movediza movable, easily moved

moverse (ue) to move

mozo/a youth, young person, kid;
    maintenance person

muchacho/a boy/girl

mucho much, a lot

mueble *m* furniture

muela molar, one of the back teeth

muerte *f* death

mujer *f* woman

multar to fine

multiplicar to multiply

mundo world

muñeca wrist

músculo muscle

museo museum

música music

muslo thigh

mutilación mutilation

mutilador(a) multilator

mutilar to mutilate

mutuo mutual, reciprocal

# N

nabo turnip

nacer to be born

nacimiento birth

nacional national

nada nothing; **de** __ you're welcome

nadie no one, nobody

nalga buttock

naranja orange

narcomanía drug addiction

nariz nose

nata whipped cream

necesario necessary

necesitar to need

negado incapable, unfit

negocio business

negro black

neoyorquino/a New Yorker

**nervioso** nervous
**neto** *adj* net
**neumático** *n* tire; *adj* pneumatic, of rubber
**neumonía** pneumonia
**neurólogo** *m + f* neurologist
**nieto/a** grandson/granddaughter
**niña** pupil (of the eye)
**niño/a** boy/girl
**niños** *pl* children
**nivel** *m* level
**noche** *f* night
**nombrar** to name; to assign
**nombre** *m* name; __ **de pila** middle name
**nómina** payroll
**nopal** *m* nopal cactus, prickly pear
**normalidad** normal
**nota** grade; note
**notar** to note, to mark; to notice
**notario público** *m + f* notary public
**noticias** *pl* news, information
**noveno** ninth
**noviembre** November
**novio/a** boyfriend/girlfriend; bridegroom/bride
**nublado** cloudy
**nuca** nape of the neck
**nudillo** knuckle
**nudo** lump
**nuera** daughter-in-law
**nuevo** new
**nuez** *f* nut
**número** number; *ab* n°

## Ñ

**ñoño** delicate; timid; whiny

## O

**obedecer** to obey
**objeto** object
**obligación** obligation
**obra** work
**obrero/a** worker
**obsequio** gift
**obvio** obvious

**octavo** eighth
**octubre** October
**oculista** *m + f* oculist, eye specialist
**ocupación** occupation
**ocupado** busy
**ocurrir** to occur
**odioso** odious, hateful
**odontólogo** *m + f* odontologist, dentist
**oferta** offer, promise
**oficial** *m + f* officer; __ **de préstamos** loan officer
**oficina** office; __ **de pagos** credit office
**ofrecer** to offer
**oftalmólogo** *m + f* opthalmologist, oculist
**oído** sense of hearing; ear
**oir** to hear
**ojo** eye; __ **morado** black eye
**oliva** olive tree; olive
**ombligo** navel
**operación** operation
**operar** to operate (on)
**óptica** optics
**optómetro** optometrist
**orden** *m* order
**ordenar** to arrange, to put in order; to order
**oreja** ear
**órgano** organ
**orgulloso** proud, haughty
**orinar** to urinate
**oro** gold
**ortopédico** orthopedic
**oscuridad** darkness
**oscuro** dark
**ostión** *m* oyster (larger and coarser than the common one)
**ostra** oyster
**otorrinolaringólogo** *m + f* ear, nose, and throat doctor
**otra vez** again
**oveja** sheep
**oxigenado** oxygenated

## P

**pabellón** *m* pavilion; ward
**paciente** *m + f* patient; __ **interno** in-patient; __ **no interno** out-patient

pachucho   under the weather (*Spain*)

padecer (de)   to suffer (from)

padrastro   stepfather

padre *m*   father; *pl* parents

pagar   to pay

página   page

pago   payment; __ de sostenimiento a hijos   child support; __ extraordinario   bonus; __ por entrenamiento   training incentive

país *m sing*   country

palabra   word

palacio de justicia   courthouse

pan *m*   bread; __ dulce   sweet roll

panqueque *m*   pancake

pantalones *m pl*   trousers, pants, slacks; __ cortos   shorts, cutoffs; __ vaqueros   jeans

pantalla   screen

pantorrilla   calf (of the leg)

papa   potato

papá *m*   papa, daddy

papel *m*   paper; __ de color   colored paper; __ de propiedad   proof of ownership

papelería   stationery shop or department

paperas *pl*   mumps

para   for, in order to

parabrisas *m sing*   windshield

parada   stop; stop sign

paraguayo/a   Paraguayan

parálisis *f sing*   paralysis

parar   to stop, to halt

parcela   plot of land

parecer   to appear, to seem

parecido   similar

pareja   pair, couple; __ casada   married couple

parentesco   blood relation; sin __   unrelated

pariente *n m*   relative

párrafo   paragraph

parrilla   luggage rack

parte *f*   part

particular *adj*   particular; private; *n m* detail; bit of news

parto   childbirth

párvulo/a   small child, tot; escuela de párvulos   nursery school, kindergarten

pasa   raisin

pasado *adj*   past; __ mañana   day after tomorrow

pasajero   temporary

pasar   to pass; to move from place to place; to happen, occur; __ lista   to take roll; __ un cheque   to cash/clear a check

pastel *m*   cake

pastilla   pill, tablet; lozenge

paterno   paternal

patio de recreo   playground

pato   duck

patrimonio   inheritance; __ de los accionistas   stockholders' equity

patrón *m*   pattern

patrón/patrona   boss, owner

patrulla   patrol

patrullar   to patrol

pavo   turkey

peatón *m*   pedestrian

peca   freckle; speck

pecho   breast; chest

pediatra *m + f*   pediatrician

pedicuro *m + f*   chiropodist

pedido *n*   order of goods or merchandise

pedir (i)   to ask (for), order; to request

pegadura   glue

pegamento   glue

pelear   to fight

peletería   fur shop or department

película   film

peligroso   dangerous, perilous

pelirrojo   redhead

pelo   hair; __ castaño   chestnut hair; __ postizo   wig

peluca   wig

pélvico   pelvic

pena   punishment, sentence; pain; __ de muerte   death penalty

pena capital   capital punishment

penal *adj*   penal, concerning punishment; *n m* prison

pendiente *m*   pendant; earring

pene *m*   penis

penicilina   penicillin

penitenciaría   penitentiary

pensar (ie)   to think; __ + *inf*   to intend (to do something)

peón *m*   day laborer

pepino   cucumber

**pequeño** little, small
**pera** pear
**perder (ie)** to lose
**pérdida** loss; damage
**perdonar** to pardon
**perejil** *m* parsley
**perfume** *m* perfume
**perfumería** perfume shop or department
**período** period
**peritonitis** *f sing* peritonitis
**perjurar** to perjure
**perjuro** perjury
**perjuro/a** perjurer
**permanecer** to stay, remain; to persist, to endure
**permanente** permanent
**permiso** permission; **con __** excuse me
**permitir** to permit, to consent
**pero** but
**perro** dog
**pérsimo** persimmon
**persistente** persistent
**persona** person
**personal** *n m* personnel; *adj* personal
**perspectiva** perspective
**peruano/a** Peruvian
**pesar** *n m* grief, sorrow; *v* to weigh
**pescado** fish
**peso** weight; Mexican currency
**pestaña** eyelash; **__ postiza** false eyelash
**pezón** *m* nipple
**picado** chopped
**picadura** puncture; bite or sting of an insect
**pie** *m* foot; **__ de atleta** athlete's foot
**piedra** stone; kidney stone
**piel** *f* skin
**pierna** leg
**pila** baptismal font; pile; **nombre de __** middle name
**píldora** pill
**pillo** vagabond; rascal
**pimiento** bell pepper
**pintura** painting; picture; paint
**piña** pineapple
**piñón** *m* pine nut
**pío** *adj* pious; *n* peep (of chickens)
**piocha** chin
**piojo** louse
**pipa** pipe (for tobacco); pipe

**pique** *n m* resentment; **irse a __** to founder, be ruined, break up
**pisar** to tread on, to trample; to step on
**piso** floor; floor of a building
**pistacho** pistachio nut
**pizarra** chalkboard
**pizarrón** *m* chalkboard
**placa** metal license plate
**plan** *m* plan; design
**planear** to plan
**planificación** planning
**planificar** to design, plan
**planta** sole (of the foot); floor (of a building)
**plástico** plastic
**plata** silver; money
**plátano** banana
**plazo** period of time given to pay; terms of payment; **a plazos** on time
**pleuresía** pleurisy
**pliegue** *m* fold or crease (in clothes); pleat
**plomero** *m + f* plumber
**pluma** feather; pen (for writing); **__ atómica** ballpoint pen; **__ fuente** fountain pen
**poco** *adv* little, infrequently; *adj* little, small quantity
**poder** *n m* power; ability
**poder (ue)** *v* to be able to
**polen** *m* pollen
**policía** *f* police force; *m* police officer; **__ de tránsito** traffic officer
**polio** infantile paralysis, polio
**poliomielitis** *m sing* infantile paralysis, polio
**política** politics
**político** political
**póliza** policy
**polvo** dust; powder
**pollo** chicken
**pomada** salve
**pomelo** grapefruit
**poner** to put; **__ en libertad** to set free; **-se** to put on (clothing); to apply to oneself; to turn on; **-se en contacto** to contact
**por** for; during; through; by; per; **__ ciento** percent; **__ completo** completely; **__ favor** please
**¿por qué?** why?

**porque** because
**portamaletas** *m sing* trunk (of a car)
**portero** porter, maintenance person
**porvenir** *m* future
**posdata** postscript
**posición** position
**postal** *f* postcard
**postizo** artificial, not natural
**potra** (*coll*) rupture, scrotal hernia
**practicar** to practice; to perform
**precedente** preceding, foregoing
**precio** price
**preciso** necessary; precise, exact
**predecir** (i) to foretell, to predict
**predominante** predominant
**preferir** (ie) to prefer
**pregunta** question
**preguntar** to question; to demand
**preliminar** preliminary
**prenda** article of clothing
**prender** to seize, to catch; to turn on (a light)
**preocuparse** to worry
**preparar** to prepare, to make ready
**prescripción** prescription
**prescrito** prescribed
**presidente** *m + f* president
**presidio** hard labor; garrison
**presión** pressure; blood pressure
**preso** prisoner
**prestador** *m* lender
**préstamo** loan
**prestar** to lend
**prestatario** borrower
**presupuesto** budget; estimate
**prima** premium; __ **de riesgo** risk premium
**primaria** *n* grade school
**primario** *adj* principal, primary
**primero** first; **primeros auxilios** first aid
**primo/a** cousin
**principal** *adj* principal, main; *n m* director
**principio** beginning
**prisa** urgency, promptness in executing
**prisión** prison, jail
**probar** (ue) to try; to try on; to taste
**procurador(a)** attorney general
**procuraduría** attorney general's office; law office
**procurar** to solicit; to try

**profesión** profession
**profesor(a)** professor, teacher
**profesorado** faculty, group of professors
**programar** to program
**prolongado** prolonged, extended
**prometido/a** person engaged to be married
**pronto** quick, soon
**propenso(a)** inclined (to), tending (to)
**propiedad** property; __ **en alquiler** rental property
**propietario/a** owner
**propina** tip, gratuity
**propio** *adj* own; proper, suitable
**proporcionar** to furnish; to provide; to adjust
**prosperar** to prosper, to thrive
**prostituta** prostitute
**prótesis** *f sing* prosthesis
**provecho** benefit
**proveer** to provide; to procure beforehand
**provisión** provisions; writ, decree
**próximo** next
**proyección** projection
**proyector** *m* projector
**prueba** exam; proof; attempt
**psiquiatra** *m + f* psychiatrist
**publicar** to publish
**público** *adj* public
**pudín** *m* pudding
**pueblo** town; people
**puente** *m* bridge
**puerco** *n* hog; *adj* filthy
**puerro** leek
**puerta** door
**puerto** port; mountain pass
**puertorriqueño/a** Puerto Rican
**pues** well, since
**puesto** *n* place, space; job; assigned post or position; stall; *adj* in place, placed; **tener __** to have on (clothing)
**pulgada** inch
**pulmón** *m* lung
**pulmonía** pneumonia
**pulsera** bracelet
**puño** fist
**pupilente** *f* contact lens
**pupitre** *m* (writing) desk
**puro** *adj* pure; *n* cigar

# Q

**que**   that, which; who, whom

**¿qué?**   which? what?; **¿__ tal?**   how are you?; **¿__ tal . . .?**   what do you think of . . .?

**¡qué lástima!**   what a shame!

**¡qué pena!**   what a shame!

**quebrado**   bankrupt

**quebrar (ie)**   to break; to burst

**quedar**   to remain, stay; to fit (with clothing); to be (with directions)

**queja**   complaint

**quejarse (de)**   to complain (of)

**quemadura**   burn; **__ de sol**   sunburn

**quequi** (*coll*) *m*   cake (*Mex*)

**querer (ie)**   to want; to like, love

**querido**   wished; dear, beloved

**quiebra**   bankruptcy

**¿quién?**   who? whom?

**quinto**   fifth

**quirófano**   operating room

**quiropráctico** *m + f*   chiropractor

**quiste** *m*   cyst

**quitar**   to take away; **-se**   to take off (clothing)

**quizá**   perhaps

# R

**rábano**   radish

**rabia**   rabies; fury

**racha**   bout

**radiografía**   X ray

**radiólogo** *m + f*   radiologist

**raíz** *f*   root

**rancho**   ranch

**raptar**   to kidnap

**rapto**   kidnapping

**raptor(a)**   kidnapper

**rasguño**   scratch

**rayo**   ray; **rayos equis**   X rays

**raza**   race

**razón** *f*   reason; **tener __**   to be right, correct

**reacción**   reaction

**readaptación**   readaptation

**rebaja**   reduction; sale

**recado**   message

**recamarera**   hotel maid (*Mex*)

**recaudo**   collection

**recepción**   reception; front desk

**receptor** *m*   receiver

**receta**   prescription; recipe

**recetar**   to prescribe

**recibir**   to receive

**recibo**   receipt; **__ de nómina**   pay stub

**reciente**   recent

**reclamar**   to demand

**recluir**   to seclude

**recluso/a**   prisoner, inmate, convict

**recoger**   to gather; to pick (up)

**recomendar (ie)**   to recommend

**reconocer**   to recognize

**reconocimiento**   examination

**recreo**   recreation; recess

**recto**   rectum

**rector(a)**   president (of a university)

**rectoría**   rectory; administration (of a school)

**recuperar**   to rescue; **-se**   to recover

**recurso**   recourse, appeal; resource

**redondo**   round

**reducción**   reduction

**reducir**   to reduce

**reembolsar**   to recover money advanced; to reimburse; to refund

**reembolso**   reimbursement; refund; **__ de impuestos**   tax refund

**reformar**   to reform

**reformatorio**   reformatory

**refresco**   refreshment; soft drink

**regalar**   to give as a gift

**regalo**   gift

**registrar**   to inspect, to search; to register; to record

**registro**   record, list

**regla**   rule, ruler

**regresar**   to return

**regular**   fair, moderate, medium

**regularidad**   regularity

**rehabilitación**   rehabilitation

**rehusar**   to refuse; to decline

**reino**   kingdom

**relación**   relation

**relacionado**   related

**reloj** *m*   clock; watch

**rellenar**   to fill out

**remate** *m*   end, conclusion, expiration; bid

**remolacha** beet
**renombre** *m* reknown, fame
**renta** rent; __ **neta** net income
**reñir (i)** to quarrel; to challenge
**reo** *m* + *f* offender, criminal, culprit, convict
**repaso** review
**repentino** sudden
**repetir (i)** to repeat
**repollo** cabbage
**reportar** to report
**reposar** to rest, to repose
**representante** *n m* + *f* representative, agent; *adj* representative
**representar** to represent
**reprobar (ue)** to fail; to reject
**reprochar** to criticize (for)
**res** *f* head of cattle
**resaca** (*coll*) hangover
**reservar** to reserve
**resfriado** (head) cold
**residencia** residence
**residente** *m* + *f* resident
**resolver (ue)** to resolve, solve
**respetable** respectable
**respiración** breathing
**respirar** to breathe
**restar** to subtract
**resto** remainder, balance
**resumen** *n* summary
**retrovisor** *m* rear-view mirror
**reuma** *m* rheumatism
**reumático** rheumatic
**reumatismo** rheumatism
**reverendo** reverend
**revisar** to check; to review, to examine
**revivir** to revive; -se to come around, recover consciousness
**rico** rich
**riesgo** risk, danger
**riña** quarrel, dispute
**riñón** *m* kidney
**río** river
**risueño** smiling, pleasant
**ritmo** rhythm
**robado** robbed
**robar** to rob
**robo** theft, robbery
**rodilla** knee
**rogar (ue)** to implore

**rojo** red
**romper** to break, to tear
**ronchas** *pl* hives
**ropa** clothing, clothes; __ **interior** underwear
**roto** broken, destroyed
**rotura** rupture, fracture; crack
**rozadura** abrasion; chafed or sore spot
**rubeola** measles, rubeola
**rubio** blond
**rueda** wheel; rim
**ruta** route

## S

**saber** to know (facts)
**sabotaje** *n m* sabotage
**saboteador(a)** saboteur
**sabotear** to sabotage
**sacapuntas** *m sing* pencil sharpener
**sacerdote** *m* priest
**saco** sack, bag; sportscoat
**sala** room; living room; __ **de emergencia/ urgencia** emergency room; __ **de espera** waiting room; __ **de operaciones** operating room; __ **del tribunal** courtroom
**salame** *m* salami
**salario** salary, wages
**salchicha** wiener; sausage
**saldo** balance of an account; amount left (of merchandise)
**salida** departure; exit
**salir** to go out; to leave
**salmón** *m* salmon
**salón** *m* large hall; lounge
**salsa** sauce; __ **de tomate** ketchup
**salud** *f* health
**saludar** to greet
**salvado** bran
**salvadoreño/a** Salvadorean
**sanar** to heal, to cure
**sanatorio** sanatorium, hospital
**sanción** sanction, penalty
**sancionar** to sanction, approve
**sandalia** sandal
**sandía** watermelon
**sangrar** to bleed
**sangre** *f* blood

**sanidad** soundness, health

**sano** sound, healthy

**sarampión** *m* measles

**sardina** sardine

**sarpullido** skin rash

**satírico** satirical, sarcastic

**secretario/a** secretary; __ **de tribunal** clerk of the court

**secuestrador(a)** kidnapper

**secuestrar** to kidnap

**secuestro** kidnapping

**secundaria** *n* high school

**secundario** *adj* secondary

**sed** *f* thirst; **tener** __ to be thirsty

**seguir (i)** to follow

**segundo** second

**seguridad** security; confidence; __ **del ingreso** supplemental income, supplemental security

**seguro** *n m* insurance; button lock (on a car door); __ **social** social security; *adj* sure, certain; __ **de desempleo** unemployment insurance; __ **por incapacidad** disability insurance

**semáforo** traffic light

**semana** week

**semanal** weekly

**semejante** similar, same

**semestre** *m* semester

**sémola** grits

**sensible** sensible; sensitive; substantial

**sentadera** seat; buttocks

**sentar (ie)** to sit; to fit; **-se** to sit down

**sentencia** sentence (of a court)

**sentenciar** to commit, sentence; to pass judgment

**sentir (ie)** to feel; to grieve; to be sorry, regret

**señal** *f* sign, mark

**señalar** to point out

**señor** *m* mister, man

**señorita** Miss, Ms., young lady

**separado** separate

**separar** to separate; to part

**septiembre** September

**séptimo** seventh

**ser** to be

**serio** serious

**servicio** service; **servicios municipales** utilities

**servir (i)** to serve; **-se** to help oneself

**seso** brain; prudence, good sense

**seta** general name for all species of mushroom

**sexo** sex

**sexto** sixth

**siempre** always

**sífilis** *f sing* syphilis

**siguiente** following, next

**sillón** *m* armchair

**símbolo** symbol, mark

**simpático** charming, nice

**sin** without

**sincero** sincere, honest

**sindicato** union, syndicate

**sintético** synthetic

**síntoma** *m* symptom

**siquiatra** *m + f* psychiatrist

**sistema** *m* system

**sitio** place

**situación** situation

**situado** situated, located

**sobaco** armpit

**sobornador(a)** briber

**sobornar** to bribe

**soborno** bribery; bribe

**sobre** *prep* on, over, above; *n m* envelope

**sobrenombre** *m* nickname, alias

**sobresaliente** outstanding

**sobretodo** overcoat

**sobrino/a** nephew/niece

**sociedad** society

**sofá** *m* sofa

**soja** soybean

**sol** *m* sun

**solanera** sunburn

**solar** *m* plot of land on which a house is built

**solicitante** *m + f* applicant

**solicitar** to solicit; to apply for

**solicitud** application; application form

**solo** *adj* alone

**sólo** *adv* only

**soltar (ue)** to untie; to loosen

**soltero/a** single, unmarried person

**sombrero** hat

**sopa** soup

**soplar** to blow

**soplón** *m + f* stool pigeon, informer

**sospechoso**  suspicious

**sospechoso/a**  suspect

**sostenimiento**  sustenance; support

**sótano**  basement

**subasta**  auction

**subir**  to mount, get on; to climb, ascend

**subvención**  grant

**suceder**  to succeed; to happen

**suceso**  event, incident

**sucursal** *m*  branch (of a store, bank, and so on)

**sudamericano/a**  South American

**suegro/a**  father-in-law/mother-in-law

**sueldo**  salary, wages; __ **en bruto**  gross salary; __ **neto**  net salary

**suelo**  ground; floor

**sueño**  dream; **tener** __  to be sleepy

**suero**  blood serum

**suerte** *f*  luck

**suéter** *m*  sweater

**sufrir**  to suffer

**suicidarse**  to commit suicide

**sujetar**  to subdue, to reduce to submission; to hold

**sumar**  to add (up)

**sumario**  summary

**superintendente** *m + f*  superintendent

**supervisar**  to supervise

**suponer**  to suppose, to surmise; to imply

**supositorio**  suppository

**sustantivo**  noun

**sustento**  food, sustenance


# T

**tabaco**  tobacco

**tabla**  (arithmetic) table

**tablón** *m*  large board; __ **de anuncias**  bulletin board

**tal**  such, as, so

**tal vez**  perhaps

**talón** *m*  heel (of the foot); stub (in a checkbook)

**talla**  size (in clothing)

**taller** *m*  shop, workshop

**tamal** *m*  Mexican corn dumpling

**tamaño**  size

**también**  also, too; likewise

**tampoco**  neither, not either

**tanto** *adv*  so, in such a manner; *adj* so much, so many

**tapa**  hubcap

**tapar**  to cover, to stop up

**tapatío/a**  person from Guadalajara, Mexico

**tardanza**  lateness

**tardar**  to be late; __ **en** + *inf*  to take long (to do something)

**tarde** *n f*  afternoon; *adv* late

**tarea**  homework

**tarjeta**  card; __ **de crédito**  credit card; __ **de inmigración**  immigration card

**tasa**  rate; __ **bancaria**  bank rate

**taza**  cup

**té** *m*  tea

**techo**  roof; top

**tejido**  texture; weaving; fabric; __ **nervioso**  nervous system

**tela**  cloth

**telefónico** *adj*  telephone, pertaining to the telephone

**teléfono**  telephone

**televisor** *m*  television set

**templado**  temperate, warm, lukewarm

**temporal**  temporary, temporal

**tender (ie)**  to make (a bed)

**tendón** *m*  tendon

**tenedor(a) de libros**  bookkeeper

**tener (ie)**  to have; __ **que** + *inf*  to have to (do something); __ **que ver con**  to have to do with

**tenis** *m*  *sing* tennis; *sing + pl* tennis shoes

**teología**  theology

**terapia**  therapy; __ **del habla**  speech therapy

**tercero**  third

**terminar**  to finish, terminate

**termómetro**  thermometer

**ternero/a**  calf, veal

**terror** *m*  terror

**terrorista** *m + f*  terrorist

**testículo**  testicle

**testigo** *m + f*  witness

**testimonio**  testimony

**tétano**  tetanus

**texano/a**  Texan

**texto**  text

**tez** *f*  skin, complexion; **de** __ **blanca**  of light complexion

**tiempo**   time; weather; __ **completo**   full time

**tienda**   store

**tifoidea**   typhoid fever

**tigre** *m*   tiger

**tijeras** *f pl*   scissors

**tintorería**   dry cleaning establishment

**tío/a**   uncle/aunt

**tipo**   type; model, kind; __ **de cambio** rate of exchange

**tirita**   band-aid

**tiroides** *m sing*   thyroid (gland)

**titular** *m*   owner, holder (of an account)

**título**   title; __ **de propiedad**   deed

**tiza**   chalk

**tobillo**   ankle

**tocar**   to touch; to play (an instrument); to sound (a horn); to be one's turn, chance

**tocólogo** *m + f*   obstetrician

**todavía**   still, yet

**todo**   all; whole

**tolerancia**   tolerance

**tolerar**   to tolerate

**tomar**   to take, to grasp; to drink; __ **lugar** to take place

**tomate** *m*   tomato

**tono**   tone, shade

**toque** *n m*   touch, feel

**torcedura**   sprain

**torcer (ue)**   to twist, to sprain

**torno**   wheel, lath; **en** __   around, about

**toronja**   grapefruit

**tortuga**   turtle

**tos** *f sing*   cough; __ **ferina**   whooping cough

**toser**   to cough

**total** *m*   total

**totalizar**   to total, add up

**trabajador(a) social**   social worker

**trabajar**   to work

**trabajo** *n*   work; job

**traer**   to bring

**traficante** *m + f*   trader, dealer

**traficar**   to traffic, to trade

**tráfico**   traffic; trade

**tragar**   to swallow

**traje** *m*   suit

**tranquilizarse**   to calm down

**tranquilo** *adj* tranquil, calm; *command* relax, stay calm

**transacción**   transaction

**transitar**   to travel

**tránsito**   transit; traffic

**transportación**   transportation

**transportar**   to transport

**transporte** *m*   transporting, transportation

**tráquea**   windpipe

**trasero** *adj*   back, rear

**tratamiento**   treatment

**tratar**   to treat; to discuss; __ **de** + *inf* to try to (do something)

**tribunal** *m*   tribunal; __ **titular de menores** juvenile court

**trigal** *m*   wheat field

**trigo**   wheat

**trigueño**   olive-skinned

**trimestre** *m*   quarter; three-month period

**tripa**   gut, intestine

**triste**   sad

**trucha**   trout

**tuberculosis** *f sing*   tuberculosis

**tubo**   pipe; __ **de escape**   exhaust pipe

**tumor** *m*   tumor

**turista** *m + f*   tourist

**turno**   turn

**turquesa**   turquoise

**tutelar** *adj*   guardian; protective

# U

**úlcera**   ulcer

**último**   last

**unido**   united

**universidad**   university

**universitario** *adj*   university

**uña**   fingernail, toenail

**urgencia**   urgency

**urinario**   urinary

**urólogo** *m + f*   urologist

**urticaria**   hives

**uruguayo/a**   Uruguayan

**usar**   to use

**uso** *n*   use, employment

**útero**   uterus, womb

**utilidad**   utility; usefulness

**uva**   grape

# V

vaca  cow

vacación  vacation

vaciar  to empty

vacuna  vaccination

vado  dip in the road

vago *adj*  errant, vagrant

vajilla  table service of dishes, plates

vale *n m*  promissory note

valer *v*  to be worth

valor *m*  valor; asset

valorar  to value

valuación  valuation, appraisal

varicela  chickenpox

vaso  tumbler, glass; vessel

vejiga  bladder

velocidad  speed, velocity

vena  vein

venado  deer; venison

venda  bandage

vendaje *m*  bandage, dressing

vender  to sell

venéreo  venereal

venezolano/a  Venezuelan

venir (ie)  to come; to advance; __
     incluído  to be included

venta  sale

ventana  window

ventanilla  teller's window (at a bank)

ver  to see

veranear  to spend or pass the summer

verano  summer

verbo  verb

verde  green

verdura  vegetable

vesícula biliar  gall bladder

vestido  dress; clothing

vestir (i)  to dress; -se  to get dressed

vez *f*  turn; time; a la __  at the same
     time; a veces  sometimes; en __ de
     instead of; otra __  again

vía  way, road, route; vías urinarias
     urinary tract; __ corta  short cut

vicepresidente *m + f*  vice president

víctima *m + f*  victim

vida  life

vidrio  glass

viejo/a *adj*  old; *n* old person

vientre *m*  belly, abdomen

viernes *m sing*  Friday

vigente *adj*  in force; up to date

vino  wine

violación  violation; rape

violador(a)  rapist; criminal

violar  to rape; to violate

virar  to turn

viruela  smallpox

visceras *pl*  inner organs

visita  visit

visitar  to visit

vitamina  vitamin

viudo/a  widower/widow

vivienda  dwelling, housing

vivir  to live

vivo *adj*  alive; bright, quick

vocabulario  vocabulary

vocación  vocation

volante *m*  steering wheel

volver (ue)  to return

vomitar  to vomit

vómito  vomit, vomiting

# Y

ya *adv*  still, already; __ que  now that

yerno  son-in-law

yodo  iodine

# Z

zanahoria  carrot

zapatilla  slipper

zapato  shoe; zapatos con tacones  high
     heels

zarcillo  earring

zarzamora  blackberry

zona  zone; __ postal  zip code

zoológico  zoo

## A

**achaque** m  health problem.
**ajo**  garlic.
**alcohol** m  alcohol.
**aluminio**  aluminum.
**angina**  angina.
**apuñalar**  to stab.
**axila**  armpit.

## B

**barbilampiño**  "peach fuzz" hair.
**bigote** m  mustach.
**borrachera**  drunkenness.
**botica**  pharmacy.

## C

**callo**  corn, callus; tripe.
**canoso** adj.  grey hair.
**carril** m  lane.
**cobre** m  copper.
**cortada**  cut.
**crucero**  crossroad.
**cuadrado** adj.  square, plaid..
**cuero**  leather, skin.

## CH

**chaparro** adj.  short (Mex.).
**chicle**  gum (chewing).

## D

**demandante**  plaintiff.
**descoyuntar**  dislocate.
**deshidratación** adj.  dehydration.
**dislocar**  dislocate.

## E

**entrecano**  "salt and pepper" hair.
**evaporada**  evaporated.

## F

**fibra**  fiber.

## J

**juicio**  judgement, sense, wisdom.
**juramento**  oath.
**jurar**  to swear.

## L

**línea**  line, lane.
**lunar** m  mole, skin blemish.

## M

**maltratar**  to mistreat, to abuse.
**mancha**  stain, spot, blot.
**matriz** f  uterus, womb.
**molida** adj.  ground up.
**morcilla**  blood sausage.
**mordida**  bite; (Mex.) bribe.
**moretón** m  bruise.

## P

**palpitación** f  palpitation, heart beat.
**pana**  corduroy.
**parachoques** m  car bumper.
**prematuro**  premature.

## Q

**quemadura**  burn.

## S

**sacar**  to take out, to release.
**seda**  silk.
**seno**  breast.
**S.I.D.A.**  AIDS.

## T

**tapacubo**  hub cap.
**tienditas**  small store, shop.
**tirita**  band-aid (Spain).
**tocino**  bacon.
**torcer**  to twist, sprain.
**tuna**  prickly pears.

## G

**vendar** to bandage.
**gárgara** gargle.
**greñudo** long-haired, snarled hair.

## H

**hierro** iron.
**hule** rubber.

## I

**insolación** sun stroke.
**inspección** inspeccion.

## V

| | |
|---|---|
| **Saludos** | **Greetings** |
| 1. ---Buenos días. | Good morning. |
| 2. ---Buenas tardes. | Good afternoon. |
| 3. ---Buenas noches. | Good evening.  Good night. |

| | |
|---|---|
| **Pidiendo informes** | **Asking for information** |
| Por favor | please? |
| ¿dónde está... | where is? |
| el aeropuerto? | the airport? |
| el avión? | the plane? |
| el banco? | the bank? |
| el correo? | the post office? |
| la embajada de EE.UU.? | USA embassy? |
| el hotel? | the hotel ? |
| el museo? | the museum? |
| el restaurante? | the restaurant? |
| el excusado / servicio? | the toilet? |
| el tren? | the train? |
| la calle? | the street? |
| la estación? | the station? |
| la plaza? | the square? |
| la iglesia? | the church? |
| la catedral? | the cathedral? |
| lléveme (llévenos) ... | take me (take us) to |

| | |
|---|---|
| **Contestaciones** | **Answers** |
| está aquí | it is here |
| está allí | it is there |
| está  lejos | it is far |
| no está lejos | it is not far |
| está cerca | it is near |
| no está cerca | it is not near |
| está a la derecha | it is to the right |
| está a la izquierda | it is to the left |
| | |
| dígame usted | tell me |
| por favor | please |
| ¿ dónde está | where is |
| el baño? | the bathroom? |
| el comedor? | the dining room? |
| el cine? | the cinema, movie? |
| el taxi? or el libre? | the taxi? |
| el teatro? | the theater? |
| el teléfono? | the telephone? |
| la entrada? | the entrance? |
| la salida? | the exit? |
| mi cuarto? | my room? |
| mi llave? | my key? |
| adelante | forward, ahead |
| al final | at the end |

| en frente | opposite |
| siga usted | keep going |
| todo derecho/seguido | straight ahead |
| gracias | thanks |
| muchas gracias | many thanks |
| de nada | you're welcome (lit. 'of nothing') |

| **Pidiendo refrescos** | **Ordering refreshments** | **La hora** | **Telling time** |
|---|---|---|---|
| usted tiene | you have | ¿qué hora es? | what time is it? |
| ¿Tiene usted? | have you, do you have | es la una | it is one o'clock |
| no tengo | I do not have | son las dos, etc. | it is two o'clock, etc. |
| Deme usted | give me | es la una y cuarto | it is a quarter past one |
| | | (quince) | (fifteen) |
| Tráigame por favor | bring me, please | es la una y veinte | it is twenty past one |
| pan | bread | son las dos y media | it is half past two |
| sopa | soup | son las tres y diez | it is ten minutes after three |
| agua caliente | hot water | son las diez menos diez | |
| agua fría | cold water | faltan diez para las diez | it is ten minutes to ten |
| agua mineral | mineral water | ¿a qué hora | at what time |
| cerveza fría | cold beer | sale el tren? | does the train leave? |
| leche caliente | hot milk | sale el avión? | does the plane leave? |
| leche fría | cold milk | llega el autobús? | does the bus arrive? |
| té helado | iced tea | llega el barco | does the boat arrive? |
| vino dulce | sweet wine | empieza el teatro? | does the theater begin? |
| vino tinto | red wine | empieza la comida | does the dinner begin? |
| una taza de | a cup of | termina el cine | does the movie end? |
| café caliente | hot coffee | sale, llega, | it leaves, arrives, |
| chocolate caliente | hot chocolate | empieza, termina | begins, ends |
| té caliente | hot tea | a las nueve y media | at half past nine |
| ¿Cuánto es? | how much is it? | a las once en punto | at eleven sharp |
| es caro | it's expensive | a las dos menos cinco | at five minutes to two |
| no es caro | it's not expensive | (or cinco para las dos) | |
| es barato | it's cheap | a las cinco | at five |
| no es barato | it's not cheap | | |
| cuesta $ | it costs $ | | |

| **Más frases útiles** | **More useful phrases** |
|---|---|
| tengo que | I must, have to |
| comprar | buy |
| dar | give |
| decir | say |
| descansar | rest |
| dormir | sleep |
| entrar | go in, enter |
| escribir | write |
| salir | go out, leave |
| quisiera | I should/would like |
| bailar | to dance |
| comer | to eat |
| conocer | to know (a person/place) |
| desayunar | to have breakfast |

| | |
|---|---|
| fumar | to smoke |
| ir a | to go |
| jugar | to play |
| pasear | to walk |
| pedir | to ask for |
| preguntar | to ask (a question) |
| regresar a | to return |
| saber | to know (a thing) |
| ver | to see |
| ¿Qué tiempo hace | what's the weather like? |
| hace buen tiempo | the weather is good |
| hace mal timepo | the weather is bad |
| hace calor | it is hot |
| hace frío | it is coild |
| hace mucho calor | it is very hot |
| hace mucho frío | it is very cold |
| llueve (está lloviendo) | it is rainig |
| no llueve | it is not raining |
| hace viento | it is windy |